James J. Treacy

Tributes of Protestant Writers to the Truth and Beauty of

Catholicity

James J. Treacy

Tributes of Protestant Writers to the Truth and Beauty of Catholicity

ISBN/EAN: 9783741183669

Manufactured in Europe, USA, Canada, Australia, Japa

Cover: Foto ©Lupo / pixelio.de

Manufactured and distributed by brebook publishing software
(www.brebook.com)

James J. Treacy

Tributes of Protestant Writers to the Truth and Beauty of Catholicity

TRIBUTES

OF

PROTESTANT WRITERS

TO THE

TRUTH AND BEAUTY

OF

CATHOLICITY.

BY

JAMES J. TREACY,

Editor of "Catholic Flowers from Protestant Gardens," Etc.

Magna est veritas, et prevalebit.

FR. PUSTET & CO.,

50 AND 52 BARCLAY ST.,	204 VINE STREET,
NEW YORK.	CINCINNATI.

TO

The Right Rev. Tobias Kirby, D.D.,
LORD BISHOP OF LITA,

AND

RECTOR OF THE IRISH COLLEGE, ROME,

This Book,

As a slight tribute to his virtues and learning, is humbly dedicated by the Editor

WITH PROFOUND SENTIMENTS OF VENERATION AND RESPECT.

PREFACE.

"How beautiful are thy tabernacles, O Jacob, and thy tents, O Israel!" Thus spoke the wicked Balaam, when, from the mountain of Phogor, he looked upon the encampment of the chosen people of God. He had been invited to come and pronounce a curse upon the Israelites, but God constrained him to change the curse into a blessing.

It has not unfrequently happened that men, who went forth to labor against God, have been compelled to act as the unwilling and almost unconscious instruments of His holy designs. Thus we see that, Julian the Apostate, when he undertook the impious task of attempting to falsify the prophecies, by rooting up the foundations of the temple of Jerusalem, and "not leaving a stone upon a stone," but helped to fulfil the prophecies to the very letter. Thus, too, Volney, the French infidel, who went to Palestine, for the express purpose of manufacturing evidence against the Christian religion, furnished, in the *data*, which he afterward gave in his works, abundant material for some of the most powerful and convincing arguments in favor of Christianity.

This idea is forced upon those, who have taken the pains to examine carefully the enormous number of books, of every size and description, which have been poured out upon the world with no other purpose than that of misrepresenting the Church of God, when they find some magnificent *tributes to the truth and beauty of Catholicity* in a vast mass of the most violent vituperation and shameless falsehood.

"For three centuries," says Count Joseph de Maistre, "history has been only one grand conspiracy against truth." The *suggestio falsi* and the *suppressio veri* have been the grand principles of most of the non-Catholic historians. Whitaker, a Protestant, says that he blushes to admit that forgery has been the characteristic of the Reformation; and Nightingale candidly acknowledges that "In scarcely a single instance has the case concerning them (Catholics) been fairly stated, or the channels of history not been grossly, not to say wickedly, corrupted." It would seem that like Nabuchodonosor, a beast's heart had been given them, and that they had no idea of moral justice, or honor, or honesty.

But the machinations of mendacious writers were in vain, and only showed more strikingly the indefectibility of the Church, and verified the predictions of the prophet Isaias that "No weapon formed against thee shall prosper, and every tongue that resisteth thee in judgment, thou shalt condemn."

While the sects that broke off from the Church, soon, like rotten branches, became subject to speedy disintegration, and fell to pieces, the Church stood, like a mighty, living, energizing oak of the forest, or rather it "stood like some majestic monument amid the desert of antiquity, just in its proportions, sublime in its associations, rich in the virtue of its saints, cemented by the blood of its martyrs, pouring forth for ages the unbroken series of its venerable hierarchy, and like the pyramid in the desert, only the more magnificent from the ruins by which it is surrounded."

"Its light is 'light from heaven'; it will assist its children through the perils of their earthly pilgrimage; and like the fiery pillar of the 'chosen' Israel, it will cheer the desert of their bondage, and light them to the land of their liberation!"

CONTENTS.

	PAGE
The Early Jesuit Missionaries in North America,	1
The Church in America,	6
The Catholic Clergy,	10
The Catacombs of Rome,	16
The Power and Primacy of the Roman Pontiff,	21
Votum pro pace,	26
The Church the Protector and Defender of the Poor and Oppressed,	30
The Triumph of the Church at the Downfall of the Roman Empire,	35
Monasticism,	38
The Influence of Religion on the Tyrolese,	40
The Influence of the Church upon Slavery,	44
The Ages of Faith,	48
The Crusades,	52
Chivalry,	54
The Sacred Structures of the Middle Ages,	57
Lying Church Historians,	61
The Studious Monks of the Middle Ages,	63
The Great Catholic Italian Republics,	65
The Debt of English to Italian Literature,	73
Leo the Tenth,	77
St. Mark's, Venice,	82

CONTENTS.

	PAGE
CHRISTIANITY THE SAVIOUR OF CIVILIZATION,	92
HOLY WEEK IN ROME,	95
ALFRED THE GREAT,	101
THOMAS CROMWELL, EARL OF ESSEX,	105
THE TRIAL AND EXECUTION OF MARY QUEEN OF SCOTS,	123
CARDINAL NEWMAN,	150
IRELAND AS THE SCHOOL OF THE WEST,	161
ELIZABETH'S REFORMATION IN IRELAND,	166
THE ACTS PASSED IN THE CATHOLIC PARLIAMENT OF JAMES II. AND THOSE PASSED BY THE PROTESTANT PARLIAMENT OF WILLIAM III.,	171
SAINT LOUIS,	174
JOAN OF ARC, THE MAID OF ORLEANS,	180
DEATH OF MARIE ANTOINETTE,	186
THE FRENCH REVOLUTION IN ITS RELATION WITH THE POPE,	188
THE IMPRISONMENT OF POPE PIUS VII.,	191
CHATEAUBRIAND,	194
ISABELLA OF CASTILE,	197
THE JESUITS,	206
RESIGNATION OF CHARLES V.,	210
THE NECESSITY OF AN INFALLIBLE GUIDE,	221
THE PRESENT STATE OF PROTESTANTISM,	226
SACRIFICE OF THE MASS,	228
THE ADORATION OF THE BLESSED SACRAMENT,	231
A PROCESSION OF THE BLESSED SACRAMENT IN THE CATHEDRAL OF AMIENS,	234
JACQUELINE,	237
PENANCE,	246
CONFESSION,	248

CONTENTS.

	PAGE
THE INVOCATION OF THE SAINTS,	251
THE SYMBOLISM OF RITUAL,	254
RELIGIOUS MEMORIALS,	257
THE BEAUTIES OF THE CATHOLIC WORSHIP,	260
CHARLES CARROLL OF CARROLLTON,	262
THE SUBVERSION OF LIBERTY IN NORTHERN EUROPE,	268
THE RELIGIOUS ORDERS OF THE ROMAN CATHOLIC CHURCH,	270
VOWS,	273
CELIBACY,	283
THE ANCIENT MONK,	287
ST. IGNATIUS LOYOLA AND HIS COMPANIONS,	289
MISSIONARY CONTRAST,	322
HOSPITALS AND SISTERHOODS,	324
THE PROFESSION OF A NUN,	336
DIVORCE,	340
THE ROMAN CATHOLIC CHURCH,	342
THE POPULATION, WEALTH, POWER, FREEDOM, AND PLENTY OF ENGLAND AND IRELAND BEFORE THE REFORMATION,	345

INDEX TO NAMES OF AUTHORS, ETC.

ALISON, SIR ARCHIBALD,
    PAGE
    Chateaubriand, ... 194
    The Influence of Religion on the Tyrolese, . . 40

BAXLEY, H. WILLIS,
    Missionary Contrast, ... 322

BELL, HENRY GLASSFORD,
    Trial and Execution of Mary Queen of Scots, . . 123

BELL, JOHN,
    Profession of a Nun, ... 336
    Holy Week in Rome, ... 95

BROUGHAM, HENRY, LORD,
    Charles Carroll of Carrollton, ... 262

BURKE, EDMUND,
    The French Revolution in its Relation with the Pope, 188

CARLYLE, THOMAS,
    Death of Marie Antoinette, ... 186
    The Ancient Monk, ... 287

CARTER, REV. T. THELLUSSON,
  Vows, ... 273

COBBETT, WILLIAM,
  The Population, Wealth, Power, Freedom, and Plenty of England and Ireland before the Reformation, ... 345

DAVY, SIR HUMPHRY,
  Religious Memorials, ... 257

DE QUINCEY, THOMAS,
  Joan of Arc, Maid of Orleans, ... 180

DE WETTE, WILHELM MARTIN LEBERECHT,
  The Present State of Protestantism, ... 226

DIX, REV. MORGAN,
  Divorce, ... 340

FREEMAN, EDWARD A.,
  Alfred the Great, ... 101

FROUDE, JAMES ANTHONY,
  Cardinal Newman, ... 150

GILES, HENRY,
  The Sacred Structures of the Middle Ages, . . 57

GROTIUS, HUGO,
  Votum pro pace, ... 26

GUIZOT, F.,
    Penance, ... 246

HILL, O'DELL TRAVERS,
    Christianity the Saviour of Civilization, . . . 92

JAMESON, MRS.,
    Hospitals and Sisterhoods, ... 324
    Studious Monks of the Middle Ages, . . . 63

KIP, REV. WILLIAM INGRAHAM,
    The Early Jesuit Missionaries in North America, . . 1

LAING, SAMUEL,
    The Catholic Clergy, ... 10
    Subversion of Liberty in Northern Europe, . . 268

LAW, WILLIAM,
    Celibacy, ... 283

LECKY, WILLIAM EDWARD HARTPOLE,
    The Church the Protector and Defender of the Poor
        and Oppressed, ... 30
    The Influence of the Church upon Slavery, . . 44

LEE, REV. FREDERICK GEORGE,
    Thomas Cromwell, Earl of Essex, ... 105

LE GEYT, CHARLES J.,
    Symbolism of Ritual, ... 254

LEIBNITZ, GOTTFRIED WILHELM VON,

	PAGE
The Power and Primacy of the Roman Pontiff,	21
Adoration of the Blessed Sacrament,	231
Invocation of the Saints,	251
Confession,	248
The Religious Orders of the Roman Catholic Church,	270
The Sacrifice of the Mass,	228

LÖBEN, COUNT ISIDORE VON,

Beauties of Catholic Worship, ... 260

LONGFELLOW, H. W.,

Jacqueline, ... 237

MACAULAY, LORD,

Great Catholic Italian Republics, ... 65
The Roman Catholic Church, ... 342

McCULLAGH, W. TORRENS,

The Triumph of the Church at the Downfall of the Roman Empire, ... 35

MACKINTOSH, SIR JAMES,

The Jesuits, ... 206

MAITLAND, REV. S. R.,

Monasticism, ... 38

MALLOCK, WILLIAM HURRELL,

Necessity of an Infallible Guide, ... 221

MAURY, SARAH MYTTON,

The Church in America, ... 6

MÜLLER, JOHN VON,
    Ages of Faith, ... 48

NEALE, REV. J. M.,
    Procession of the Blessed Sacrament in the Cathedral of Amiens, ... 234

PALGRAVE, SIR FRANCIS,
    Lying Church Historians, ... 61

PHILLIPS, CHARLES,
    Imprisonment of Pope Pius the Seventh, . . . 191

PRESCOTT, WILLIAM H.,
    Isabella of Castile, ... 197

ROBERTSON, WILLIAM,
    Chivalry, ... 54
    Resignation of the Emperor Charles the Fifth, . 210

ROSCOE, WILLIAM,
    Leo the Tenth, ... 77

RUSKIN, JOHN,
    St. Mark's, Venice, ... 82

SMILES, SAMUEL,
    Elizabeth's Reformation in Ireland, ... 166
    The Acts passed in the Catholic Parliament of James the Second, and those passed in the Protestant Parliament of William the Third, ... 171

STEPHEN, SIR JAMES,
                PAGE
 Saint Louis, ... 174
 St. Ignatius Loyola and his Companions, . . . 289

SYMONDS, JOHN ADDINGTON,
 The Debt of English to Italian Literature, . . 173

TRENCH, ARCHBISHOP,
 The Crusades, ... 52

WITHROW, REV. W. H.,
 The Catacombs of Rome, ... 16

WORDSWORTH, BISHOP,
 Ireland as the School of the West, ... 161

THE EARLY JESUIT MISSIONARIES IN NORTH AMERICA.

THERE is no page of our country's history more touching and romantic, than that which records the labors and sufferings of Jesuit Missionaries. In these western wilds they were the earliest pioneers of civilization and faith. The wild hunter or the adventurous traveller, who, penetrating the forests, came to new and strange tribes, often found that years before, the disciples of Loyola had preceded him in that wilderness. Traditions of the "Black Robes" still lingered among the Indians. On some moss-grown tree they pointed out the traces of their work, and in wonder they deciphered, carved side by side on its trunk, the emblem of our salvation and the lilies of the Bourbons. Amid the snows of Hudson's Bay, among the woody islands and beautiful inlets of the St. Lawrence, by the council fires of the Hurons and the Algonquins, at the source of the Mississippi, where, first of the white men, their eyes looked upon the Falls of St. Anthony, and traced down the course of the bounding river, as it rushed onward to earn its title of "Father of Waters"—on the vast prairies of Illinois and Missouri, among the blue hills which hem in the salubrious dwellings of the Cherokees, and in the thick canebrakes of Louisiana—everywhere were found the members of the "Society of Jesus." Marquette, Joliet, Brebeuf, Jogues, Lallemand, Rasles, and Marest, are the names which the West should ever hold in remembrance. But it was only by suffering and trial that these early laborers won their triumphs. Many of them, too, were men who had stood high in camps and courts, and could contrast their desolate state in the solitary wigwam with the refinement and affluence which had waited on them in their early years. But now all these were gone. Home, the love of kindred, the golden ties of relationship, all were to be forgotten by these stern and high-wrought men, and they were often to go forth into the wilderness without an adviser on their way, save their God. Through long and sorrowful years they were obliged to "sow in tears" before they could "reap in joy." Every self-denial gathered around them which could wear upon the spirit and cause the heart to fail. Mighty forests were to be threaded on foot, and the great lakes of the West passed in the feeble bark canoe. Hunger and cold and disease were to be encountered, until nothing but the burning zeal within could keep alive the wasted and sinking frame. Most of them, too, were martyrs to their faith. It will be noticed in reading their lives how few of their number "died the common death of all men," or slept at last in the ground which their Church had consecrated. Some, like Jogues, and du Poisson, and Souel, sunk beneath the blows of the infuriated savages, and their bodies were thrown out to feed the vulture, whose shriek, as he flapped his wings above them, had been their only requiem. Others, like Brebeuf and Lallemand and Sanet, died at the stake, and their ashes "flew, no marble tells us whither," while the dusky sons of the forest stood around, and mingled their wild yells of triumph with the martyrs' dying prayers. Others again, like the aged Marquette, sinking beneath years of toil, fell asleep in the wilderness, and their sorrowing companions dug their graves in the green turf, where for many years the rude forest ranger stopped to invoke their names, and bow in prayer before the cross which marked the spot. But did these things stop the progress of the Jesuits? The sons of Loyola never retreated. The mission they founded in a tribe ended only with the extinction of the tribe itself. Their lives were made up of fearless devotedness and self-sacrifice. Though sorrowing for the dead, they pressed forward at once to occupy their places, and if needs be, share their fate. "Nothing," wrote Father le Petit after describing the martyrdom of two of his brethren, "nothing has happened to these two excellent missionaries for which they were not prepared, when they devoted themselves to the Indian Missions." If the flesh trembled, the spirit seemed never to falter. Each one, indeed, felt that he was "baptized for the dead," and that his own blood, poured out in the mighty forests of the West, would bring down perhaps greater blessings on those for whom he died, than he could win for them by the labors of a life. He realized that he was "appointed unto death." "*Ibo, et non redibo,*" were the prophetic words of Father Jogues, when, for the last time, he departed to the Mohawks. When Lallemand was bound to the stake, and for seventeen hours his excruciating agonies were prolonged, his words of encouragement to his companions were, "Brothers, we are made a spectacle unto the world, and to angels, and to men." When Marquette was setting out for the source of the Mississippi, and the friendly Indians who had known him, wished to turn him from his purpose by declaring,

"Those distant nations never spare the stranger," the calm reply of the missionary was, "I shall gladly lay down my life for the salvation of souls." And then the red sons of the wilderness bowed with him in prayer, and before the simple cross of cedar, and among the stately groves of elm and maple which line the St. Lawrence, there rose that old chant which the aged man had been accustomed to hear in the distant Cathedrals of his own land—

> "*Vexilla Regis prodeunt;*
> *Fulget Crucis mysterium.*" *

But how little is known of all these men! The history of their bravery and sufferings, touching as it is, has been comparatively neglected.

REV. WILLIAM INGRAHAM KIP,
Early Jesuit Missions in North America.

---

* The banner of Heaven's king advance,
   The mystery of the Cross shines forth.
   BANCROFT'S UNITED STATES, Vol. iii., 156.

THE CHURCH IN AMERICA.

AND looking round in anxious and inquiring solicitude, for dear, unutterably dear to me is that America where my children's children will be reared, I behold, with grateful heart, provision made by the Supreme Regulator of human things against these ripening dangers; dangers which the mind dares scarcely pause to look upon. A scheme of infinite Mercy has been divulged and committed to the wisdom and energy of appointed messengers to be fulfilled. THE CLERGY OF THE CATHOLIC CHURCH OF EUROPE, THE HEIRS OF THE FIRST PILGRIMS OF THE CROSS IN THE WESTERN HEMISPHERE, SEEK THEIR INHERITANCE; they rest their claims upon the Gospel which they preach, upon the services which they render, and the example which they give; taking neither purse nor scrip across the ocean, they carry with them the inestimable boon which maketh men wise unto Salvation. They have laid the foundation-stone of real education—education of the heart; the formation of character, *without which liberty is licentiousness;* and compared to which the mere accomplishments of the mind and fingers are airy nothings, unsubstantial in possession and useless in application. In the numerous and crowded Catholic schools of the United States are taught the exercise of prayer, the practice of morality, the laws of obedience and responsibility, and self-sacrifice, and moral and spiritual humility, and GOOD WORKS as well as *saving faith*, and charity, and brotherly love; and here the strong hand of DISCIPLINE is felt and respected. Many well-judging persons of different religious persuasions have assured me that the one really *useful* and *corrective* education is that of the Catholic schools and colleges. So far as I have known, these Seminaries are crowded not only with pupils of their own Creed, but with those of other Sects. And I have high official authority for saying that the ministers and missionaries of the Roman Catholic Church are at this moment doing more good for the cause of virtue and morality throughout the whole continent of America, than those of any other religious denomination whatever.

The Hierarchy of the Catholic Church in the United States seek not endowment; they love their independence; they seek not power; they prize their purity; they seek not sinecures; they value their high prerogative of usefulness. And thus as saintly men do they pursue their steady way, void of offence before God and man, approved on earth and registered in Heaven. I am an Episcopalian, or Protestant of the Church of England. But I am not, can not be blinded to the many excellences of the Catholic Church; and especially as its institutions regard America; they are, beyond comparison, the best adapted to curb the passions of a young, impetuous, intelligent, generous, and high-minded Democracy; to protect the religion of the Republic from annihilation; to subdue the struggling and discordant interests of an immense territory into harmony, and to enchain the sympathies of a whole people in one magnificent scheme of morality and devotion. "They shall be one fold under one Shepherd."

The Institutions besides, of this Church, are themselves based upon that very *equality* which their *discipline* so efficiently modifies. There is one common law, and one alone, for all—in the words of the Old Testament, so admirably adapted to the description of the Catholic Faith: "Here the wicked cease from troubling, and here the weary are at rest; here the prisoners rest together; they hear not the voice of the oppressor. The small and the great are there; and the servant is free from his master." These words can not be said to the same extent of any other Church whatever.

The celibacy of the Catholic clergy is another great advantage in the wilds of this great continent, and in her populous cities. No domestic or personal anxieties distract or lead them from their flock. "*Dèsqu'un Prêtre se marie, il n'est plus Prêtre?*" observed the Marquis de Talaru to me one day upon the Mississippi. And I frequently experienced the truth of the remark.

I yield this tribute of just and high commendation to the professors of this faith with pleasure mingled with pain; for I owe them much excuse; I blush for my former weak and contemptible intolerance. I was reared in the vulgar prejudices of ignorance against Catholic teachers and their disciples: in England I knew them not; sought them not; loved them not; but among the many benefits derived from my visit to America, has been that one of exceeding value, the acquaintance and friendship of the excellent and enlightened Bishop of New York,* who holds so high a place in his adopted country.

SARAH MYTTON MAURY,
The Statesmen of America in 1846.

---
* Bishop Hughes.

THE CATHOLIC CLERGY.

CATHOLICISM has certainly a much stronger hold over the human mind than Protestantism. The fact is visible and undeniable, and perhaps not unaccountable. The fervor of devotion among these Catholics, the absence of all worldly feelings in their religious acts, strikes every traveller who enters a Roman Catholic country abroad. They seem to have no reserve, no false shame, false pride or whatever the feeling may be, which, among us, Protestants, makes the individual exercise of devotion private, hidden—an affair of the closet. Here, and everywhere in Catholic countries, you see well-dressed people, persons of the higher as well as of the lower orders, on their knees upon the pavement of the church, totally regardless of, and unregarded by, the crowd of passengers in the aisles moving to and fro. In no Protestant place of worship do we witness the same intense abstraction in prayer, the unaffected devotion of mind. The beggar-woman comes in here and kneels down by the side of the princess, and evidently no feeling of intrusion suggests itself in the mind of either. Their churches are God's houses, open alike to all rational creatures, without distinction of high or low, rich or poor. All who have a soul to be saved come freely to worship.

In the Catholic Church the clergyman is more of a sacred character than it is possible to invest him with in our Protestant Church, and more cut off from all worldly affairs. It is very up-hill work in the Church of England, and still more so in the Church of Scotland, for the clergyman to impress his flock with the persuasion that he is a better man, and more able to instruct them, than any other equally pious and equally well educated man in the parish, whose worldly circumstances have given him equal opportunity and leisure to cultivate his mind; and in every parish, owing to the diffusion of knowledge, good education, and religious feeling among our upper and middle classes, there are now such men. The Scotch country clergyman in this generation does not, as in the last, stand in the position of being the only regularly educated, enlightened, religious man perhaps in his whole congregation. He has also the cares of a family, of a housekeeping, of a glebe in Scotland, of tithe in England, and, in short, the business and toils, the motives of action, and objects of interest that other men have. It is difficult, or in truth impossible, in our state of society, to impress on his flock that he is in any way removed from their condition, from their failings or feelings; and it would be but a delusion if he succeeded, for he is a human being in the same position with themselves, under the influences of the same motives and objects with themselves in his daily life.

In the Roman Catholic Church it is altogether different, and produces a totally different result. The clergyman is entirely separated from individual interests, or worldly objects of ordinary life, by his celibacy. This separates him from all other men. Be their knowledge, their education, their piety, what it will, they belong to the rest of mankind in feelings, in interests, and motives of action, —he to a peculiar class. The Catholics, who receive the elements as transubstantiated by the consecration, require very naturally and properly that the priest should be of a sanctified class, removed from human impurity, contamination, or sensual lust, as well as from all worldly affairs, as far as human nature can be.

But our Scotch clergy, placed by the Reformation in such a totally different religious position as to the nature of their functions, are wrong in expecting a peculiar veneration, and in challenging a peculiar sanctity for their order. As a sacred order, or class, they ceased to exist, or to have influence founded upon any sound religious grounds, when the distinction which made them a peculiar class in the eyes and feelings of mankind, the distinction in their sacramental function, and consequent separation in all worldly affairs between their class and other men, ceased and was removed. They have an elevated, and if they will so apply the word, a sacred duty to perform along with the ordinary duties of life; but they form no distinct sacred class, or corporation, like the tribe of Levi among the Israelites, or like the Catholic clergy among the Catholics, having religious duties or functions which none can perform but its members, and to which they are essential.

Our clergy, especially in Scotland, have a very erroneous impression of the state of the Catholic clergy. In our country churches we often hear them prayed for as men wallowing in luxury, and sunk in gross ignorance. This is somewhat injudicious, as well as uncharitable; for when the youth of their congregations, who, in this travelling age, must often come in contact abroad with the Catholic clergy so described, find them, in learning, liberal views, and genuine piety, so very different from the description and describers, there will unavoidably arise comparisons by no means edifying or flattering to their clerical teachers at home.

The education of the regular clergy of the Catholic Church is, perhaps, positively higher, and, beyond doubt, comparatively higher than the education of the Scotch clergy. Education is in reality not only not repressed, but is encouraged by the Catholic Church, and is a mighty instrument in its hands, and ably used. In every street in Rome, for instance, there are, at short distances, public primary schools for the education of the children of the lower and middle classes in the neighborhood. Rome, with a population of 158,678 souls, has 372 public primary schools, with 482 teachers, and 14,099 children attending them. Has Edinburgh so many public schools for the education of these classes? I doubt it. Berlin, with a population about double that of Rome, has only 264 schools. Rome has also her university, with an average attendance of 660 students; and the Papal States, with a population of two and one-half millions, contain seven universities. Prussia, with a population of fourteen millions, has but seven. These are amusing statistical facts—and instructive as well as amusing—when we remember the boasting and glorying carried on a few years back, and even to this day, about the Prussian educational system for the people, and the establishment of governmental schools, and enforcing by police regulation the school attendance of the children of the lower classes. The statistical fact, that Rome has above a hundred schools more than Berlin, for a population little more than half that of Berlin, puts to flight a world of humbug about systems of national education carried on by governments, and their moral effects on society.

SAMUEL LAING,
Notes of a Traveller.

THE CATACOMBS OF ROME.

"Among the cultivated grounds not far from the city of Rome," says the Christian poet Prudentius, "lies a deep crypt, with dark recesses. A descending path, with winding steps, leads through the dim turnings, and the daylight, entering by the mouth of the cavern, somewhat illumes the first part of the way. But the darkness grows deeper as we advance, till we meet with openings, cut in the roof of the passages, admitting light from above. On all sides spreads the densely-woven labyrinth of paths, branching into caverned chapels and sepulchral halls; and throughout the subterranean maze, through frequent openings, penetrates the light."

This description of the Catacombs in the fourth century is equally applicable to their general appearance in the nineteenth. Their main features are unchanged, although time and decay have greatly impaired their structure and defaced their beauty These Christian cemeteries are situated chiefly near the great roads leading from the city, and, for the most part, within a circle of three miles from the walls. From this circumstance they have been compared to the "encampment of a Christian host besieging Pagan Rome, and driving inward its mines and trenches with an assurance of final victory." The openings of the Catacombs are scattered over the Campagna, whose mournful desolation surrounds the city; often among the mouldering mausolea that rise, like stranded wrecks, above the rolling sea of verdure of the tomb-abounding plain. On every side are tombs—tombs above and tombs below—the graves of contending races, the sepulchres of vanished generations: "*Piena di sepoltura è la Campagna.*" *

How marvellous that beneath the remains of a proud pagan civilization, exist the early monuments of that power before which the myths of paganism faded away as the spectres of darkness before the rising sun, and by which the religions and institutions of Rome were entirely changed. Beneath the ruined palaces and temples, the crumbling tombs and dismantled villas, of the august mistress of the world, we find the most interesting relics of early Christianity on the face of the earth.

---

* Ariosto, *Orlando Furioso*.

In traversing these tangled labyrinths we are brought face to face with the primitive ages; we are present at the worship of the infant Church; we observe its rites; we study its institutions; we witness the deep emotions of the first believers as they commit their dead, often their martyred dead, to their last resting-place; we decipher the touching records of their sorrow, of the holy hopes by which they were sustained, of "their faith triumphant over their fears," and of their assurance of the resurrection of the dead and the life everlasting.

We read in the testimony of the Catacombs the confession of faith of the early Christians, sometimes accompanied by the record of their persecution, the symbols of their martyrdom, and even the very instruments of their torture. For in these halls of silence and gloom slumbers the dust of many of the martyrs and confessors, who sealed their testimony with their blood during the sanguinary ages of persecution; of many of the early bishops and pastors of the Church, who shepherded the flock of Christ amid the dangers of those troublous times; of many who heard the words of life from teachers who lived in or near the apostolic age, perhaps from the lips of the apostles themselves. Indeed, if we would accept ancient tradition, we would even believe that even the bodies of St. Peter and St. Paul were laid to rest in those hallowed crypts—a true *terra sancta*, inferior in sacred interest only to the rock-hewn sepulchre consecrated evermore by the body of Our Lord.

As the pilgrim to this shrine of the primitive faith visits these chambers of silence and gloom, accompanied by a serge-clad, sandaled monk, he seems like the Tuscan poet wandering through the realms of darkness with his shadowy guide.

> "Ora sen' va per un segreto calle
> Tra l' muro della terra."*

His footsteps echo strangely down the distant passages and hollow vaults, dying gradually away in the solemn stillness of this valley of the shadow of death. The graves yawn weirdly as he passes, torch in hand. The flame struggles feebly with the thickening darkness, vaguely revealing the unfleshed skeletons on either side, till its redness fades to sickly white. Deep mysterious shadows crouch around, and the dim perspective, lined with the sepulchral niches of the silent community of the dead, stretches on in an apparently unending

---

* "And now through narrow, gloomy paths we go,
   'Tween walls of earth and tombs."—*Inferno*.

vista. The vast extent and population of this great necropolis overwhelm the imagination. Almost appalling in its awe and solemnity is the sudden transition from the busy city of the living to the silent city of the dead; from the golden glory of the Italian sunlight to the funereal gloom of these sombre vaults. The sacred influence of the place subdues the soul to tender emotions. The fading pictures on the walls and the pious epitaphs of the departed breathe on every side an atmosphere of faith and hope. We speak with bated breath and in whispered tones, and thought is busy with the past. It is impossible not to feel strangely moved, while gazing on the crumbling relics of mortality committed years ago, with pious care and many tears, to their last, long rest. In this silent city of the dead we are surrounded by a "mighty cloud of witnesses," "a multitude which no man can number," whose names, unrecorded on earth, are written in the Book of Life. "It is scarcely known," says Prudentius, "how full Rome is of buried saints—how richly her soil abounds in holy sepulchres."

REV. W. H. WITHROW,
Catacombs of Rome.

THE POWER AND PRIMACY OF THE ROMAN PONTIFF.

THE Sacrament of Orders, or of the Ecclesiastical Hierarchy, is that by which the ecclesiastical or spiritual office or power, distinguished into its several grades, is conferred on certain individuals, whose ministry God uses for the purpose of dispensing the grace of His Sacraments, and of instructing, ruling, and retaining others in the unity of the faith and the obedience of charity, superadding thereto a certain power of jurisdiction, which is comprehended chiefly in the use of the keys. To the Hierarchy of Pastors of the Church, belong, not only Priesthood and its preparatory grades, but also Episcopacy, and even the Primacy of the Sovereign Pontiff, *all of which we must believe to be of divine right*. As Priests are ordained by a Bishop, the Bishop, *and especially that Bishop to whom the care of the entire Church is committed*, has power to moderate and limit the office of the Priest, so that in certain cases he is restrained from exercising the power of the keys, not only lawfully, but even validly. Moreover, the Bishop, *and especially the Bishop who is called Œcumenical, and who represents the entire Church*, has the power of excommunicating and depriving of the grace of the Sacraments, of binding and retaining sins, of loosing and restoring again. For it is not merely that voluntary jurisdiction which belongs to the Priest in the confessional, that is contained under the power of the keys; but the Church, moreover, has power to proceed against the unwilling; and he "*who does not hear the Church*," and does not, so far as is consistent with the salvation of his soul, keep her commandments, "*should be held as the heathen and the publican*"; and as the sentence on earth is regularly confirmed by that of heaven, such a man draws on himself, at the peril of his own soul, the weight of ecclesiastical authority, to which God himself lends that which is last and highest in all jurisdiction—execution.

In order, however, that the power of the Hierarchy may be better understood, we must recollect that every state and commonwealth, and therefore the commonwealth of the Church, should be considered as a civil body, or one moral person. For there is this difference between an assembly of many and one body: that an assembly, of itself, does not form a single person out of many individuals; whereas a body constitutes a person, to which person may belong various properties and rights, distinct from the rights of the individuals; whence it is that the right of a body, or college, is vested in one individual, while that of an assembly is necessarily in the hands of many. Now it is of the nature of a person, whether natural or moral, to have a will, in order that its wishes may be known. Hence, if the form of government is a monarchy, the will of the monarch is the will of the state; but if it be a polycracy, we regard as the will of the state the will of some College or Council, whether this consists of a certain number of the citizens, or of them all, ascertained either by the number of votes, or by certain other conditions.

Since, therefore, our merciful and sovereign God has established His Church on earth, as a sacred "*city placed upon a mountain,*" His immaculate spouse, and the interpreter of His will,—and has so earnestly commended the universal maintenance of her unity in the bonds of love, and has commanded that she should be heard by all who would not be esteemed "*as the heathen and the publican*"; it follows that He must have appointed some mode by which the will of the Church, the interpreter of the Divine will, could be known.

What this mode is, was pointed out by the Apostles, who, in the beginning, represented the body of the Church. For at the council which was held in Jerusalem, in explaining their opinion, they use the words, "*It hath seemed good to the Holy Ghost and to us.*" Nor did this privilege of the assistance of the Holy Ghost cease in the Church with the death of the Apostles; it is to endure "*to the consummation of the world,*" and has been propagated throughout the whole body of the Church by the Bishops, as successors of the Apostles. Now as, from the impossibility of the Bishops frequently leaving the people over whom they are placed, it is not possible to hold a council continually, or even frequently, while at the same time the person of the Church must always live and subsist, in order that its will may be ascertained, it was a necessary consequence, by the Divine law itself, insinuated in Christ's most memorable words to Peter (when He committed to him specially the keys of the kingdom of heaven), as well as when He thrice emphatically commanded him to "*feed His sheep,*" and uniformly believed in the Church, that one among the Apostles, and the successor of this one among the Bishops, was invested with pre-eminent power; in order that by him, as the visible centre of unity, the body of the

Church might be bound together; the common necessities be provided for; a council, if necessary, be convoked, and when convoked, directed; and that, in the interval between councils, provision might be made lest the commonwealth of the faithful sustain any injury. And as the ancients unanimously attest that the Apostle Peter governed the Church, suffered martyrdom, and appointed his successor, in the city of Rome, the capital of the world; and as no other Bishop has ever been recognized under this relation, we justly acknowledge the Bishop of Rome to be the chief of all the rest. *This, at least, therefore, must be held as certain, that in all things which do not admit the delay necessary for the convocation of a general council, the power of the chief of the Bishops, or Sovereign Pontiff, is, during the interval, the same as that of the whole Church. We are to obey the Sovereign Pontiff as the only Vicar of God on earth.*

GOTTFRIED WILHELM VON LEIBNITZ,
Systema Theologicum.

VOTUM PRO PACE.

NURTURED from my youth in sacred literature, and taught by masters not holding the same opinions on divine things, it was easy for me to see the will of Christ, that all who desired to bear His name, and through Him attain blessedness, should be one among themselves as He is one with the Father (John 17). And that, not one in spirit merely, but likewise in a communion which can be seen, and is specially seen in the bonds of government and the participation of sacraments. For the Church is one, or ought to be, a certain Body (Rom. xii.; Ephes. i. 4, 5; Colos. i.); which Body, Christ, the Head given to it by God, has willed to be jointed together by the ligaments of various offices (Ephes. iv. 11); and individuals to be baptized in it, that they may become one body (1 Cor. xii.). And they are to feed on one consecrated Bread, that they may grow more and more unto each other, and show themselves to be one Body (1 Cor. x. 17). I was strangely captivated by the beauty of that ancient Church, on whose Catholicity there is no controversy; when all Christians, save fragments torn off, and therefore easy to be recognized, were knit together by the intercourse of ecclesiastical letters from the Rhine to Africa and Egypt, from the British ocean to the Euphrates, or beyond. I saw that it was for this very reason that schisms and separations in that conspicuous Body were severally interdicted (Rom. xvi. 17; 1 Cor. i. 10, 11; iii. 3; xi. 18; xii. 25; Gal. v. 20); and that this was the special subject in the letters of Paul, and Clement of Rome to the Corinthians, and in many writings of Optatus of Milan, and Augustine against the Donatists. Moreover, I began to reflect that not only my ancestors, but those of many others, had been pious men, hating superstition and wickedness; men who brought up their families well, in the worship of God and the love of their neighbor; whom I had ever deemed to have departed from this life in a state of salvation; nor had Francis Junius taught me otherwise—a man of such fair and mild opinions, that the more heated Protestants disliked and abused him. I was also aware from the report of my elders, and the histories I had read, that men afterwards arose who were altogether for deserting the Church in which our ancestors had been; and who not only themselves deserted it—some even before they were excommunicated—but made new assemblies too, which they were for calling Churches, made new presbyteries in them, taught and administered sacraments, and that in many places against the edicts of kings and bishops, and alleged, in defence of this, that they must obey God rather than man, just as if they had had such a charge from Heaven as the Apostles had. Nor had they halted in their daring at this point; but traducing kings as idolaters and slaves of the Pope, had stirred up the mob to armed meetings, seditions against the magistrates, breaking of the images of saints, of holy tables and shrines, and finally to civil war and open rebellion. I saw that much Christian blood had thus been everywhere shed, that morals, looking generally, especially where they had prospered, had so far from improved, that long wars had made men savage, and the contact of foreign vices infected them. My sorrow at these things increasing with my years, I began to reflect myself, and consider with others on the cause of calamities so great. *The seceders, to cover their own deed, stoutly maintained that the doctrine of the Church united with the chief See had been corrupted by many heresies, and by idolatry.* This was the occasion of my inquiring into the dogmas of that Church, of reading the books written on both sides, reading also what has been written of the present state and doctrine of the Church in Greece, and of those joined to it in Asia and Egypt.

I found that the East held the same dogmas which had been defined in the West by universal councils; and that their judgments agreed on the government of the Church (save the controversies with the Pope), and on the rites of the Sacraments unbrokenly handed down. I went further, and chose to read the chief writers of ancient times, as well Greek as Latin, among whom are Gauls and Africans; and those of the three next centuries I read both all and often; but the later ones, as much as my occupations and circumstances allowed, especially Chrysostom and Jerome, because I saw that they were considered happier than the rest in the exposition of the Holy Scriptures. Applying to these writings the rules of Vincentius of Lerins, which I saw to be approved by the most learned, I deduced what were the points which had been everywhere, always, and perseveringly handed down, by the testimony of the ancients, and by the traces of them remaining to the present day. *I saw that these remained in that Church which is bound to the Roman.*

HUGO GROTIUS,
Votum pro pace Ecclesiastica.

THE CHURCH THE PROTECTOR AND DEFENDER OF THE POOR AND OPPRESSED.

THE enthusiasm of charity, manifested in the Church, speedily attracted the attention of the Pagans. The ridicule of Lucian, and the vain effort of Julian to produce a rival system of charity within the limits of Paganism, emphatically attested both its pre-eminence and its catholicity. During the pestilences that desolated Carthage in A.D. 326, and Alexandria in the reigns of Gallienus and of Maximian, while the Pagans fled panic-stricken from the contagion, the Christians extorted the admiration of their fellow-countrymen by the courage with which they rallied around their bishops, consoled the last hours of the sufferers, and buried the abandoned dead. In the rapid increase of pauperism arising from the emancipation of numerous slaves, their charity found free scope for action, and its resources were soon taxed to the utmost by the horrors of the barbarian invasions. The conquest of Africa by Genseric, deprived Italy of the supply of corn upon which it almost wholly depended, arrested the gratuitous distribution by which the Roman poor were mainly supported, and produced all over the land the most appalling calamities. The history of Italy became one monotonous tale of famine and pestilence, of starving populations and ruined cities. But everywhere amid this chaos of dissolution we may detect the majestic form of the Christian priest mediating between the hostile forces, straining every nerve to lighten the calamities around him. When the Imperial city was captured and plundered by the hosts of Alaric, a Christian church remained a secure sanctuary, which neither the passions nor the avarice of the Goths transgressed. When a fiercer than Alaric had marked out Rome for his prey, the Pope St. Leo, arrayed in his sacerdotal robes, confronted the victorious Hun, as the ambassador of his fellow-countrymen, and Attila, overpowered by religious awe, turned aside in his course. When, twelve years later, Rome lay at the mercy of Genseric, the same Pope interposed with the Vandal conqueror, and obtained from him a partial cessation of the massacre. The Archdeacon Pelagius interceded with similar humanity and similar success, when Rome had been captured by Totila. In Gaul, Troyes is said to have been saved from destruction by the influence of St.

Lupus, and Orleans by the influence of St. Agnan. In Britain an invasion of the Picts was averted by St. Germain of Auxerrois. The relations of rulers to their subjects, and of tribunals to the poor, were modified by the same intervention. When Antioch was threatened with destruction on account of its rebellion against Theodosius, the anchorites poured forth from the neighboring deserts to intercede with the ministers of the emperor, while the Archbishop Flavian went himself as a suppliant to Rome. St. Ambrose imposed public penance on Theodosius, on account of the massacre of Thessalonica. Synesius excommunicated for his oppression a governor named Andronicus; and two French Councils, in the sixth century, imposed the same penalty on all great men who arbitrarily ejected the poor. St. Abraham, St. Epiphanius, and St. Basil are all said to have obtained the remission or reduction of oppressive imposts. To provide for the interest of the widows and orphans was part of the ecclesiastical duty, and a Council of Macon anathematized any ruler who brought them to trial without first apprising the bishop of the diocese. A Council of Toledo, in the fifth century, threatened with excommunication all who robbed priests, monks, or poor men, or refused to listen to their expostulations. As time rolled on, charity assumed many forms, and every monastery became a centre from which it radiated. By the monks the nobles were overawed, the poor protected, the sick tended, travellers sheltered, prisoners ransomed, the remotest spheres of suffering explored.

There is no fact of which an historian becomes more speedily or more painfully conscious than the great difference between the importance and the dramatic interest of the subjects he treats. Wars or massacres, the horrors of martyrdom or the splendors of individual prowess, are susceptible of such brilliant coloring, that with but little literary skill they can be so portrayed that their importance is adequately realized, and they appeal to the emotions of the reader. But this vast and unostentatious movement of charity, operating in the village hamlet and in the lonely hospital, staunching the widow's tears, and following all the windings of the poor man's griefs, presents few features the imagination can grasp, and leaves no deep impression upon the mind. The greatest things are often those which are most imperfectly realized; and surely no achievements of the Christian Church are more truly great than those which have been effected in the sphere of charity. For the first time in the history of mankind, it has inspired many thousands of men and women, at the sacrifice of all worldly interests, and often under circumstances of extreme discomfort or danger, to devote their entire lives to the single object of assuaging the sufferings of humanity.

WILLIAM EDWARD HARTPOLE LECKY,
History of European Morals.

THE TRIUMPH OF THE CHURCH AT THE DOWNFALL OF THE ROMAN EMPIRE.

'TWAS the solemnest epoch in the lifetime of man—that, when the civilization of two thousand years, unionized into one gigantic fabric by the power of Rome, so that the whole trust and worth of nations was by compulsion made to rest thereon, began visibly to break down. 'Twas the sultriest hour of time. The sweat-drops of terror fell, and made echo in their fall. The loosing of the chariot-steeds of barbarism was heard afar, and men knew not what it meant, for they had never heard the like before. Vague feelings of their helplessness and danger—vague forebodings of unknown evils, overcast their sapless hearts. They had time to fly, but whither? They had hands and brains, but the hands were nerveless, and "the formidable *pilum*, which had subdued the world, dropt from them,"—the brains were crammed full of controversial logic, so that there was no room in them for manly thoughts. Men had been bent and bowed for centuries to believe the lie, that one arch of power is enough for all Mankind—that it is safest and best for many nations to trust all to one. All rivalry or competition was not only dead, but it was a thing forgotten; it had come to be a rude, uncivilized, unenlightened thing. There stood but one world-spanning arch—but one only tolerated or known bridge over anarchy. . . . . Downward it totters—crumbling down, with its multitudinous load. They sink wailing; sink with whatever they possess of valuables—valuables as they called them; and doubtless dragging with them much also of true value into the unwritten grave. Yet is not *all* lost. Christianity remained a refuge for the drowning civilization of antiquity. The Church sank not. Since the unannalled days of the first flood, when the primitive science, art, and knowledge of mankind were destroyed, there had been nought within comparison so appalling to this unsheltered world as this Scythian tide; and, as in the elder tempest, there was no salvation but in an ark of safety of no human providence or contriving. The Church alone outrode the storm. When its surging crest of ruin rose most high, the cross rose with it, and above it still. The barbarians embraced Christianity; and when the vanquished felt that between them and their conquerors was one tie—that of a common faith—they said within themselves, "Surely the bitterness of death is passed." It was the Church that saved whatever could be rescued from the universal wreck: in her sanctuary were preserved for succeeding times, the laws, and a few hastily snatched up records of a drowned antiquity. On, on, with force as if forever, the gush of Scythia and Burgundia roars. All political power is overwhelmed in its weltering wave. The Church alone sinks not. It alone presumes to beard and to reprove—to rebuke and to restrain its rage. Immortal faith saves human hope from dying. All this is assuredly no scoffing matter. Sceptic, sarcastic Gibbon was no man to write its history; when next it shall be written, pray that it fall into far different hands. Can we imagine anything so crushing of all hope of progress, as the state of things that would have been, had antiquity been entirely lost? Can we conceive a more exalting proof of a superintending wisdom in the affairs of men, than the provision whereby religion was made to guard that perilled treasure?

W. TORRENS McCULLAGH,
The Use and Study of History.

MONASTICISM.

It is quite impossible to touch the subject of *Monasticism* without rubbing off some of the dirt which has been heaped upon it. It is impossible to get even a superficial knowledge of the mediæval history of Europe, without seeing how greatly the world of that period was indebted to the Monastic Orders; as a quiet and religious refuge for helpless infancy and old age, a shelter of respectful sympathy for the orphan maiden and the desolate widow—as central points whence agriculture was spread over bleak hills, and barren downs, and marshy plains, and dealt its bread to millions perishing with hunger and its pestilential train—as repositories of the learning which then was, and the well-springs for the learning which was to be—as nurseries of art and science, giving the stimulus, the means, and the reward to invention, and aggregating around them every head that could devise, and every hand that could execute—as the nucleus of the city which in after-days of pride should crown its palaces and bulwarks with the towering cross of its cathedral.

This, I think, no man can deny. I believe it is true, and I love to think of it. I hope that I see the good hand of God in it, and the visible trace of His mercy that is over all His works. But if it is only a dream, however grateful, I shall be glad to be awakened from it; not indeed by the yelling of illiterate agitators, but by a quiet and sober proof that I have misunderstood the matter. In the meantime, let me thankfully believe that thousands of the persons at whom Robertson and Jortin and other such very miserable second-hand writers, have sneered, were men of enlarged minds, purified affections, and holy lives—that they were justly reverenced by men—and, above all, favorably accepted by God, and distinguished by the highest honor which He vouchsafes to those whom He has called into existence, that of being the channels of His love and mercy to their fellow-creatures.

Rev. S. R. Maitland,
Dark Ages.

THE INFLUENCE OF RELIGION ON THE TYROLESE.

Perhaps the most remarkable feature in the character of the Tyrolese, is their uniform *Piety*, a feeling which is nowhere so universally diffused as among their sequestered valleys. Chapels are built almost at every half mile on the principal roads, in which the passenger may perform his devotions, or which may awaken the thoughtless mind to a recollection of its religious duties. Even in the higher parts of the mountains, where hardly any vestiges of human cultivation are to be found, in the depth of the untrodden forests, or on the summit of seemingly inaccessible cliffs, the symbols of devotion are to be found, and the cross rises everywhere amidst the wilderness as if to mark the triumph of Christianity over the greatest obstacles of nature.

In ancient times, we are informed, these mountains were inhabited by the Rhætians, the fiercest and most barbarous of the tribes, who dwelt in the fastnesses of the mountains, and of whose savage manners Livy has given so striking an account in his description of Hannibal's passage of the Alps. Many Roman legions were impeded in their progress, or thinned of their numbers, by these cruel barbarians; and even after they were reduced to subjection, by the expedition of Drusus, it was still esteemed a service of the utmost danger to leave the high-road, or explore the remote recesses of the country.

What is it, then, which has wrought so wonderful a change in the manners, the habits, and the condition of the inhabitants of those desolate regions? What is it which has spread cultivation through wastes, deemed in ancient times inaccessible to human improvement, and humanized the manners of a people remarkable only, under the Roman sway, for the ferocity and barbarism of their institutions? From what cause has it happened that those savage mountaineers, who resisted all the arts of civilization by which the Romans established their sway over mankind, and continued, even to the overthrow of the empire, impervious to all the efforts of ancient improvement, should, in later times, have so entirely changed their character, and have appeared, even from the first dawn of modern civilization, mild and humane in their character and manners? From what but from the influence of *Religion*—of that religion which calmed the savage feeling of the human mind, and spread its beneficial influence among the remotest habitations of men; and which prompted its disciples to leave the luxuries and comforts of southern climates, to diffuse knowledge and humanity through inhospitable realms, and spread, even amidst the regions of winter and desolation, the light and blessings of a spiritual faith.

Universally it has been observed throughout the whole extent of the Alps, that the earliest vestiges of civilization, and the first traces of order and industry which appeared after the overthrow of the Roman empire, were to be found in the immediate neighborhood of the religious establishments; and it is to the unceasing efforts of the clergy, during the centuries of barbarism which followed that event, that the judicious historian of Switzerland ascribes the early civilization and humane disposition of the Helvetic tribes. We would not, perhaps, be inclined to credit the accounts of the heroic sacrifices which were then made by numbers of great and good men who devoted themselves to the conversion of the Alpine tribes, did not their institutions remain to this day as a monument of their virtue; and did we not still see a number of benevolent men who seclude themselves from the world, and dwell in the regions of perpetual snow, in the hope of rescuing a few individuals from a miserable death. When the traveller on the summit of the St. Bernard reads the warm and touching expressions of gratitude with which the Roman travellers recorded their gratitude for having escaped the dangers of the pass, even in the days of Adrian and the Antonines, and reflects on the perfect safety with which he can now traverse the remotest recesses of the Alps, he will think with thankfulness of the religion by which this wonderful change has been effected, and with veneration of the saint whose name has for a thousand years been affixed to the pass where his influence first reclaimed the people from their barbarous life.

Sir Archibald Alison,
Miscellaneous Essays.

THE INFLUENCE OF THE CHURCH UPON SLAVERY.

WHILE Christianity broke down the contempt with which the master had regarded his slaves, and planted among the latter a principle of moral regeneration which expanded in no other sphere with an equal perfection, its action in procuring the freedom of the slave was unceasing. The law of Constantine, which placed the ceremony under the superintendence of the clergy, and the many laws that gave special facilities of manumission to those who desired to enter the monasteries or the priesthood, symbolized the religious character the act had assumed.

It was celebrated on Church festivals, especially on Easter. St. Melania was said to have emancipated 8,000 slaves; St. Ovidius, a rich martyr of Gaul, 5,000; Chromatius, a Roman prefect under Diocletian, 1,400; Hermes, a prefect in the reign of Trajan, 1,250; Pope St. Gregory, and many of the clergy at Hippo, under the rule of St. Augustine, and great numbers of private individuals, freed their slaves as an act of piety. It became customary to do so on occasions of national or personal thanksgiving, on recovery from sickness, on the birth of a child, at the hour of death, and above all, in testamentary bequests. Numerous charters and epitaphs still record the gift of liberty to slaves throughout the middle ages. In the thirteenth century, when there were no slaves to emancipate in France, it was usual in many churches to release caged pigeons on the ecclesiastical festivals, in memory of the ancient charity, and that prisoners might still be freed in the name of Christ.

Closely connected with the influence of the Church in destroying hereditary slavery, was its influence in redeeming captives from servitude. In no other form of charity was its beneficial character more continually and more splendidly displayed. During the long and dreary trials of the barbarian invasions, when the whole structure of society was dislocated, when vast districts and mighty cities were in a few months almost depopulated, and when the flower of the youth of Italy were mowed down by the sword or carried away into captivity, the bishops never desisted from their efforts to alleviate the sufferings of the prisoners. St. Ambrose, disregarding the outcries of the Arians, who denounced his act as atrocious sacrilege, sold the rich church ornaments of Milan to rescue some captives who had fallen into the hands of the Goths, and this practice—which was afterward formally sanctioned by St. Gregory the Great—became speedily general.

When the Roman army had captured, but refused to support, seven thousand Persian prisoners, Acacius, Bishop of Amida, undeterred by the bitter hostility of the Persians to Christianity, sold all the rich church ornaments of his diocese, rescued the unbelieving prisoners, and sent them back unharmed to their king. During the horrors of the Vandal invasion, Deogratias, Bishop of Carthage, took a similar step to ransom the Roman prisoners. St. Augustine, St. Gregory the Great, St. Cæsarius of Arles, St. Exuperius of Toulouse, St. Hilary, St. Remi, all melted down or sold their church vases to free prisoners. St. Cyprian sent a large sum for the same purpose to the Bishop of Nicomedia. St. Epiphanius and St. Avitus, in conjunction with a rich Gaulish lady named Syagria, are said to have rescued thousands. St. Eloi devoted to this object his entire fortune. St. Paulinus of Nola displayed a similar generosity. When, long afterward, the Mohammedan conquests in a measure reproduced the calamities of the barbarian invasions, the same unwearied charity was displayed. The Trinitarian monks, founded by John of Matha, in the twelfth century, were devoted to the release of Christian captives, and another society was founded with the same object by Peter Nolasco, in the following century.

WILLIAM EDWARD HARTPOLE LECKY,
History of European Morals.

THE AGES OF FAITH.

Those were brilliant and glorious times, when Europe formed one Christian country, when one Christendom inhabited this civilized portion of the globe; and one common interest bound together the most remote provinces of this widely-extended spiritual empire. Without great secular possessions, one head guided and united the great political powers. A numerous corporation, to which every one had access, stood in subordination to this head, and executed his mandates, and zealously strove to consolidate his power. Every member of this order was universally respected.

A filial confidence attached men to their instructions. How serenely could each one perform his daily task, when by these holy men a secure futurity was prepared for him, and every transgression was forgiven, and every dark passage of life was blotted out and effaced. They were the experienced pilots on the great unknown sea, under whose guidance we might safely disregard all storms, and confidently expect a secure landing on the coast of our true country.

The most savage, impetuous passions were compelled to bend with awe and submission to their words. Peace went out from them. They preached nothing but love for the holy marvellous Virgin of Christianity, who, endowed with heavenly power, was prepared to rescue every believer from the most fearful dangers. They spoke of long-departed men of God, who, by their attachment and fidelity to that blessed mother and her divine child, had withstood the temptations of the world, had attained unto heavenly honors, and were now become tutelary and beneficent powers to their brethren on earth, willing helpers in their wants, intercessors for human frailty, and efficacious friends to humanity at the throne of God. With what serenity of mind did men leave the beautiful assemblies in those mysterious churches, which were adorned with heart-stirring pictures, filled with the sweetest odors, and enlivened by a holy and exalting music. In them were gratefully preserved, in costly vessels, the sacred relics of those venerable servants of God. And in these churches, too, glorious signs and miracles attested as well the efficacious beneficence of these happy saints, as the Divine goodness and omnipotence. In the same way as tender souls preserve locks of hair, or autographs of their departed loves, and nourish thereby the sweet flame of affection, down to the reuniting hour of death; so men then gathered with pious assiduity whatever belonged to these holy souls, and every one esteemed himself happy, who could possess, or even touch, such consoling relics. Here and there the grace of heaven lighted down on some favored image or tombstone. Thither men flocked from all countries to proffer their fair donations, and brought back in return those celestial gifts—peace of mind, and health of body.

This powerful but pacific society zealously sought to make all men participators in its beautiful faith, and sent forth its missionaries to announce everywhere the gospel of life, and make the kingdom of heaven the only kingdom in this world.

At the Court of the Head of the Church, the most prudent and most venerable men in Europe were assembled. The destroyed Jerusalem had avenged herself, and Rome had become Jerusalem —the holy abode of God's government on earth. Princes submitted their disputes to the arbitration of the common Father of Christendom, willingly laid down at his feet their crowns and their regal pomp, and esteemed it a glory to become members of the great clerical fraternity, and pass the evening of their lives in divine contemplation within

THE TRUTH AND BEAUTY OF CATHOLICITY. 51

the walls of a cloister. How very beneficial, how well adapted to the exigencies of human nature, were these religious institutions, is proved by the vigorous expansion of all human energies—by the harmonious development of all moral and intellectual faculties, which they promoted—by the prodigious height which individuals attained to in every department of art and science, and by the universally prosperous condition of trade, whether in intellectual or material merchandise, throughout the whole extent of Europe, and even to the remotest India.

JOHN VON MÜLLER,
Travels of the Popes.

THE CRUSADES.

A MIGHTY tempest of elevating, purifying emotions swept over Christendom. It is not easy for those who have never known, to understand what it must be for an age receptive of noble impressions to have a purpose and aim set before it, which claim all its energies, meet all its peculiar conditions, while, at the same time, lifting it above the commonplace and the mean, they are far loftier than any which men's minds have hitherto entertained. Such a purpose and aim was the Crusades, during well-nigh two centuries, for Europe; and the answer which Christian Europe made to the appeal is a signal testimony of the preparedness of the Middle Ages for noble thoughts and noble deeds.

To the high thoughts which they kindled in so many hearts, to the religious consecration which they gave to the bearing of arms, we are indebted for some of the fairest aspects of chivalry, as it lives on a potent and elevating tradition to the present day. Thus to them we owe the stately courtesies of gallant foes able to understand and to respect one another, with much else which has lifted up modern warfare into something better than a mere mutual butchery, even into a school of honor in which some of the gentlest and noblest men have been trained. The "Happy Warrior" of Wordsworth could never have been written, for such an ideal of the soldier could never have been conceived except for them.

ARCHBISHOP TRENCH,
Lectures on Mediæval Church History.

CHIVALRY.

The same spirit of enterprise which had prompted so many gentlemen to take arms in defence of the oppressed pilgrims of Palestine, incited others to declare themselves the patrons and avengers of injured innocence at home. When the final reduction of the Holy Land under the dominion of infidels put an end to these foreign expeditions, the latter was the only employment left for the activity and courage of adventurers. To check the insolence of overgrown oppressors; to rescue the helpless from captivity; to protect or to avenge women, orphans, and ecclesiastics, who could not bear arms in their own defence; to redress wrongs and remove grievances: were deemed acts of the highest prowess and merit. Valor, humanity, courtesy, justice, honor, were the characteristic qualities of chivalry. Men were trained to knighthood by a long previous discipline; they were admitted into the Order by solemnities no less devout than pompous; every person of noble birth courted that honor; it was deemed a distinction superior to royalty; and monarchs were proud to receive it from the hands of private gentlemen.

The singular institution, in which valor, gallantry, and religion were so strangely blended, was wonderfully adapted to the taste and genius of martial nobles: and its effects were soon visible in their manners. War was carried on with less ferocity when humanity came to be deemed the ornament of knighthood no less than courage. More gentle and polished manners were introduced when courtesy was recommended as the most amiable of knightly virtues. Violence and oppression decreased when it was reckoned meritorious to check and to punish them. A scrupulous adherence to truth, with the most religious attention to fulfil every engagement, became the distinguishing characteristic of a gentleman; because chivalry was regarded as the school of honor, and inculcated the most delicate sensibility with respect to these points. The admiration of those qualities, together with the high distinctions and prerogatives conferred on knighthood in every part of Europe, inspired persons of noble birth on some occasions with a species of military fanaticism, and led them to extravagant enterprises. But they deeply imprinted on their minds the principles of generosity and honor. These were strengthened by everything that can affect the senses or touch the heart. The wild exploits of those romantic knights who sallied forth in quest of adventures are well known. The political and permanent effects of the spirit of chivalry have been less observed. Perhaps the humanity which accompanies all the operations of war, the refinements of gallantry, and the point of honor—the three chief circumstances which distinguish modern from ancient manners—may be ascribed in a great measure to this institution, which has appeared whimsical to superficial observers, but by its effects has proved of great benefit to mankind. The sentiments which chivalry inspired had a wonderful influence on manners and conduct during the twelfth, thirteenth, fourteenth, and fifteenth centuries. They were so deeply rooted, that they continued to operate after the vigor and reputation of the institution itself began to decline.

WILLIAM ROBERTSON,
History of the Reign of the Emperor Charles V.

THE SACRED STRUCTURES OF THE MIDDLE AGES.

As we advance into the Middle Ages, we observe the Christian idea unfolding itself in art of imposing majesty and of exceeding beauty. First, naturally in architecture. The architecture which ultimately prevailed in the sacred buildings of Western Europe was that which we call the Gothic. I enter into no discussion on its name, its origin, its varieties, and its transitions. The distinctive spirit which pervades all its forms, is what we have to consider. That, I would say, was the spirit of mystery and of aspiration. A Gothic cathedral seemed an epitome of creation. In its vastness it was a sacramental image of the universe; in its diversity it resembled nature, and in its unity it suggested God. But it suggested man too. It was the work of man's hands, shaping the solemn visions of his soul into embodied adoration. It was, therefore, the grandest symbol of union between the divine and human which imagination ever conceived, which art ever moulded; and it was in being symbolic of such union, that it had its Christian peculiarity. The mould of its structure was a perpetual commemoration of Christ's sufferings, and a sublime publication of His glory. Its ground plan in the figure of a cross was emblematic of Calvary. Its pinnacles, which tapered through the clouds and vanished into light, pointed to those heavens to which the Crucified had ascended. Here is the mystery of death and sorrow. And that mystery is intensified in the sufferings of Christ; hence is the aspiration of life and hope, as it is exalted in the victory of Christ.

In yet other ways mystery and aspiration are suggested in the sacred structures of Gothic architecture. I particularly refer to structures of ancient and majestic greatness. The mere bulk of one of those seems at the same time to overpower the mind, and yet lift it up to heaven. The mere personal presence of a human being seems lost in its mighty space; but while the body is dwarfed, the soul is magnified. As we look and wonder, the thought ever comes that man it was who conceived, consolidated, upreared those monuments of immensity; and the spirit of his immortal being seems to throb in every stone. Here, then, is the mystery of man in his lowliness and his grandeur, in his dust and dignity, touching earth and heaven—feeble as an insect, and mighty as an angel. Again, if we look through a vast cathedral in its many and dim-lit passages, our sight "in wandering mazes lost," finds no end and no beginning. Then does the thought occur to us, that, if we can not with the eye take in the windings of a church, how infinitely less can we with the mind discover all the ways of God. And while the cathedral gives us in one aspect a sense of sacred mystery, in another it gives us an impression of the boundless. Its awful spaces of naves and aisles carry our thoughts away into the amplitude of God's dominion. Its bold and lofty arches lift them up to the battlements of His throne. Was it not the soul, reaching to its sublimest strivings, which placed turret above tower and spire above turret, until the cross, over all, seemed to melt away into immortal light? I love with the strength of early love the sacred structures of the Middle Ages. Ireland, the country of my birth and of my youth, is covered with the ruins of olden sanctuaries, and in their sombre silence many an hour of my early life was passed. The rustic parish church, the pontifical cathedral, though all unroofed, were even in their desolation lovely; and more days than I can now remember they were my lonely shelter from the sun of summer noontide. Then, in such visions as under the spells of hoary Time the young imagination dreams, I have built these ruins up again—flung out the sound of matin chimes upon the morning air — awakened once more, at sunset, the vesper hymn—called from the sleeping dust prelates, priests, choristers, congregations—bade the long procession move—caused the lofty altar to blaze with light—listened to the chanted Mass—heard the swelling response of surpliced singers, and thrilled with the reverberation of the mighty organ. Even now, in hours of idle musing, the dream comes back, and the form of a pine-tree, projected on the sunshine of Maine, or of New Hampshire, or of Massachusetts, can still cheat me for a moment to believe it is the shadow of an ancient spire. Such temples, though silent, had a language of deep meaning ; silent to the ear, their language was to the soul. They told me of the power, the earnestness of faith. They told me of men in other days, strong in conviction, patient in hope, and persevering in believing work. They told me of the ancient dead. They told me how generations have come and passed away like the changes of a dream—how centuries are less than seconds on the horologe of the universe. They proclaimed eternity in the presence of the tomb, and announced immortality on the ashes of the grave.

HENRY GILES,
Lectures and Essays.

LYING CHURCH HISTORIANS.

ABSTRACTEDLY from all the influences which we have sustained in common with the rest of the civilized commonwealth, our British disparagement of the Middle Ages has been exceedingly enhanced by our grizzled ecclesiastical or church historians of the sixteenth and seventeenth centuries. These "standard works," accepted and received as Canonical Books, have tainted the nobility of our national mind. An adequate parallel to their bitterness, their shabbiness, their shirking, their habitual disregard of honor and veracity, is hardly afforded even by the so-called "Anti-Jacobin" during the revolutionary and Imperial wars. The history of Napoleon, his Generals, and the French nation, collected from these exaggerations of selfish loyalty, rabid aversion, and panic terror, would be the match of our popular and prevailing ideas concerning Hildebrand, or Anselm, or Becket, or Innocent III., or mediæval Catholicity in general, grounded upon our ancestral traditionary "Standard ecclesiastical authorities," such as Burnet's *Reformation*, or Fox's *Book of Martyrs*.

The scheme and intent of mediæval Catholicity was to render Faith the all-actuating and all-controlling vitality. So far as the system extended, it had the effect of connecting every social element with Christianity. And Christianity being thus wrought up into the mediæval system, every mediæval institution, character, or mode of thought afforded the means or vehicle for the vilification of Christianity. Never do these writers, or their school, whether in France or in Great Britain, Voltaire or Mably, Hume, Robertson, or Henry, treat the Clergy or the Church with fairness; not even with common honesty. If historical notoriety enforces the allowance of any merit to a Priest, the effect of this extorted acknowledgment is destroyed by a clever insinuation, or a coarse innuendo. Consult, for example, Hume when compelled to notice the Archbishop Hubert's exertions in procuring the concession of the Magna Charta; and Henry, narrating the communications which passed between Gregory the Great and Saint Austin.

Sir Francis Palgrave,
History of Normandy and England.

THE STUDIOUS MONKS OF THE MIDDLE AGES.

MONACHISM in art, taken in a large sense, is historically interesting, as the expression of a most important era of human culture. We are outliving the gross prejudices which once represented the life of the cloister as being from first to last a life of laziness and imposture; we know that, but for the monks, the light of liberty, and literature and science had been forever extinguished; and for six centuries there existed for the thoughtful, the gentle, the inquiring, the devout spirit, no peace, no security, no home but the cloister. There, learning trimmed her lamp; there, contemplation plumed her wings; there, the traditions of art preserved from age to age by lonely, studious men, kept alive in form and color the idea of a beauty beyond that of earth—of a might beyond that of the spear and the shield—of a divine sympathy with suffering humanity. To this we may add another and a stronger claim to our respect and moral sympathies. The protection and the better education given to women in these early communities; the venerable and distinguished rank assigned to them, when as governesses of their order, they became in a manner dignitaries of the Church; the introduction of their beautiful and saintly effigies, clothed with all the insignia of sanctity and authority into the decoration of places of worship and books of devotion, did more, perhaps, for the general cause of womanhood than all the boasted institutions of chivalry.

Mrs. Jameson,
Legends of the Monastic Orders.

THE GREAT CATHOLIC ITALIAN REPUBLICS.

During the gloomy and disastrous centuries which followed the downfall of the Roman Empire, Italy had preserved, in a far greater extent than any other part of Western Europe, the traces of ancient civilization. The night which descended upon her was the night of an Arctic summer—the dawn began to reappear before the last reflection of the preceding sunset had faded from the horizon. It was in the time of the French Merovingians, and of the Saxon Heptarchy, that ignorance and ferocity seem to have done their worst. Yet even then the Neapolitan provinces, recognizing the authority of the Eastern Empire, preserved something of Eastern knowledge and refinement. Rome, protected by the sacred character of its Pontiffs, enjoyed at least comparative security and repose. Even in those regions where the sanguinary Lombards had fixed their monarchy, there was incomparably more of wealth, of information, of physical comfort, and of social order, than could be found in Gaul, Britain, or Germany.

That which most distinguished Italy from the neighboring countries was the importance which the population of the towns, from a very early period, began to acquire. Some cities, founded in wild and remote situations, by fugitives who had escaped from the rage of the barbarians, preserved their freedom by their obscurity till they became able to preserve it by their power. Others seemed to have retained, under all the changing dynasties of invaders, under Odoacer and Theodoric, Narses and Alboin, the municipal institutions which had been conferred on them by the liberal policy of the Great Republic. In provinces which the central government was too feeble either to protect or to oppress, these institutions first acquired stability and vigor. The citizens, defended by their walls, and governed by their own magistrates and their own by-laws, enjoyed a considerable share of republican independence. Thus a strong democratic spirit was called into action. The generous policy of Otho encouraged it. In the twelfth century it attained its full vigor, and, after a long and doubtful conflict, it triumphed over the abilities and courage of the Swabian Princes.

This liberty revisited Italy; and with liberty

came commerce and empire, science and taste, all the comforts and all the ornaments of life. The Crusades brought the rising commonwealth of the Adriatic and Tyrrhene seas a large increase of wealth, dominion, and knowledge. Their moral and their geographical position enabled them to profit alike by the barbarism of the West and the civilization of the East. Their ships covered every sea. Their factories rose on every shore. Their money-changers set their tables in every city. Manufactures flourished. Banks were established. The operations of the commercial machine were facilitated by many useful and beautiful inventions. We doubt whether any country of Europe has at the present time reached so high a point of wealth and civilization as some parts of Italy had attained four hundred years ago. Historians rarely descend to those details from which alone the real state of a community can be collected. Hence posterity is too often deceived by the vague hyperboles of poets and rhetoricians, who mistake the splendors of a court for the happiness of a people. Fortunately John Villani has given us an ample and precise account of the state of Florence in the earlier part of the fourteenth century. The revenue of the republic amounted to three hundred thousand florins—a sum which, allowing for the depreciation of the precious metals, was at least equivalent to six hundred thousand pounds sterling; a larger sum than England and Ireland, two centuries ago, yielded annually to Elizabeth—a larger sum than, according to any computation which we have seen, the Grand Duke of Tuscany now derives from a territory of much greater extent. The manufacture of wool alone employed two hundred factories and thirty thousand workmen. The cloth annually produced sold, at an average, for twelve hundred thousand florins; a sum fairly equal, in exchangeable value, to two millions and a half of our money.* Four hundred thousand florins were annually coined. Eighty banks conducted the commercial operations, not of Florence only, but of all Europe. The transactions of these establishments were sometimes of a magnitude which may surprise even the contemporaries of the Barings and the Rothschilds. Two houses advanced to Edward the Third of England upwards of three hundred thousand marks, at a time when the mark contained more silver than fifty shillings of the present day, and when the value of silver was more than quadruple of what it now is. The progress of elegant literature and

---

* Twelve and a half million dollars.

of the fine-arts was proportioned to that of the public prosperity. Under the despotic successors of Augustus all the fields of the intellect had been turned into arid wastes, still marked out by formal boundaries, still retaining the traces of old cultivation, but yielding neither flowers nor fruit. The deluge of barbarism came. It swept away all the landmarks. It obliterated all the signs of former tillage. But it fertilized while it devastated. When it receded, the wilderness was as the garden of God, rejoicing on every side, laughing, clapping its hands, pouring forth in spontaneous abundance everything brilliant, or fragrant, or nourishing. A new language, characterized by simple sweetness and simple energy, had attained its perfection. No tongue ever furnished more gorgeous and vivid tints to poetry; nor was it long before a poet appeared who knew how to employ them. Early in the fourteenth century came forth the "Divine Comedy," beyond comparison the greatest work of imagination which had appeared since the poems of Homer. The following generation produced, indeed, no second Dante; but it was eminently distinguished by general intellectual activity.

From this time the admiration of learning and genius became almost an idolatry among the people of Italy. Kings and republics, cardinals and doges, vied with each other in honoring and flattering Petrarch. Embassies from rival States solicited the honor of his instructions. His coronation agitated the court of Naples and the people of Rome as much as the most important political transactions could have done. To collect books and antiques, to found professorships, to patronize men of learning, became almost universal fashions among the great. The spirit of literary research allied itself to that of commercial enterprise. Every place to which the merchant princes of Florence extended their gigantic traffic, from the bazaars of the Tigris to the monasteries of the Clyde, was ransacked for medals and manuscripts. Architecture, painting, and sculpture were munificently encouraged. Indeed it would be difficult to name an Italian of eminence during the period of which we speak, who, whatever may have been his general character, did not at least affect a love of letters and of the arts. Knowledge and public prosperity continued to advance together. Both attained their meridian in the age of Lorenzo the Magnificent.

The Roman Pontiffs exhibited in their own persons all the austerity of the early anchorites of Syria. Paul IV. brought to the Papal throne the same fervent zeal which had carried him into the

Theatine convent. Pius V., under his gorgeous vestments, wore day and night the hair shirt of a simple friar; walked barefoot in the streets at the head of processions; found, even in the midst of his most pressing avocations, time for private prayer; often regretted that the public duties of his station were unfavorable to growth in holiness; and edified his flock by innumerable instances of humility, charity, and forgiveness of personal injuries; while, at the same time, he upheld the authority of his See, and the unadulterated doctrines of his Church with all the vehemence of Hildebrand. Gregory XIII. exerted himself to imitate Pius in the severe virtues of his sacred profession.

It is delightful to turn to the opulent and enlightened States of Italy—to the vast and magnificent cities, the ports, the arsenals, the villas, the museums, the libraries, the marts filled with every article of comfort and luxury, the manufactories swarming with artisans, the Appenines covered with rich cultivation up to their very summits, the Po wafting the harvests of Lombardy to the granaries of Venice, and carrying back the silks of Bengal and the furs of Siberia to the palaces of Milan. With peculiar pleasure, every cultivated mind must repose on the fair, the happy, the glorious Florence, on the halls which rung with the mirth of Pulci, the cell where twinkled the midnight lamp of Politian, the statues on which the young eye of Michael Angelo glared with the frenzy of a kindred inspiration.

LORD MACAULAY,
Critical and Miscellaneous Essays.

THE DEBT OF ENGLISH TO ITALIAN LITERATURE.

To the Englishman one of the chief interests of the study of Italian literature is derived from the fact that between England and Italy an almost uninterrupted current of intellectual intercourse had been maintained throughout the last five centuries. Italy has formed the dreamland of the English fancy, inspiring poets with their most delightful thoughts, supplying them with subjects, and implanting in their minds that sentiment of Southern beauty which, engrafted on our less passionately imaginative Northern nature, has borne rich fruit in the works of Chaucer, Spencer, Marlowe, Shakespeare, Milton, and the poets of this century.

It is not strange that Italy should thus in matters of culture have been the guide and mistress of England. Italy, of all the European nations, was the first to produce high art and literature in the dawn of modern civilization. Italy was the first to display refinement in domestic life, polish of manners, civilities of intercourse. In Italy the commerce of courts first developed a society of men and women educated by the same traditions of humanistic culture. In Italy the principles of government were first discussed and reduced to theory. In Italy the zeal for the classics took its origin; and scholarship, to which we owe our mental training, was at first the possession of none almost but Italians. It therefore followed that during the age of Renaissance any man of taste or genius who desired to share the newly discovered privileges of learning had to seek Italy. Every one who wished to be initiated into the secrets of science or philosophy had to converse with Italians in person or through their books. Every one who was eager to polish his native language, and to render it the proper vehicle of poetic thought, had to consult the masterpieces of Italian literature. To Italians the courtier, the diplomatist, the artist, the student of state-craft and military tactics, the political theorist, the merchant, the man of laws, the man of arms, and the churchman turned for precedents and precepts. The nations of the North, still torpid and somnolent in their semi-barbarism, needed the magnetic touch of Italy before they could awake to intellectual life. Nor was this all. Long before the thirst for culture possessed the English mind, Italy had appropriated and assimilated all that Latin literature contained of strong or splendid to arouse the thought and fancy of the modern world; Greek, too, was rapidly becoming the possession of the scholars of Florence and Rome; so that English men of letters found the spirit of the ancients infused into a modern literature; models of correct and elegant composition existed for them in a language easy, harmonious, and not dissimilar in usage to their own.

The importance of this service, rendered by Italians to the rest of Europe, can not be exaggerated. By exploring, digesting, and reproducing the classics, Italy made the labor of scholarship comparatively light for the Northern nations, and extended to us the privilege of culture without the peril of losing originality in the enthusiasm for erudition. Then, in addition to this benefit of instruction, Italy gave to England a gift of pure beauty, the influence of which, in refining our national taste, harmonizing the roughness of our manners and our language, and stimulating our imagination, has been incalculable. It was not an unfrequent custom for young men of ability to study at the Italian universities, or at least to undertake a journey to the principal Italian cities. From their sojourn in that land of loveliness and intellectual life they returned with their Northern brains more powerfully stimulated. To produce, by masterpieces of the imagination, some work of style that should remain as a memento of that glorious country, and should vie on English soil with the art of Italy, was their generous ambition. Consequently the substance of the stories versified by our poets, the forms of our metres, and the cadences of our prose periods reveal a close attention to Italian originals.

JOHN ADDINGTON SYMONDS,
Sketches and Studies in Southern Europe.

LEO THE TENTH.

By no circumstance in the character of an individual is the love of literature so strongly evinced, as by the propensity for collecting together the writings of illustrious scholars, and compressing "the soul of ages past" within the narrow limits of a library. Few persons have experienced this passion in an equal degree with Leo X., and still fewer have had an equal opportunity of gratifying it. We have already seen, that in the year 1508, whilst he was yet a cardinal, he had purchased from the monks of the convent of St. Marco, at Florence, the remains of the celebrated library of his ancestors, and had transferred it to his own house in Rome. Unwilling, however, to deprive his native place of so invaluable a treasure, he had not, on his elevation to the pontificate, thought proper to unite this collection with that of the Vatican; but had entrusted it to the care of the learned Varino Camerti; intending again to remove it to Florence, as to the place of its final destination. This design, which he was prevented from executing by his death, was afterward carried into effect by the cardinal Giulio de' Medici, who before he attained the supreme dignity, had engaged the great artist, Michael Angelo Buonarotti, to erect the magnificent and spacious edifice near the church of St. Lorenzo, at Florence, where these inestimable treasures were afterward deposited; and where, with considerable additions from subsequent benefactors, they yet remain, forming an immense collection of manuscripts of the Oriental, Greek, Roman, and Italian writers, now denominated the "Bibliotheca Mediceo-Laurentiana."

The care of Leo X. in the preservation of his domestic library did not, however, prevent him from bestowing the most sedulous attention in augmenting that which was destined to the use of himself and his successors in the palace of the Vatican. This collection, begun by that excellent and learned sovereign, Nicholas V., and greatly increased by succeeding pontiffs, was already deposited in a suitable edifice, erected for that purpose by Sixtus IV., and was considered as the most extensive assemblage of literary productions in all Italy. The envoys employed by Leo X. on affairs of State in various parts of Europe, were directed to avail themselves of every opportunity of obtaining these precious remains of antiquity, and men of learning were frequently dispatched to remote and barbarous countries for the sole purpose of discovering and rescuing these works from destruction. Nor did the pontiff hesitate to render his high office subservient to the promotion of an object which he considered of the utmost importance to the interest of literature, by requiring the assistance of the other sovereigns of Christendom in giving effect to his researches. In the year 1517 he dispatched as his envoy, John Heytmers de Zonvelben, on a mission to Germany, Denmark, Sweden, and Gothland, for the sole purpose of inquiring after literary works, and particularly historical compositions. This envoy was furnished with letters from the Pope to the different sovereigns through whose dominions he had to pass, earnestly entreating them to promote the object of his visit by every means in their power. Some of these letters yet remain, and afford a decisive proof of the ardor with which Leo X. engaged in this pursuit. With a similar view he dispatched to Venice the celebrated Agostino Beazzano, whom he furnished with letters to the doge Loredano, directing him to spare no expense in the acquisition of manuscripts of the Greek authors. Efforts so persevering could not fail of success; and the Vatican library, during the pontificate of Leo X., was augmented by many valuable works, which without his vigilance and liberality would probably have been lost to the world.

After the pages which have been already devoted to enumerate the services rendered by Leo X. to all liberal studies, by the establishment of learned seminaries, by the recovery of the works of the ancient writers, and the publication of them by means of the press, by promoting the knowledge of the Greek and Latin languages, and the munificent encouragement bestowed by him on the professors of every branch of science, of literature, and of art; it would surely be as superfluous to recapitulate his claims, as it would be unjust to deny his pretensions to an eminent degree of merit.

That an astonishing proficiency in the improvement of the human intellect was made during the pontificate of Leo X. is universally allowed. That such proficiency is principally to be attributed to the exertions of that pontiff, will now perhaps be thought equally indisputable. Of the predominating influence of a powerful, and accomplished, and fortunate individual on the character and manners of the age, the history of mankind furnishes innumerable instances; and happy it is for the world, when the pursuits of such individuals, instead of being devoted, through blind ambition, to the subjugation or destruction of the human race, are directed toward those beneficent and generous ends, which amid all his avocations, *Leo The Tenth* appears to have kept continually in view.

WILLIAM ROSCOE,
Life and Pontificate of Leo X.

4*

ST. MARK'S, VENICE.

AND well may they fall back, for beyond those troops of ordered arches there rises a vision out of the earth, and all the great square seems to have opened from it in a kind of awe, that we may see it far away; a multitude of pillars and white domes, clustered into a long, low pyramid of colored light; a treasure-heap, it seems, partly of gold, and partly of opal and mother-of-pearl, hollowed beneath into five great vaulted porches, ceiled with fair mosaic, and beset with sculpture of alabaster, clear as amber and delicate as ivory; sculpture fantastic and involved, of palm leaves and lilies, and grapes and pomegranates, and birds clinging and fluttering among the branches, all twined together into an endless network of buds and plumes; and in the midst of it, the solemn forms of angels, sceptred and robed to the feet, and leaning to each other across the gates, their figures indistinct among the gleaming of the golden ground through the leaves beside them, interrupted and dim, like the morning light as it faded back among the branches of Eden, when first its gates were angel-guarded long ago. And round the walls of the porches there are set pillars of variegated stones, jasper and porphyry, and deep-green serpentine, spotted with flakes of snow, and marbles that half refuse and half yield to the sunshine, Cleopatra-like, "their bluest veins to kiss," the shadow, as it steals back from them, revealing line after line of azure undulation, as a receding tide leaves the waved sand; their capitals rich with interwoven tracery, rooted knots of herbage, and drifting leaves of acanthus and vine and mystical signs, all beginning and ending in the Cross; and above them in the broad archivolts, a continuous chain of language and of life—angels and the signs of heaven, and the labors of men, each in its appointed season upon the earth; and above these, another range of glittering pinnacles, mixed with white arches edged with scarlet flowers,—a confusion of delight, amidst which the breasts of the Greek horses are seen blazing in their breadth of golden strength, and the St. Mark's Lion lifted on a blue field covered with stars, until at last, as if in ecstasy, the crests of the arches break into a marble foam, and toss themselves into the blue sky, in flashes and wreaths of sculptured spray, as if the breakers on the Lido shore had been frost-bound before they fell, and the sea-nymphs had inlaid them with coral and amethyst.

A large atrium or portico is attached to the two sides of the church, a space which was especially reserved for unbaptized persons and new converts. It was thought right that, before their baptism, these persons should be led to contemplate the great facts of the Old Testament history; the history of the Fall of Man, the lives of the Patriarchs up to the period of the Covenant by Moses; the order of the subjects in this series being very nearly the same as in many Northern churches, but significantly closing with the Fall of the Manna, in order to mark to the catechumen the insufficiency of the Mosaic covenant for salvation,—"Our fathers did eat manna in the wilderness, and are dead,"—and to turn his thoughts to the true Bread of which that manna was the type.

Then, when after his baptism he was permitted to enter the church, over its main entrance he saw, on looking back, a mosaic of Christ enthroned, with the Virgin on one side and St. Mark on the other, in attitudes of adoration. Christ is represented as holding a book open upon his knee, on which is written: "I AM THE DOOR; BY ME IF ANY MAN ENTER IN, HE SHALL BE SAVED." On the red marble moulding which surrounds the mosaic is written: "I AM THE GATE OF LIFE; LET THOSE WHO ARE MINE ENTER BY ME." Above on the red marble fillet which forms the cornice of the west end of the church, is written, with reference to the figure of Christ below: "WHO HE WAS, AND FROM WHOM HE CAME, AND AT WHAT PRICE HE REDEEMED THEE, AND WHY HE MADE THEE, AND GAVE THEE ALL THINGS, DO THOU CONSIDER."

Now observe, this was not to be seen and read only by the catechumen when he first entered the church; every one who at any time entered, was supposed to look back and to read this writing; their daily entrance into the church was thus made a daily memorial of their first entrance into the spiritual church; and we shall find that the rest of the book which was opened for them upon its walls, continually led them in the same manner to regard the visible temple as in every part a type of the invisible Church of God.

Therefore the mosaic of the first dome, which is over the head of the spectator as soon as he has entered by the great door (that door being the type of baptism), represents the effusion of the Holy Spirit, as the first consequence and seal of the entrance into the Church of God. In the centre of the cupola is the Dove. From the central symbol of the Holy Spirit twelve streams of fire descend upon the heads of the twelve apostles, who are represented standing around the dome; and below them, between the windows which are pierced in its walls, are represented, by groups of two figures for each separate people, the various nations who heard the apostles speak at Pentecost, every man in his own tongue. Finally, on the vaults, at the four angels which support the cupola, are pictured four angels, each bearing a tablet upon the end of a rod in his hand: on each of the tablets of the first three angels is inscribed the word "Holy"; on that of the fourth is written "Lord"; and the beginning of the hymn being thus put into the mouths of the four angels, the words of it are continued around the border of the dome, uniting praise to God for the gift of the Spirit, with welcome to the redeemed soul into His Church.

"HOLY, HOLY, HOLY, LORD GOD OF THE SABAOTH:
HEAVEN AND EARTH ARE FULL OF THY GLORY.
HOSANNA IN THE HIGHEST:
BLESSED IS HE THAT COMETH IN THE NAME OF THE LORD."

After thus hearing praise rendered to God by the angels for the salvation of the newly-entered soul, it was thought fittest that the worshipper should be led to contemplate, in the most comprehensive forms possible, the past evidence and the future hopes of Christianity, as summed up in three facts without assurance of which all faith is vain ; namely, that Christ died, that He rose again, and that He ascended into heaven, there to prepare a place for His elect. On the vault between the first and second cupolas are represented the crucifixion and resurrection of Christ, with the usual series of intermediate scenes—the treason of Judas, the judgment of Pilate, the crowning with thorns, the descent into Hades, the visit of the women to the Sepulchre, and the apparition to Mary Magdalene. The second cupola itself, which is the central and principal one of the church, is entirely occupied by the subject of the Ascension. At the highest point of it Christ is represented as rising into the blue heaven, borne up by four angels, and throned upon a rainbow, the type of reconciliation. Beneath Him, the twelve apostles are seen upon the Mount of Olives, with the Madonna, and, in the midst of them, the two men in white apparel who appeared at the moment of the Ascension, above whom, as uttered by them, are inscribed the words, " Ye men of Galilee, why stand ye gazing up into heaven ? This Christ, the Son of God, as He is taken from you, shall so come, the arbiter of the earth, trusted to do judgment and justice."

Beneath the circle of the apostles, between the windows of the cupola, are represented the Christian virtues, as sequent upon the crucifixion of the flesh, and the spiritual ascension together with Christ. Beneath them, on the vaults which support the angels of the cupola, are placed the four Evangelists, because on their evidence our assurance of the facts of the ascension rests; and, finally, beneath their feet, as symbols of the sweetness and fulness of the Gospel which they declared, are represented the four rivers of Paradise, Pison, Gihon, Tigris, and Euphrates.

The third cupola, that over the altar, represents the witness of the Old Testament to Christ; showing Him enthroned in its centre, and surrounded by the patriarchs and prophets. But this dome was little seen by the people; their contemplation was intended to be chiefly drawn to that of the centre of the church, and thus the minds of the worshippers was at once fixed on the main groundwork and hope of Christianity, — "Christ is risen," and "Christ shall come." If he had time to explore the minor lateral chapels and cupolas, he would find in them the whole series of the New Testament history, the events of the Life of Christ, and the Apostolic miracles in their order, and, finally, the scenery of the Book of Revelation; but if he only entered, as often the common people do to this hour, snatching a few moments before beginning the labor of the day to offer up an ejaculatory prayer, and advanced but from the main entrance as far as the altar screen, all the splendor of the glittering nave and variegated dome, if they smote upon his heart, as they might often, in strange contrast with his reed cabin among the shallows of the lagoon, smote upon it only that they may proclaim the two great messages — "Christ is risen," and "Christ shall come." Daily, as the white cupolas rose like wreaths of sea-foam in the dawn, while the shadowy campanile and frowning palace were still withdrawn into the night, they rose with the Easter Voice of Triumph, — "Christ is risen"; and daily, as they looked down upon the tumult of the people, deepening and eddying in the wide square that opened from their feet to the sea, they uttered above them the sentence of warning,—" Christ shall come."

And this thought may surely dispose them to look with some change of temper upon the gorgeous building and wild blazonry of that shrine of St. Mark's. He now perceives that it was in the hearts of the old Venetian people far more than a place of worship. It was at once a type of the Redeemed Church of God, and a scroll for the written word of God. It was to be to them, both an image of the Bride, all glorious within, her clothing of wrought gold; and the actual Table of the Law and the Testimony, written within and without. And whether honored as the Church or as the Bible, was it not fitting that neither the gold nor the crystal should be spared in the adornment of it? that, as the symbol of the Bride, the building of the wall thereof should be of jasper, and the foundations of it garnished with all manner of precious stones; and that, as the channel of the Word, that triumphant utterance of the Psalmist should be true of it,—"I have rejoiced in the way of thy testimonies as much as in all riches." And shall we not look with changed temper down the long perspective of St. Mark's Place toward the sevenfold gates and glowing domes of its temple, when we know with what solemn purpose the shafts of it were lifted above the pavement of the populous square? Men meet there from all countries of the earth, for traffic or for pleasure; but, above the crowd swaying forever to and fro in the restlessness of avarice or thirst of delight, was seen perpetually the glory of the temple, attesting to them, whether they would hear or whether they would forbear, that there was one treasure which the merchantmen might buy without a price, and one delight better than all others, in the word and statutes of God. Not in the wantonness of wealth, not in the vain ministry to the desire of the eye or the pride of life, were those marbles hewn into transparent strength, and those arches arrayed in the colors of the iris. There is a message written in the dyes of them that once was written in blood; and a sound in the echoes of their vaults that one day shall fill the vault of heaven,—"He shall return, to do judgment and justice."

JOHN RUSKIN,
The Stones of Venice.

CHRISTIANITY THE SAVIOUR OF CIVILIZATION.

It is a remarkable fact in history that it was nothing but Christianity saved Rome from utter extinction. Had she not been the chosen home of this rising faith and new glory, the barbarians would scarcely have left one stone upon another: she would have been to us what Nineveh, Babylon, Thebes, and many other cities are, a tradition grand, yet almost beyond conception. As over the great solitudes of the sites of those mighty cities, wild beasts wander and howl by night, so it would have been with Rome when her glory fell, had not another and brighter glory settled upon her ruins. In fact, the remains of her ancient social life were never completely dispersed; and when the first dawn of the new religion appeared, and the old luminaries of pagan night receded before the rays of a brighter day, its votaries instinctively settled at Rome. Popes followed in the wake of Cæsars; the glory of the Flavian amphitheatre gave way before the new splendors of a Vatican; gladiators and games were supplanted by religious processions and masses; unable to destroy feudalism, it created chivalry; in its convents persecuted innocence always found an asylum, and against the ambition of tyrants it opposed the power of its thunders. But it was at Rome that the vicarial head of the Church had taken up his abode; toward Rome were bent periodically the footsteps of thousands of pilgrims; and from Rome as from a centre emanated all the influences which the new religion exercised over the nations who had enlisted under the cross. That every stage of her history, and more especially of her future destiny, should be intensely interesting to Europe and all the outlying colonies, the rising new worlds of European planting, is not to be wondered at, for she is the foster-mother of modern civilization. When the wolf and the jackal roamed over the very sites of our proudest cities, when offerings were made to strange gods by a Druidical priesthood, and the inhabitants of this country were but a band of painted savages, Rome was in the very zenith of civilized life. When the migration of the northern hordes toward the South, extinguished the just kindling torch of civilization, and overwhelmed in its dark flood all the evidences of refinement in Europe, Rome suffered last and least;

in her temples were gathered, as in a sanctuary, learning, science, and art; there was kept burning, dimly enough, yet still cherished with tender care, the trembling lamp of genius, until the better time should come when it might be reproduced and its genial rays diffused; and when the time did come, and the nations awoke from a long slumber to a new life, it was from Rome and Roman traditions that the new order of things drew its laws, its language, and its faith. In nearly every part of Europe traces are to be found of Roman life; it has permeated through the very aspect of the country, the blood of the races, their thought, their laws, their idiom, so that civilization seems to have been concentrated into a focus at Rome, and thence radiated over all the world. It is from the fountains of her lore that all modern law has been derived, and she may well be called the lawgiver of Europe.

O'DELL TRAVERS HILL,
English Monasticism: Its Rise and Influence.

HOLY WEEK IN ROME.

The service opens by a portion of the Lamentations of Jeremiah sung by the choristers, after which the Pope recites the pater-noster in a low voice; then being seated on the throne, and crowned with the mitre, the theme is continued, sung loud and sweet by the first soprano, in a tone so long sustained, so high, so pure, so silvery and so mellifluous, as to produce the most exquisite effect, in contrast with the deep choruses, answering in rich harmony at the conclusion of every strophe; and again the lamenting voice is heard, tender and pathetic, repeating one sweet prolonged tone, sounding clear and high in the distance, till brought down again by the chorus. It is as if a being of another world were heard lamenting over a ruined city, with the responses of a dejected people, and forms a grand and mournful preparation for the Miserere.

The last light being extinguished, the chorus, in hurried sounds, proclaims that our Saviour is betrayed; then, for a moment, as a symbol of the darkness in which the moral world is left, the deepest obscurity prevails; at the words "*Christus est mortuus*," the Pope, the whole body of clergy and the people knelt, and all was silent, when the solemn pause was broken by the commencing of the Miserere, in low, rich, exquisite strains, rising softly on the ear, and gently swelling into powerful sounds of seraphic harmony.

The effect produced by this music is finer and greater than that of any admired art; no painting, statue, or poem, no imagination of man, can equal its wonderful power on the mind. The silent solemnity of the scene, the touching import of the words, "Take pity on me, O God," passes to the inmost soul, with a thrill of the deepest sensation, unconsciously moistening the eye, and paling the cheek. The music is composed of two choruses of four voices; the strains begin low and solemn, rising gradually to the clear tones of the first soprano, which at times are heard alone; at the conclusion of the verse, the second chorus joins, and then by degrees the voices fade and die away. The soft and almost imperceptible accumulation of sound, swelling in mournful tones of rich harmony, into powerful effect, and then receding, as if in the distant sky, like the lamenting song of angels and spirits, conveys, beyond all conception to those who have heard it, the idea of darkness, of desolation, and of the dreary solitude of the tomb. A solemn silence ensues, and not a breath is heard, while the inaudible prayer of the kneeling Pope continues. When he rises, slight sounds are heard, by degrees breaking on the stillness, which has a pleasing effect, restoring, as it were, the rapt mind to the existence and feelings of the present life. The effect of those slow, prolonged, varied, and truly heavenly strains will not easily pass from the memory.

The service on Easter Sunday is grand and most imposing, insensibly raising the feelings to a true accord with the scene. There under the superb dome built by Michael Angelo, the solemn mass is sung in deep silence, amidst the assembly of priests and princes. The morning was serene and lovely, the sun shone clear and bright through the edifice, giving to its imposing dimensions, and noble architecture, a more than usual splendor. At the end of the great cross, terminating in the grand altar, the Pope is seated, supported on either side by the cardinals and bishops, with their attendant priests. The marble balustrade encircling the altar, is lined within by the guards, and spreading out at the further ends, galleries are extended, destined for royal visitors, princes, and ambassadors, on the one hand, and on the other for strangers of all classes. The vast height of the dome, rising superbly overhead; the magnificent lower altar of fine bronze, relieved by a beautiful railing of white marble, and lighted by lamps which burn continually; the fine effect produced by the gigantic statues lessening in the distant vista, as the eye traverses along the immense space of this noble structure, form a coup d'œil very striking, and singularly fine. At the conclusion of the service, the Pope advancing to kneel at the lower altar, recites the pater-noster, and then proceeded from the church to the balcony in front of St. Peter's, to perform the benediction. The sacred character of this ceremony receives an additional dignity from the fine and commanding aspect of the surrounding scenery. The approach to St. Peter's is very grand, the space within the court immense, and the columns and colonnades most magnificent; while the noble and high buildings of the Vatican are seen towering on the right hand in a broad style of irregular but fine architecture. The long, flat steps, ascending to the wide-spreading gates of the church, run the whole length of the edifice, producing, from their vast extent one of its most striking features; while over the low, square-roofed, and not unpicturesque buildings, in front of St. Peter's, the eye wanders abroad to the distant prospect, to the blue hills, and far-seen glaciers,—the effect being altogether solemn, and fine beyond imagination.

The ample steps of St. Peter's were peopled by thousands of the peasantry, who crowded from every distant part of the Campagna; those of the higher classes, forming rich and showy groups, were seen on each side, covering the fine, flat-roofed colonnades. Below, on the level ground, the whole body of the Papal guards was drawn out in array. Beyond, stood like a deep dark phalanx, the carriages and innumerable equipages, the vivid tints of the brilliant midday sun giving every variety of color, by deepened shade or added brightness. In the central balcony of the church, awaiting the approach of the Pope, were seated the cardinals and prelates, overlooking the numbers in the space below. Expectation prevailed throughout, till his Holiness approached, when in a moment all was still; every eye turned from the sunny scene to the dark front of St. Peter's, lying deep in the shade, from its massive columns; not a breath, not a sound reached the ear. The deep silence that reigned amid such a concourse was most impressive; the whole scene excited feelings of the deepest interest, as we contemplated the pale, benign, mild countenance and venerable aspect of him who was now bending forward with anxious zeal to bless the surrounding multitude. The deep-toned bell of St. Peter's announced the conclusion of the benediction—solemn sounds, which were instantly answered by the loud-pealing cannon of Castle St. Angelo, as likewise by the voices of the musicians, and the clamorous rejoicings of the people.

When night approaches, and the dome of this magnificent temple is hung with lights, all the grandeur of its architecture is displayed. Each frieze and cornice, arch, and gate, and pillar, is enriched with lines of splendid fires, and every steeple, tower, and bulky dome, glittering with light, seems to hang in a firmament of its own, high in the clear dark sky. The long sweeping colonnades form, as it were, a golden circle, enclosing the dark mass of people below, filling the spacious basin of the court, while the waters of the superb fountains, sparkling in the partial gleams of light, are heard dashing amid the hum and murmur of the busy throng; when suddenly, in an instant, the form is changed, the red distinct stars are involved in one blaze of splendid flame, as if the vast machine were moved by the hand of some master spirit.

JOHN BELL,
Observations on Italy.

ALFRED THE GREAT.

ALFRED is a singular instance of a prince, who has become a hero of romance, who, as such, has had countless exploits and imaginary institutions attributed to him, but to whose character romance has done no more than justice, and who appears in exactly the same light in history and in fable. No other man on record has ever so thoroughly united all the virtues, both of the ruler and of the private man. In no other man on record were so many virtues disfigured by so little alloy. A scholar without ostentation, a warrior all of whose wars were fought in the defence of his country, a conqueror whose laurels were never stained by cruelty, a prince never cast down in adversity, never lifted up to insolence in the day of triumph—there is no other name in history to compare with his. With an inquiring spirit which took in the whole world, for purposes alike of scientific inquiry and of Christian benevolence, Alfred never forgot that his first duty was to his own people. He forestalled our own age in sending expeditions to explore the Northern Ocean, and in sending alms to the distant churches of India. The same union of zeal for religion and learning with the highest gifts of the warrior and the statesman is found, on a wider field of action, in Charles the Great. But even Charles can not aspire to the pure glory of Alfred. Amidst all the splendors of conquest and legislation, we can not be blind to an alloy of personal ambition. Among our later princes, the great Edward alone can bear for a moment comparison with his glorious ancestor. And, when tried by such a standard, even the great Edward fails. Even in him we do not see the same union of gifts which so seldom meet together. The times indeed were different; Edward had to tread the path of righteousness and honor in a time of far more tangled policy, and amidst temptations, not harder indeed, but far more subtle. The legislative merits of Edward are greater than those of Alfred; but this is a difference in the times rather than the men. It is perhaps, after all, in his literary aspect, that the distinctive beauty of Alfred's character shines forth most clearly. As a rule, literary kings have not been a class deserving of much honor. They have, for the most part, stepped out of their natural sphere only to display the least honorable characteristics of another calling. But it was not so with Alfred. In Alfred there is no sign of literary pedantry, ostentation, or jealousy; nothing is done for his own glory; he writes, just as he fights and legislates, with a single eye to the good of his people. He shows no signs of original genius; he is simply an editor and translator, working honestly for the improvement of the subjects whom he loved. This is really a purer fame, and one more in harmony with the other features of Alfred's character, than the highest achievements of the poet, the historian, or the philosopher. Alfred was specially happy in handing on a large share of his genius and his virtue to those who came after him. The West Saxon Kings, for nearly a century, form one of the most brilliant royal lines on record. From Aethelred the Saint to Eadgar the Peaceful, the short and wretched reign of Eadwig is the only interruption to the one continued display of valor under the guidance of wisdom. The greatness of the dynasty, obscured under the second Aethelred, flashes for a moment in the short and glorious career of the second Eadmund. It then becomes more permanently eclipsed under the rule of the Danes, Normans, and Angevin, till it shines forth once more in the first of the new race whom we can claim as English at heart, and the greatest of the West-Saxons seems to rise again to life in the Greatest of the Plantagenets.

EDWARD A. FREEMAN,
Norman Conquest.

THOMAS CROMWELL, EARL OF ESSEX.

It would have been morally impossible for a monarch so arbitrary and tyrannical as Henry the Eighth to have successfully compassed the total destruction of the monastic system in England, and the subversion of the ancient religion, unless he had first obtained the tacit co-operation of the impoverished nobility; and further secured, by the appointment of Thomas Cranmer to the Archbishopric of Canterbury, a pliant servant of the highest ecclesiastical rank, who would do his royal master's will with due subservience ; and such an unscrupulous lay-tool as Thomas Cromwell, to second and carry out the project.

When it is in the power of kings and rulers to perpetrate gross acts of injustice; when the principle that "might is right" is tolerated and approved, and when able and unscrupulous coadjutors have been found to co-operate in doing injustice, those who may have planned it, are at no great loss for pretence to justify their course of proceedings.

To turn the life-owners of estates out of their estates; to uproot and overturn institutions which had existed for eight centuries, and were deservedly valued and venerated by the English people from their childhood; to set all law, human and divine, at defiance; to make a monarch's will law, for the time being; to violate every true principle on which property rested; to rob those who had deliberately and solemnly consecrated themselves to God; to deface and destroy religious houses and sanctuaries of retirement and rest, where the worship of the Blessed Trinity had been piously rendered for centuries, needed the services of a suitable agent. This was found in Thomas Cromwell, the son of Walter Cromwell, a blacksmith, of Putney, who was born at or about the year 1490, and through whose sister who married a Welshman named Williams, another tyrant of a later age, Oliver Cromwell, claimed descent from the family at Putney.

He is said to have been first employed in the English factory at Antwerp, and was afterward engaged in the service of the Duke of Bourbon as a soldier; though some writers affirm that prior to this he had been, when a mere youth, a page or body-servant to Thomas, Lord Cardinal Wolsey; anyhow he was present when Pope Clement VII.

was made prisoner at the disastrous sack of the city of Rome in 1527; and by his intercourse with various continental people and places had obtained the usual advantages of travel and experience.

On his return to England he was again employed by Wolsey, by whom he appears to have been much esteemed for his vigor and boldness.

When, in the year 1529, that eminent prince of the Church and Prelate fell, Cromwell certainly had the courage and honesty to stand by his friend and master—the single redeeming feature in his otherwise detestable character.

This feature, attracting the attention of the king, as was reported, induced his Majesty to command Cromwell's services, which were given with such dexterous servility, unscrupulous tactics, and commanding resolution, that the road to the highest honors in the State shortly presented an unimpeded course for his ambition.

King Henry having assumed the style, title, dignity, and powers of "the only Protector and Supreme Head of the Church and Clergy of England"—and this immediately after the spirituality, in 1531, had granted him a heavy subsidy, equivalent to two million pounds of our present money,—almost immediately delegated his new and unprecedented authority to Thomas, Lord Cromwell.

This person was to exercise "all the spiritual authority belonging to the king, for the due administration of justice in all cases touching the ecclesiastical jurisdiction, and the godly reformation and redress of errors, heresies, and abuses in the said church."

Prior to this event and its immediate consequences, however, the various stages in what is commonly called the "Reformation of religion" had been taken with steady resolve and a most determined purpose by the king and his selected coadjutors. In the spring of 1532, the illustrious and high-minded Sir Thomas More resigned the Lord High Chancellorship; while about four months later, the king raised his mistress, Anne Boleyn, to the dignity of Marchioness of Pembroke. Thomas Cranmer was appointed to the Archbishopric of Canterbury, by a Papal Bull dated 21st February, 1533. In the following year the clergy were forbidden to make canons or constitutions; while none of those existing were to be enforced contrary to the king's prerogative, and all appeals to Rome were absolutely abolished. The payment of the first-fruits was also declared illegal and strictly forbidden, and that generally-recognized

Papal power of hearing appeals, which had existed since the mission of St. Augustine, first Archbishop of Canterbury, and by which local churches were visibly bound and banded together both in faith and polity, was formally set aside by Act of Parliament. The customary and reasonable confirmation of Bishops by the Primate of Christendom was abolished—persons so regarding or seeking it henceforth being subject to all the penalties of the statutes of *præmunire*. In 1534, the king's marriage with Queen Catherine of Arragon was declared invalid; she was henceforth to be styled "the Princess Dowager"; and any one found maintaining the contrary, viz., that she was the king's lawful wife, incurred the penalties of high treason, *i. e.*, hanging, drawing, and quartering.

All these steps were taken under the advice and with the active and efficient co-operation of Thomas Cromwell. But there was still much to be done. Difficulties standing in the way of robbery and reformation were considerable, but by no means insuperable. Those irons, already put in the fire, were likely, in due course, to be used largely for breaking down the spirit, independence, and power of the secular clergy. But the influence of the regulars was still very great, and this must be at once circumscribed, if not wholly stamped out, by *their* "reformation," likewise, if anything permanent was to be accomplished.

In order suitably and with reasonable tactics to commence this new step in a "godly" work, a visitation of the religious houses was determined on. This resolve appears to have been finally taken, after due consideration with the king's chief advisers, at or about the 15th of January, 1535, when his Grace formally assumed the title of "Only Supreme Head on Earth of the Church of England," which had been granted by a statute recently passed. The clergy generally had acknowledged that title, with such personal explanations and reservations as seemed lawful or expedient to them; but the religious houses were held to be the strongholds of the king's foes.

As it was impossible that one Vicar-General could properly investigate the state of these sacred and venerable institutions, Cromwell appointed several deputies to aid him practically in making the visitation. The selection of these was his own work; though their formal commissions were, of course, under the king's hand and signet. For the purpose of this visitation, the country was divided into appointed districts, and two or more of these official deputies were sent to inquire into the state of the religious houses in each. Some of the deputies were men of notoriously infamous characters; some of them had been branded, having been convicted of heinous crimes. On arriving at the gates of the houses, they appear to have demanded an immediate production of money, jewels, Church-plate and vestments; but specially of the title-deeds of their property.

To quote from an able and forcible writer as to their general doings and customary processes: "The monks and nuns, who had never dreamed of the possibility of such proceedings, who had never had any idea that Magna Charta and all the laws of the land could be set aside in a moment, and whose recluse and peaceful lives rendered them wholly unfit to cope with at once crafty and desperate villainy, fell before these ruffians as chickens fall before the kite. The report made by these villains met with no contradiction; the accused parties had no means of making a defence; there was no court for them to appear in; they dared not, even if they had the means, offer a defence or make a complaint, for they had seen the horrible consequences, the burnings, the rippings up of all those of their brethren who ventured to whisper their dissent from any dogma or decree of the Tyrant. The project was to deprive the people of their property; and yet the parties from whom the property was to be taken were to have no court in which to plead their cause, no means of obtaining a hearing, could make even no complaint but at the peril of their lives. They, and those who depended on them, were to be at once stripped of this great mass of property, without any other ground than that of reports made by men sent for the express purpose of finding a pretence for the dissolution of the monasteries, and for the king's taking to himself property that had never belonged to him or his predecessors."

In the spring of the same year, that is, in 1535, Cromwell, in order not to forget the secular clergy, and at the same time not to allow them to forget him, suggested to the king the desirability of compelling those bishops and ecclesiastical authorities who appeared at all backward in their duties to recommend the same kind of subserviency to the inferior clergy under them as they had shown to the Supreme Head and ordinary, and to his Vicar-General. By consequence official letters were dispatched to all the English Bishops, enjoining them to preach the newly-adopted Gospel of Erastianism with zeal and devotion. They were to put in the forefront of their homilies the novel title and ecclesiastical dignity of the king, now formally assumed, and to see that on all Sundays and feast-days the preachers under them did the same in plain and unmistakable terms. They were at the same time strictly enjoined to erase from the service-books of the Church every prayer, rule, and rubric in which the name of the Pope occurred, so that, as the phrase ran, the "memory of the Bishop of Rome, except to his contumely and reproach, might be extinct, suppressed, and obscured." A new form of bidding the beads before sermons was also enjoined by Cromwell, the clergy being required to pray "for the king, only Supreme Head of the Catholic Church of England, and for Queen Anne." It was also required, among other precise directions, that every preacher should preach once on the usurped power of the Bishop of Rome, and refrain from siding with his Grace's wife, Queen Catherine; that collects for the king and for the lady known as "Queen Anne" should be used at all High Masses in every Cathedral and parish church, as well as in the churches of all the religious houses throughout the land; while, as a still more practical stir-up of their flagging energies, the clergy were furthermore furnished with a kind of outline of a special sermon upon the history of the king's divorce case, in which ready-made arguments and royal reasons were abundantly provided to uphold the policy and morals of the Supreme Head, all furthermore—perhaps with a dash of irony—were expressly required "to preach only the Scripture and the pure word of Christ."

Within five weeks most of the prelates had sent in their replies. But some few of them, and many of the inferior clergy, were not quite so obedient and subservient to the royal Defender of the Faith as they perhaps might have been. A few were silent and sullen, as was reported to Cromwell by his active and inquisitorial agents; others were outspoken and plain-spoken in opposition, both to the Supreme Head and his Vicar-General. So, within ten days of the dispatch of the order regulating the preaching of the clergy, a circular letter was sent to all the Justices of the Peace throughout the country, commanding them to make immediate and diligent search, and insist that the Bishops did their duty as required without diminution or omission. This took place on the 9th of June. To place the Bishops and clergy under the town and country magistrates, though perhaps something of a novelty in Church government, was quite worthy of a lay Vicar-General and the king's other advisers. If default or dissimulation were found, it was to be reported without delay to the king's council; and if this were not done promptly and efficiently by the Justices of the Peace—if, for example, they should halt or stumble, they were to be assured that the king, like a prince of justice, would so severely punish them for their inexcusable apathy that all the world beside would take warning and beware, contrary to their due allegiance, how they disobeyed the lawful commandment of their Sovereign Lord and Prince in such things. On the other hand, if they were true and faithful in the execution of their duty, it was authoritatively and right royally asserted that "they should thus advance the honor of God Almighty," and, what was obviously of more importance, "the imperial dignity of their High and Mighty Sovereign Lord."

Three priors of three Carthusian Monasteries were foremost in boldly resisting the claim of the spiritual supremacy made by the king when the oath was legalized. One was John Houghton, prior of London; another Robert Lawrence, prior of Beauvalle; and the third Augustine Webster, prior of Axholme. The charge against them was that they had asserted that "the king, our Sovereign Lord, is not Supreme Head on Earth of the Church of England." This was reported generally, and, reaching the ears of King Henry, made him not simply angry, but furious.

On hearing this, the three priors, in their simplicity, sought an interview with Cromwell, asking his aid, as Vicar-General, in obtaining some mitigation of the terms of the oath. In reply to this request he at once ordered them to the Tower. After they had been there a week, the Vicar-General arrived to tender the oath anew, to urge upon them an immediate acceptance of the new royal supremacy, and a formal renunciation of the Pope's ancient and hitherto recognized authority.

They promised to accept everything which was in harmony with, and permitted by the law of God.

"I will have no exceptions," replied the Vicar-General. "It must be done whether the law of God allows it or not."

"But the Church Universal teaches quite a contrary doctrine," replied the spokesman of the priors.

"What care I for the Church Universal?" was Cromwell's retort. "Will you take the oath or not?"

They declined, quietly and firmly, to do so, and were consequently put on their trial for high treason.

This took place at Westminster, on the 29th of April, 1535, when they were speedily convicted, drawn to the gallows, hanged, cut down alive, dismembered, and then quartered.

The death of the holy and faithful man, Cardinal John Fisher, Bishop of Rochester, and that of the upright and noble Sir Thomas More, some time Lord Chancellor, two men most favored for learning, integrity, and true religion in England, gave a shock to the people which was both acute and severe. The zeal on behalf of, and personal devotion to the king shown by Fisher had been great. He nobly rebuked the king, both as regards religion and morals. The absurd and ridiculous supremacy recently invented he utterly condemned; to the divorce of Queen Katherine he gave the most uncompromising resistance, in return for which, after fifteen months' imprisonment, where he was treated like a common felon, buried in filth, and almost destitute of food and clothing, he perished nobly at the block.

As regards Sir Thomas More, after trial had, he was condemned as a traitor and a rebel. On the 6th of July he suffered death. When on the scaffold, after prayer, he called the people to witness that he died in the Catholic faith, and pardoned the executioner, there rose a chilling shudder through the crowd (though many of the myrmidons of Cromwell were there), which represented the general feeling of alarm, sorrow, and shame which the people of England experienced when they heard of the tragedy. Foreign nations, likewise, were utterly horrified at the frightful brutalities of the royal monster.

Cromwell's early experience of, and intercourse with, the lower classes of the continent with whom he had mixed freely during his sojourn there, as well as his observance of the ruder, but dexterous, tactics of the first foreign reformers, no doubt led him to take several leaves out of their books in his work of reformation. He had noticed that the popular ballad-singers of foreign countries exercised a vast influence over the people, more especially in periods of religious and political excitement; and that certain irreligious innovators there, by the use of lewd parodies, jocose verses, and ribald ballads, sung in street, tavern, and ale-house, had succeeded in efficiently weakening the old faith, which they had by these means brought into disrepute, and had so ridiculed sacred practices which the Church of God had enjoined and Christians had obediently and profitably observed for centuries, that Cromwell resolved to adopt the use of such literature and co-operators for the purpose of "reform" in England.

This man, then, was the great patron of ribaldry,

and the protector of the ribald, of the low jester, the filthy ballad-monger, the ale-house singers and hypocritical mockers in feasts; in short, in an indirect but yet efficient mode, of all the blasphemous mocking and scoffing which disgraced the Protestant party at the time of the Reformation. "It is of great consequence," wrote the late Dr. Maitland, "in our view of the times, to consider that the vile publications, of which too many remain, while most have rotted, and the profane pranks which were performed were not the outbreak of low, ignorant artisans, a rabble of hungry dogs, such as is sure to run after a party in spite even of sticks and stones bestowed by those whom they follow and disgrace. It was the result of design and policy, earnestly and elaborately pursued by the man possessing, for all such purposes, the highest place and power in the land."

At the same time the ungodly and the frivolous in provincial cities and country towns were systematically enlisted on the side of the innovators. In many places where interest in the old and popular miracle plays had been weakened or lost, by which the many had been taught by the eye as well as by the ear, Cromwell's perambulating allies became active in supplying a new kind of public entertainment more in harmony with the current depraved taste. Satire of the religious orders, a most popular subject for discussion, became common, and might be heard in ordinary conversation on all sides. Consequently, when plays, interludes, and farces, caricaturing the monks and religion, were performed in churchyards and sometimes even in churches by strolling players, equipped at head-quarters, the dialogues of which performances were often gross and the phrases of double-meaning numerous, the excited people flocked to witness the novel entertainments and to applaud and fee the actors.

As Jeremy Collier put on record in his "Ecclesiastical History of England": "The clergy complained, as they had reason, against such licentious sport. This, they said, was the way to let in atheism, and make all religion a jest; for, if people were allowed to burlesque devotion and make themselves merry with the ceremonies of the Church, they would proceed to further extremities and laugh the nation out of their creed at last."

Like his master, Wolsey, Cromwell had risen rapidly to fame and distinction; and like him was doomed to become an example of the instability and uncertainty of human greatness, attained, as in his case, by an utter sacrifice of true and noble principles.

Those who were most observant saw unmistakable tokens of Cromwell's fall. The king's manner toward him had changed altogether. His majesty now showed marked signs of contempt, which were noticed by many of the courtiers. The people, who had lost so much by his policy, were loud in their murmurings; nor were the aristocracy otherwise than heartily indignant with him. It was noticed that he was frequently alone. Old allies avoided him. He was often left silent and solitary —suitable prelude of his fall and death.

The king, ever capricious, was eminently so in this case. Cromwell, self-willed, resolute, and unscrupulous as he was, had been only too ready a tool in all his grace's dark and questionable designs, and certainly deserved better and fairer treatment from his royal master. But the arm of God Almighty was not shortened; and punishment from on high, so well deserved, was soon to fall upon him.

On the 10th of June, 1540, he was arrested by the Duke of Norfolk at the Council Chamber, when least expecting any such proceeding; and he was at once committed to the Tower.

Cromwell exerted all his interest to prolong a life spent in crime. In prison his conduct was the very reverse of that of those noble victims of his shameful policy, who with uplifted hands prayed fervently to God for their persecutors. From his own lips came little else but curses and imprecations for his enemies.

The day of vengeance was slowly drawing near. The desolated sanctuaries cried to heaven for Cromwell's due punishment. The woes and sorrows of outcast monks and nuns, wandering and weary, were not forgotten by an all-just and righteous God. "Vengeance is Mine; I will repay, saith the Lord." Within forty-eight days of the Earl's arrest, he received his due reward.

He laid his head on the block. At the executioner's second stroke it was severed from his body, and rolled on to the straw around, leaving a bloody track. So died this man; the crowd witnessed his end without sorrow or sympathy. No man who has thus suffered, suffered more properly. England was well rid of one who thoroughly deserved his fate.

REV. FREDERICK GEORGE LEE,
Historical Sketches of the Reformation.

THE TRIAL AND EXECUTION OF MARY QUEEN OF SCOTS.

On the 25th of September, 1586, Mary had been taken from Chartley to the castle of Fotheringay, in Northamptonshire, where she was more strictly watched than ever by Sir Amias Paulet, who was a harsh and inflexible jailor. On the 11th of October, Elizabeth's commissioners arrived, the great hall of the castle having been previously fitted up as a court-room for their reception. They would have proceeded with the trial immediately; but a difficulty occurred, which, though they scarcely can have failed to anticipate, they were not prepared to obviate. Mary refused to acknowledge their jurisdiction, denying that they possessed any right to either arraign or try her. "I am no subject to Elizabeth," she said, "but an independent queen as well as she; and I will consent to nothing unbecoming the majesty of a crowned head. Worn out as my body is, my mind is not yet so enfeebled as to make me forget what is due to myself, my ancestors, and my country. Whatever the laws of England may be, I am not subject to them; for I came into the realm only to ask assistance from a sister queen, and I have been detained an unwilling prisoner." For two days the commissioners labored in vain to induce Mary to appear before them; and as she assigned reasons for refusing which it was impossible for fair argument to invalidate, recourse was at length had to threats. They told her that they would proceed with the trial whether she consented to be present or not; and that, though they were anxious to hear her justification, they would nevertheless conclude that she was guilty, and pronounce accordingly, if she refused to defend herself. It would have been well had Mary allowed them to take their own way; but conscious that she was accused unjustly, she could not bear to think that she excited suspicion by refusing the opportunity of establishing her innocence. Actuated by this honorable motive, she at length yielded, after solemnly protesting that she did not, and never would, acknowledge the authority which Elizabeth arrogated over her.

On the 14th of October the trial commenced. The upper half of the great hall of Fotheringay Castle was railed off, and at the higher end was placed a chair of state under a canopy, for the Queen of England. Upon both sides of the room benches were arranged in order, where the Lord Chancellor Bromley, the Lord Treasurer Burleigh, fourteen earls, thirteen barons and knights, and members of the privy council sat. In the centre was a table, at which the lord chief-justice, several doctors of the civil law, Popham, the queen's attorney, her solicitors, sergeants, and notaries, took their places. At the foot of this table, and immediately opposite Elizabeth's chair of state, a chair without any canopy was placed for the Queen of Scots. Behind was the rail which ran across the hall, the lower part of which was fitted up for the accommodation of persons who were not in the commission.

There was never, perhaps, an occasion throughout the whole of Mary's life on which she appeared to greater advantage than this. In the presence of all the pomp, learning, and talents of England, she stood alone and undaunted; evincing, in the modest dignity of her bearing, a mind conscious of its own integrity, and superior to the malice of fortune. Elizabeth's craftiest lawyers and ablest politicians were assembled to probe her to the quick,—to press home every argument against her which ingenuity could devise and eloquence embellish,—to dazzle her with a blaze of erudition, or involve her in a maze of technical perplexities.

Mary had no counsellor—no adviser—no friend. Her very papers to which she might wish to refer had been taken from her; and there was not one to plead her cause, or to defend her innocence. Yet she was not dismayed. She knew that she had a higher judge than Elizabeth; and that great as was the array of lords and barons that appeared against her, posterity was greater than they, and that to its decision all things would be finally referred. Her bodily infirmities imparted only a greater lustre to her mental pre-eminence; and not in all the fascinating splendor of her youth and beauty—in the morning of her first bridal day, when Paris rang with acclamations in her praise—was Mary Stuart so much to be admired, as when, weak and worn out, she stood calmly before the myrmidons of a rival queen to hear and refute their unjust accusations, her eye radiant once more with the brilliancy of earlier years, and the placid benignity of a serene conscience lending to her countenance its undying grace.

Elizabeth's attorney-general opened the pleadings. He began by referring to the act of Parliament in which it was made capital to be the person *for* whom any design was undertaken against the life of the queen. He then described the late conspiracy, and attempted to establish Mary's connection with it, by producing copies of letters which he alleged she had written to Babington himself and several of his accomplices. To these having added letters from Babington to her, and the declarations and confessions which had been extorted from her secretaries, he asserted that the cause was made out, and wound up his speech with a labored display of legal knowledge and forensic oratory.

Mary was now called on for defence; and she entered on it with composure and dignity. She denounced all connection with Babington's conspiracy, in so far as she entertained any design injurious to Elizabeth's safety or the welfare of her kingdom; she allowed that the letters which he was said to have addressed to her might be genuine, but it had not been proved that she ever received them; she maintained that her own letters were all garbled or fabricated; that as to the confessions of her secretaries, they had been extorted by fear, and were therefore not to be credited; but that if they were in any particulars true, these particulars must have been disclosed at the expense of the oath of fidelity they had come under to her when they entered her service, and that men who would perjure themselves in one instance were not to be trusted in any; she objected besides that they had not been confronted with her according to an express law enacted in the thirteenth year of Elizabeth's reign, "that no one should be arraigned for intending the destruction of the prince's life, but by the testimony and oath of two lawful witnesses, *to be produced face to face before him*"; she maintained, that even supposing she were to allow the authenticity of many of the papers adduced against her, they would not prove her guilty of any crime; for she was surely doing no wrong, if, after a calamitous captivity of nineteen years, in which she had lost forever her youth, her health, and her happiness, she made one last effort to regain the liberty of which she had been so unfairly robbed; but as to scheming against the life of the queen her sister, it was an infamy she abhorred; "I would disdain," she said, "to purchase all that is most valuable on earth by the assassination of the meanest of the human race; and worn out, as I now am, with cares and suffering, the prospect of a crown is not so inviting that I should ruin my soul in order to obtain it. Neither am I a stranger to the feelings of humanity, nor unacquainted with the duties of religion, and it is more in my nature to be more inclined to the devotion of Esther than to the sword of Judith. If ever I have given consent by my words, or even by my thoughts, to any attempt against the life of the Queen of England, far from declining the judgment of men, I shall not even pray for the mercy of God."

Elizabeth's advocates were not a little surprised at the eloquent and able manner in which Mary conducted her defence. They had expected to have everything their own way, and to gain an easy victory over one unacquainted with the forms of legal procedure, and unable to cope with their own professional talents. But they were disappointed and baffled; and in order to maintain their ground even plausibly, they were obliged to protract the proceedings for two whole days. Nor after all did the commissioners venture to pronounce judgment, but adjourned the court to the star-chamber at Westminster, where they knew that Mary would not be present, and consequently they would have no opposition to fear.* On the 25th of October, they assembled there, and having again examined the secretaries Nau and Curl,

---

* It deserves notice, that no particulars of the trial at Fotheringay have been recorded, either by Mary herself, or any of her friends, but are all derived from the narrative of two of Elizabeth's notaries. If Mary's triumph was so decided, even by their account, it may easily be conceived that it would have appeared still more complete had it been described by less partial writers.

who appear to be persons of little fidelity or constancy, and who confirmed their former declarations, a unanimous judgment was delivered, that "Mary, commonly called Queen of Scots and dowager of France, was accessory to Babington's conspiracy, and had compassed and imagined divers matters within the realm of England, tending to the hurt, death, and destruction of the royal person of Elizabeth, in opposition to the statute framed for her protection."

In the meantime messengers had been sent to the Queen of Scots, to report to her the sentence of the commissioners, and to prepare her for the consequences which might be expected to follow. So far from receiving the news with dismay, Mary solemnly raised her hands to heaven, and thanked God that she was so soon to be relieved from her troubles. They were not yet, however, at a close; and even during the short remainder of her life, she was still further insulted. Her keepers, Sir Amias Paulet and Sir Drue Drury, refused to treat her any longer with the reverence and respect due to her rank and sex. The canopy of state, which she had always ordered to be put up in her apartment wherever she went, was taken down, and every badge of royalty removed. It was intimated to her that she was no longer to be regarded as a princess, but as a criminal; and the persons who came into her presence stood before her without uncovering their heads or paying her any obeisance. The attendance of a Catholic priest was refused, and an Episcopalian bishop sent in his stead, to point out and correct the errors of her way. Mary bore all these indignities with a calm spirit, which rose superior to them and which proved their unworthiness, by bringing them into contrast with her own elevation of mind. "In spite of your sovereign and her subservient judges," she said, "I will die a queen. My royal character is indelible, and I will surrender it with my spirit to the Almighty God, from whom I received it, and to whom my honor and my innocence are fully known." In December, 1586, she wrote her last letter to Elizabeth; and though from an unfriended prisoner to an envied and powerful sovereign, it evinces so much magnanimity and calm consciousness of mental serenity, that it is impossible to peruse it without confessing Elizabeth's inferiority and Mary's triumph. It was couched in the following terms:

"Madam, I thank God from the bottom of my heart that, by the sentence which has been passed against me, he is about to put an end to my tedious pilgrimage. I would not wish it prolonged, though it were in my power, having had enough of time to experience its bitterness. I write at present only to make three last requests, which, as I can expect no favour from your implacable ministers, I should wish to owe to your majesty and to no other. *First*, as in England I can not hope to be buried according to the solemnities of the Catholic Church (the religion of the ancient kings, your ancestors and mine, being now changed), and as in Scotland they have already violated the ashes of my progenitors, I have to request, that as soon as my enemies have bathed their hands in my innocent blood, my domestics may be allowed to inter my body in some consecrated ground; and above all, that they be permitted to carry it to France, where the bones of the queen, my most honoured mother, repose. Thus, that poor frame which has never enjoyed repose so long as it has been joined to my soul, may find it at last when they will be separated. *Second*, as I dread the tyranny of the harsh men to whose power you have abandoned me, I entreat your majesty that I may not be executed in secret, but in the presence of my servants and other persons who may bear testimony of my faith and fidelity to the true church, and guard the last hours of my life and my last sighs from false rumours which my adversaries may spread abroad. *Third*, I request that my domestics, who have served me through so much misery and with so much constancy, may be allowed to retire without molestation wherever they choose, to enjoy for the remainder of their lives the small legacies which my poverty has enabled me to bequeath to them. I conjure you, madam, by the blood of Jesus Christ, by our consanguinity, by the memory of Henry VII., our common father, and by the royal title which I carry with me to death, not to refuse these reasonable demands, but to assure me, by a letter under your own hand, that you will comply with them, and I shall then die as I have lived, your affectionate sister and prisoner, Mary Queen of Scots."

Whether Elizabeth ever answered this letter does not appear; but it produced so little effect, that epistles from her to Sir Amias Paulet still exist, which prove that in her anxiety to avoid taking upon herself the responsibility of Mary's death, she wished to have her privately assassinated or poisoned. Paulet, however, though a harsh and violent man, positively refused to sanction so nefarious a scheme. Yet in the very act of instigating murder, Elizabeth could close her eyes against her own iniquity, and affect indignation at the alleged offences of another. But perceiving, at length, that no alternative remained, she ordered her secretary, Davidson, to bring her the warrant for Mary's execution, and after perusing it, she deliberately affixed her signature. She then desired him to carry it to Walsingham, saying, with an ironical smile, and in a "merry tone," that she feared he would die of grief when he saw it. Walsingham sent the warrant to the chancellor, who affixed the great seal to it, and dispatched it by Beal, with a commission to the Earls of Shrewsbury, Kent, Derby, and others, to see it put in execution. Davidson was afterward made the victim of Elizabeth's artifice,—who, to complete the solemn farce she had been playing, pretended he had obeyed her orders too quickly, and doomed him in consequence to perpetual imprisonment.

On the 7th of February, 1578, the earls who had been commissioned to superintend Mary's execution arrived at Fotheringay. After dinner together, they sent to inform the queen that they desired to speak with her. Mary was not well, and in bed; but as she was given to understand that it was an affair of moment, she arose, and received them in her own chamber. Her six waiting-maids, together with her physician, her surgeon, and apothecary, and four or five male servants, were in attendance. The Earl of Shrewsbury, and the others associated with him, standing before her respectfully with their heads uncovered, communicated, as gently as possible, the disagreeable duty with which they had been entrusted. Beal was then desired to read the warrant for Mary's execution, to which she listened patiently; and making the sign of the cross, she said, that though she was sorry it came from Elizabeth, she had long been expecting the mandate for her death, and was not unprepared to die. "For many years," she added, "I have lived in continual affliction, unable to do good to myself or to those who are dear to me; as I shall depart innocent of the crime laid to my charge, I can not see why I should shrink from the prospect of immortality." She then laid her hand on the New Testament, and solemnly protested that she had never either devised, compassed, or consented to the death of the Queen of England. The Earl of Kent, with more zeal than wisdom, objected to the validity of this protestation, because it was made on a Catholic version of the Bible; but Mary replied, that it was the version in the truth of which she believed, and that her oath should be therefore only the less liable to suspicion. She was advised to hold some godly conversation with the Dean of Peterborough, whom they had brought with them to console her; but she declined the offer, declaring that she would die in the faith in which she had lived, and beseeching them to allow her to see her Catholic confessor, who had been for some time debarred her presence. This, however they in their turn positively refused.

Other topics were introduced, and casually discussed. Before leaving the world, Mary felt a natural curiosity to be informed upon several subjects of public interest, which, though connected with herself, and generally known, had not penetrated the walls of her prison. She asked if no foreign princess had interfered in her behalf,—if her secretaries were still alive,—if it was intended to punish them as well as her,—if they brought no letters from Elizabeth or others; and, above all, if her son, the King of Scotland, was well, and had evinced any interest in the fate of a mother who had always loved and never wronged him. Being satisfied upon these points, she proceeded to inquire when her execution was to take place. Shrewsbury replied that it was fixed for the next morning at eight. She appeared startled and agitated for a few minutes, saying that it was more sudden than she had anticipated, and that she had yet to make her will, which she had hitherto deferred, in expectation that the papers and letters which had been forcibly taken from her would be restored. She soon, however, regained her self-possession ; and informing the commissioners that she desired to be left alone to make her preparations, she dismissed them for the night.

During the whole of this scene, astonishment, indignation, and grief overwhelmed her attendants, all of whom were devoted to her. As soon as the earls and their retinue retired, they gave full vent to their feelings, and Mary herself was the only one who remained calm and undisturbed. Mary told them that she must submit with resignation to her fate, and learn to regard it as the will of God. She then requested her attendants to kneel with her, and she prayed fervently for some time in the midst of them. Afterward, while supper was preparing, she emptied all the money she had by her into separate purses, and affixed to each, with her own hand, the name of the person for whom she intended it. At supper, though she sat down to table, she ate little. Her mind, however, was in perfect composure; and during the repast, though she spoke little, placid smiles were frequently observed to pass over her countenance. The calm magnanimity of their mistress only increased the distress of her servants. They saw her sitting among them in her usual health, and with almost more than her usual cheerfulness, partaking of the viands that were set before her; yet they knew that it was the last meal at which they should ever be present together; and that the interchange of affectionate service upon their part, and condescending attention and endearing gentleness on hers, which had linked them to her for so many years, was now about to terminate forever.

Far from attempting to offer her consolation, they were unable to discover any for themselves. As soon as the melancholy meal was over, Mary desired that a cup of wine should be given to her; and putting it to her lips, drank to the health of each of her attendants by name. She requested that they would pledge her in like manner; and each, falling on his knee, and mingling tears with the wine, drank to her, asking pardon at the same time for all the faults he had ever committed. In the true spirit of Christian humility, she not only willingly forgave them, but asked their pardon also, if she had ever forgotten her duty toward them. She besought them to continue constant to their religion, and to live in peace and charity together, and with all men. The inventory of her wardrobe and furniture was then brought to her; and she wrote in the margin opposite each article the name of the person to whom she wished it should be given. She did the same with her rings, jewels, and all her most valuable trinkets; and there was not one of her friends or servants, either present or absent, to whom she forgot to leave a memorial.

These duties being discharged, Mary sat down to her desk to arrange her papers, to finish her will, and write several letters. She previously sent to her confessor, who, though in the castle, was not allowed to see her, entreating that he would spend the night in prayer for her, and that he would inform her what parts of the Scripture he considered most suited for her perusal at this juncture. She then drew up her last will and testament; and without ever lifting her pen from the paper, or stopping at intervals to think, she covered two large sheets with close writing, forgetting nothing of any moment, and expressing herself with all that precision and clearness which distinguished her style in the very happiest moments of her life. She named as her four executors—the Duke of Guise, her cousin-german; the Archbishop of Glasgow, her ambassador to France; Lesley, Bishop of Ross; and Monsieur de Ruysseau, her chancellor. She next wrote to her brother-in-law, the King of France, in which she apologized for not being able to enter into her affairs at greater length, as she had only an hour or two to live, and had not been informed till that day after dinner that she was to be executed next morning. " Thanks be unto God, however," she added, " I have no terror at the idea of death, and solemnly declare to you, that I meet it innocent of every crime. The bearer of this letter, and my other servants, will recount to you how I comported myself in my last moments." The letter concluded with earnest entreaties that her faithful followers should be protected and rewarded. Her anxiety on their account at such a moment indicated all that amiable generosity of disposition which was one of the leading features of Mary's character.* About two in the morning she sealed up all her papers, and said she would now think no more of the affairs of this world, but would spend the rest of her time in prayer and commune with her own conscience. She went to bed for some hours, but did not sleep. Her lips were observed in continual motion, and her hands were frequently folded and lifted up toward heaven.

On the morning of Wednesday, the 8th of February, Mary rose with the break of day ; and her domestics, who had watched and wept all night,

---

* "Mary's testament and letters," says Ritson, the antiquarian, "which I have seen, blotted with her tears, in the Scotch College, Paris, will remain perpetual monuments of her singular abilities, tenderness, and affection.'

immediately gathered round her. She told them that she had made her will, and requested that they would see it safely deposited in the hands of her executors. She likewise besought them not to separate until they had carried her body to France; and she placed a sum of money in the hands of her physician to defray the expenses of the journey. Her earnest desire was to be buried either in the church of St. Denis, in Paris, beside her first husband, Francis, or at Rheims, in the tomb which contained the remains of her mother. She expressed a wish, too, that besides her friends and servants, a number of poor people and children from the different hospitals should be present at her funeral, clothed in mourning at her expense, and each, according to the Catholic custom, carrying in his hand a lighted taper.

She now renewed her devotions, and was in the midst of them, when a messenger from the commissioners knocked at the door, to announce that all was ready. She requested a little longer time to finish her prayers, which was granted. As soon as she desired the door to be opened, the sheriff, carrying in his hand the white wand of office, entered to conduct her to the place of execution. Her servants crowded round her, and insisted on being allowed to accompany her to the scaffold.

But a contrary order having been given by Elizabeth, they were told that she must proceed alone. Against such a piece of arbitrary cruelty they remonstrated loudly, but in vain; for as soon as Mary passed into the gallery, the door was closed, and believing that they were separated from her forever, the shrieks of the women and the scarcely less audible lamentations of the men were heard in distant parts of the castle.

At the foot of the staircase leading down to the hall below, Mary was met by the Earls of Kent and Shrewsbury; and she was allowed to stop to take farewell of Sir Anthony Melvil, the master of her household, whom her keeper had not allowed to come into her presence for some time before. With tears in his eyes Melvil knelt before her, kissed her hand, and declared that it was the heaviest hour of his life. Mary assured him that it was not so with her. "I now feel, my good Melvil," she said, "that this world is vanity. When you speak of me hereafter, mention that I died firm in my faith, willing to forgive my enemies, conscious that I had never disgraced Scotland, my native country, and rejoicing in the thought that I had been true to France, the land of my happiest years. Tell my son," she added,—and when she named her only child, of whom she had been so proud in his infancy, but in whom all her hopes had been so fatally blasted, her feelings for the first time overpowered her, and a flood of tears flowed from her eyes,—" tell my son that I thought of him in my last moments, and that I have never yielded, either by word or deed, to aught that might lead to his prejudice; desire him to preserve the memory of his unfortunate parent, and may he be a thousand times more happy and more prosperous than she has been."

Before taking leave of Melvil, Mary turned to the commissioners, and told them that her three last requests were, that her secretary Curl, whom she blamed less for his treachery than Nau, should not be punished; that her servants should have free permission to depart for France; and that some of them should be allowed to come down from the apartments above to see her die. The earls answered, that they believed the two former of these requests would be granted; but that they could not concede the last, alleging, as their excuse, that the affliction of her attendants would only add to the severity of her suffering. But Mary was resolved that some of her own people should witness her last moments. "I will not submit to the indignity," she said, "of permitting my body to fall into the hands of strangers. You are the servants of a maiden queen, and she herself, were she here, would yield to the dictates of humanity, and permit some of those who have been so long faithful to me, to assist me at my death. Remember, too, that I am cousin to your mistress, and the descendant of Henry VII.; I am the dowager of France, and the anointed queen of Scotland." Ashamed of any further opposition, the earls allowed her to name four male and two female attendants, whom they sent for, and permitted to remain beside her for the short time she had yet to live.

The same hall in which the trial had taken place was prepared for the execution. At the upper end was the scaffold, covered with black cloth, and elevated about two feet from the floor. A chair was placed on it for the Queen of Scots. On one side of the block stood two executioners, and on the other the Earls of Kent and Shrewsbury; Beal and the sheriff were immediately behind. The scaffold was railed off from the rest of the hall, in which Sir Amias Paulet with a bodyguard, the other commissioners, and some gentlemen of the neighborhood, amounting altogether to about two hundred persons, were assembled. Mary entered, leaning on the arm of her physician, while Sir Andrew Melvil carried the train of her robe. She was in full dress, and looked as if she were about to hold a drawing-room, not to lay her head beneath the axe. She wore a gown of black silk, bordered with crimson velvet, over which was a satin mantle; a long veil of white crape, stiffened with wire, and edged with rich lace, hung down almost to the ground; round her neck was suspended an ivory crucifix, and the beads which Catholics use in their prayers were fastened to her girdle. The symmetry of her fine figure had long been destroyed by her sedentary life; and years of care had left many a trace on her beautiful features. But the dignity of the queen was still apparent; and the calm grace of mental serenity imparted to her countenance at least some share of its former loveliness. With a composed and steady step she passed through the hall, and ascended the scaffold—and as she listened unmoved while Beal read aloud the warrant for her death, even the myrmidons of Elizabeth looked upon her with admiration.

Beal having finished, the Dean of Peterborough presented himself at the foot of the scaffold, and with more zeal than humanity addressed Mary on the subject of her religion. She mildly told him that she was resolved to die a Catholic, and requested that he would not annoy her any longer with useless reasonings. But finding that he would not be persuaded to desist, she turned away from him, and falling on her knees, prayed fervently aloud—repeating, in particular, many passages from the Psalms. She prayed for her own soul, and that God would send His Holy Spirit to comfort her in the agony of death; she prayed for all good monarchs, for the Queen of England, for the king her son, for her friends, and for all her enemies. She spoke with a degree of earnest vehemence and occasional strength of gesticulation which deeply affected all who heard her. She held a small crucifix in her hands, which were clasped and raised to heaven; and at intervals a convulsive sob choked her voice. As soon as her prayers were ended, she prepared to lay her head on the block. Her two female attendants, as they assisted her to remove her veil and headdress, trembled so violently that they were hardly able to stand. Mary gently reproved them—"Be not thus overcome," she said; "I am happy to leave the world, and you also ought to be happy to see me die so willingly." As she bared her neck, she took from around it a gold cross, which she wished to give to Jane Kennedy; but the executioner with brutal coarseness objected, alleging that it was one of his perquisites. "My good friend," said Mary, "she will pay you more than its value"; but his only answer was, to snatch it rudely from her hand. She turned from him to pronounce a parting benediction on all her servants, and bid them affectionately farewell. Being now ready, she desired Jane Kennedy to bind her eyes with a rich handkerchief, bordered with gold, which she had brought with her for the purpose; and laying her head upon the block, her last words were, "O Lord, in Thee I have hoped, and into Thy hands I commit my spirit." The executioner, either from a want of skill, or from agitation, or because the axe he used was blunt, struck three blows before he separated her head from her body. His comrade then lifted the head by the hair (which falling in disorder, was observed to be quite gray), and called out, "God save Elizabeth, Queen of England!" The Earl of Kent added, "Thus perish all her enemies"; but, overpowered by the solemnity and horror of the scene, none were able to respond, "Amen!"

Mary's remains were immediately taken from her servants, who wished to pay them the last sad offices of affection, and were carried into an adjoining apartment, where a piece of green baize, taken from a billiard-table, was thrown over that form which had once lived in the light of a nation's eyes. It lay thus for some time; but was at length ordered to be embalmed, and buried with royal pomp in the cathedral at Peterborough—a vulgar artifice used by Elizabeth to stifle the gnawing remorse of her own conscience, and make an empty atonement for her cruelty. Twenty-five years afterward, James VI., wishing to perform an act of tardy justice to the memory of his mother, ordered her remains to be removed from Peterborough to Henry VII.'s chapel in Westminster Abbey.

Mary Stuart, Queen of Scots, died in the forty-fifth year of her age. The estimate which is to be formed of her character can not be a matter of much doubt. The deliberate judgment of calm impartiality, not of hasty enthusiasm, must be, that, illustrious as her birth and rank were, she possessed virtues and talents which not only made her independent of the former, but raised her above them. In her better days, the vivacity and sweetness of her manners, her openness, her candor, her generosity, her polished wit, her extensive information, her cultivated taste, her easy affability, her powers of conversation, her native dignity and grace were all conspicuous, though too little appreciated by the less refined frequenters of the Scottish Court. Nor did she appear to less advantage in the season of calamity. On the contrary, she had an opportunity of displaying in adversity a fortitude and nobility of soul, which she herself might not have known that she possessed had she been always prosperous. Her piety and her constancy became more apparent in a prison than on a throne; and of none could it be said more truly than of her, "*ponderibus virtus innata resistit.*" In the glory of victory and the pride of success, it is easy for a conquering monarch to float down the stream of popularity; but it is a far more arduous task to gain a victory over the natural weaknesses of one's own nature, and in the midst of sufferings to triumph over one's enemies. Mary did this, and was a thousand times more to be envied when kneeling at her solitary devotions in the castle of Fotheringay, than Elizabeth surrounded with all the heartless splendor of Hampton Court. As she laid her head upon the block, the dying graces threw upon her their last smiles; and the sublime serenity of her death was an argument in her favor, the force of which must be confessed by incredulity itself. Mary was not destined to obtain the crown of England, but she gained instead the crown of martyrdom.

HENRY GLASSFORD BELL,
Life of Mary Queen of Scots.

CARDINAL NEWMAN.

My Dear ——: My present letter will be given to a single figure. When I entered at Oxford, John Henry Newman was beginning to be famous. The responsible authorities were watching him with anxiety; clever men were looking with interest and curiosity on the apparition among them of one of those persons of indisputable genius who was likely to make a mark upon his time. His appearance was striking. He was above the middle height, slight and spare. His head was large, his face remarkably like that of Julius Cæsar. The forehead, the shape of the ears and nose were almost the same. The lines of the mouth were very peculiar, and I should say exactly the same. I have often thought of the resemblance, and believed that it extended to the temperament. In both there was an original force of character which refused to be molded by circumstances, which was to make its own way, and become a power in the world; a clearness of intellectual perception, a disdain for conventionalities, a temper imperious and wilful, but along with it a most attaching gentleness, sweetness, singleness of heart and purpose. Both were formed by nature to command others, both had the faculty of attracting to themselves the passionate devotion of their friends and followers.

When I first saw him he had written his book upon the Arians. An accidental application had set him upon it, at a time, I believe, when he had half resolved to give himself to science and mathematics, and had so determined him into a theological career. He had published a volume or two of parochial sermons. A few short poems of his had also appeared in the *British Magazine,* under the signature of "Delta," which were reprinted in the "Lyra Apostolica." They were unlike any other religious poetry which was then extant. It was hard to say why they were so fascinating. They had none of the musical grace of the "Christian Year." They were not harmonious; the metre halted, the rhymes were irregular, yet there was something in them which seized the attention, and would not let it go. Keble's verses flowed in soft cadence over the mind, delightful, as sweet sounds are delightful, but are forgotten as the vibrations die away. Newman's had pierced into the heart and mind, and there remained. The literary critics of the day were puzzled. They saw that he was not an ordinary man; what sort of an extraordinary man he was they could not tell. "The eye of Melpomene had been cast upon him," said the omniscient (I think) Athenæum; "but the glance was not fixed or steady." The eye of Melpomene had extremely little to do in the matter. Here were thoughts like no other man's thoughts, and emotions like no other man's emotions. Here was a man who really believed his creed, and let it follow him into all his observations upon outward things. He had been travelling in Greece; he had carried with him his recollections of Thucydides, and, while his companions were sketching olive gardens and old castles and picturesque harbors at Corfu, Newman was recalling the scenes which those harbors had witnessed thousands of years ago in the civil wars which the Greek historian has made immortal. There was nothing in this that was unusual. Any one with a well-stored memory is affected by historical scenery. But Newman was oppressed with the sense that the men who had fallen in that desperate strife were still alive, as much as he and his friends were alive.

> Their spirits live in awful singleness,

he says,

> Each in its self-formed sphere of light or gloom.

We should all, perhaps, have acknowledged this in words. It is happy for us that we do not all realize what the words mean. The minds of most of us would break down under the strain.

Other conventional beliefs, too, were quickened into startling realities. We had been hearing much in those days about the benevolence of the Supreme Being, and our corresponding obligation to charity and philanthropy. If the received creed was true, benevolence was by no means the only characteristic of that Being. What God loved we might love; but there were things which God did not love; accordingly we found Newman saying to us:

> Christian, would'st thou learn to love;
> First learn thee how to hate.
> . . . . . .
> Hatred of sin and zeal and fear
> Lead up the Holy Hill;
> Track them, till charity appear
> A self-denial still.

It was not austerity that made him speak so. No one was more essentially tender-hearted; but he took the usually accepted Christian account of man and his destiny to be literally true, and the terrible character of it weighed upon him.

> Sunt lacrymæ rerum et mentem mortalia tangunt.

He could be gentle enough in other moods.

"Lead, kindly Light," is the most popular hymn in the language. Familiar as the lines are they may here be written down once more:

> Lead, kindly Light, amid the encircling gloom
>   Lead Thou me on.
> The night is dark, and I am far from home,
>   Lead Thou me on.
> Keep Thou my feet; I do not ask to see
> Far distant scenes—one step, enough for me.
>
> I was not ever thus, nor prayed that Thou
>   Should'st lead me on.
> I loved to choose and see my path; but now
>   Lead Thou me on.
> I loved the garish day, and, spite of fears,
> Pride ruled my will. Remember not past years.
>
> So long Thy power has blest us, sure it will
>   Still lead us on.
> O'er moor and fen, o'er crag and torrent, till
>   The night is gone,
> And with the morn those angel faces smile
> Which I have loved long since, and lost awhile.

It has been said that men of letters are either much less or much greater than their writings. Cleverness and the skilful use of other people's thoughts produce works which take us in till we see the authors, and then we are disenchanted. A man of genius, on the other hand, is a spring in which there is always more behind than flows from it. The painting or the poem is but a part of him inadequately realized, and his nature expresses itself, with equal or fuller completeness, in his life, his conversation, and personal presence. This was eminently true of Newman. Greatly as his poetry had struck me, he was himself all that the poetry was, and something far beyond. I had then never seen so impressive a person. I met him now and then in private; I attended his church and heard him preach Sunday after Sunday; he is supposed to have been insidious, to have led his disciples on to conclusions to which he designed to bring them, while his purpose was carefully veiled. He was, on the contrary, the most transparent of men. He told us what he believed to be true. He did not know where it would carry him. No one who has ever risen to any great height in this world refuses to move till he knows where he is going. He is impelled in each step which he takes by a force within himself. He satisfies himself only that the step is a right one, and he leaves the rest to Providence. Newman's mind was world-wide. He was interested in everything which was going on in science, in politics, in literature. Nothing was too large for him, nothing too trivial, if it threw light upon the central question, what man really was, and what was his destiny. He was careless about his personal prospects. He had no ambition to make a career, or to rise to rank and power. Still less had pleasure any seductions for him. His natural temperament was bright and light; his senses, even the commonest, were exceptionally delicate. He could admire enthusiastically any greatness of action and character, however remote the sphere of it from his own. Gurwood's "Dispatches of the Duke of Wellington" came out just then. Newman had been reading the book, and a friend asked him what he thought of it. "Think?" he said, "it makes one burn to have been a soldier." But his own subject was the absorbing interest with him.

With us undergraduates, Newman, of course, did not enter on important questions. He, when we met him, spoke to us about subjects of the day, of literature, of public persons, and incidents, of everything which was generally interesting. He seemed always to be better informed on common topics of conversation than any one else who was present. He was never condescending with us, never didactic or authoritative; but what he said carried conviction along with it. When we were wrong he knew why we were wrong, and excused our mistakes to ourselves while he set us right. Perhaps his supreme merit as a talker was that he never tried to be witty or to say striking things. Ironical he could be, but not ill-natured. Not a malicious anecdote was ever heard from him. Prosy he could not be. He was lightness itself—the lightness of elastic strength—and he was interesting because he never talked for talking's sake, but because he had something real to say.

Thus it was that we, who had never seen such another man, and to whom he appeared, perhaps, at special advantage in contrast with the normal college don, came to regard Newman with the affection of pupils (though pupils, strictly speaking, he had none) for an idolized master. The simplest word which dropped from him was treasured as if it had been an intellectual diamond.

Personal admiration, of course, inclined us to look to him as a guide in matters of religion. No one who heard his sermons in those days can ever forget them. They were seldom directly theological. We had theology enough and to spare from the select preachers before the university. Newman, taking some Scripture character for a text, spoke to us about ourselves, our temptations, our experiences. His illustrations were inexhaustible. He seemed to be addressing the most secret consciousness of each of us—as the eyes of a portrait appear to look at every person in a room. He never exaggerated; he was never unreal. A sermon from him was a poem, formed on a distinct idea, fascinating by its subtlety, welcome — how welcome !—from its sincerity, interesting from its originality, even to those who were careless of religion; and to others who wished to be religious, but had found religion dry and wearisome, it was like the springing of a fountain out of the rock.

The hearts of men vibrate in answer to one another like the strings of musical instruments. These sermons were, I suppose, the records of Newman's own mental experience. They appear to me to be the outcome of continued meditation upon his fellow-creatures and their position in this world; their awful responsibilities; the mystery of their nature strangely mixed, of good and evil, of strength and weakness. A tone, not of fear, but of infinite pity, runs through them all, and along with it a resolution to look facts in the face; not to fly to evasive generalities about infinite mercy and benevolence, but to examine what revelation really has added to our knowledge, either of what we are or of what lies before us. We were met on all sides with difficulties; for experience did not confirm, it rather contradicted, what revelation appeared distinctly to assert. I recollect a sermon from him—I think in the year 1839; I have never read it since; I may not now remember the exact words, but the impression left is ineffaceable. It was on the trials of faith, of which he gave different illustrations. He supposed, first, two children to be educated together, of similar temperament and under similar conditions, one of whom was baptized and the other unbaptized. He represented them as growing up equally amiable, equally upright, equally reverent and God-fearing, with no outward evidence that one was in a different spiritual condition from the other; yet we were required to believe not only that their condition was totally different, but that one was a child of God, and his companion was not.

Again, he drew a sketch of the average men and women who made up society, whom we ourselves encountered in daily life, or were connected with, or read about in newspapers. They were neither special saints nor special sinners. None seemed good enough for heaven, none so bad as to deserve to be consigned to the company of evil spirits, and to remain in pain and misery forever. Yet all these people were, in fact, divided one from the other by an invisible line of separation. If they were to die on the spot as they actually were, some would be saved, the rest would be lost—the saved to have eternity of happiness, the lost to be with the devils in hell.

Again, I am not sure whether it was on the same

occasion, but it was in following the same line of thought, Newman described closely some of the incidents of our Lord's passion; he then paused. For a few moments there was a breathless silence. Then, in a low, clear voice, of which the faintest vibration was audible in the farthest corner of St. Mary's, he said: "Now, I bid you recollect that He to whom these things were done was Almighty God." It was as if an electric stroke had gone through the church, as if every person present understood for the first time the meaning of what he had all his life been saying. I suppose it was an epoch in the mental history of more than one of my Oxford contemporaries.

JAMES ANTHONY FROUDE,
Short Studies.

IRELAND AS THE SCHOOL OF THE WEST.

MORE than a thousand years ago the Church of Ireland was the *burning and shining light* of the Western World. Her Candlestick was seen from afar, diffusing its rays like the luminous beacon of some lofty lighthouse, planted on a rock amid the foaming surge of the ocean, and casting its light over the dark sea to guide the mariner in his course. Such was the Church of Ireland then. Such she was specially to *us*. We, we of this land, must not endeavor to conceal our obligations to her. We must not be ashamed to confess, that with regard to learning—and especially with regard to *sacred* learning—Ireland was in advance of England at that time. The sons of our nobles and gentry were sent for education thither. Ireland was the University of the West. She was rich in libraries, colleges, and schools. She was famous, as now, for hospitality. She received those who came to her with affectionate generosity, and provided them with books and instructors. She trained them in sound learning, especially in the Word of God.

Nor is this all. We, my brethren, are bound to remember that the Christianity of England and of Scotland was, in a great measure, reflected upon them from the West, by the instrumentality of Irish missionaries, especially of those who came from the Scriptural School of Iona. That school was founded in the sixth century by St. Columba. He came from Ireland. He was from her ancient line of kings. He is justly regarded as the Apostle of the Highlands and Western Isles of Scotland. He preached the Gospel there thirty years before St. Austin landed in England.

Many, doubtless, who are here present, have stood on the sea-girt cliff of Iona, and have viewed with religious interest and veneration the mouldering remains of ancient Christianity which still survive on its solitary shore. The name of Iona has been coupled with that of Marathon by one of our most celebrated writers, in a passage familiar to all;* and they who are versed in the history of Christianity in their own land (and who ought not to study it?), will gladly and gratefully confess, that the peaceful conquests achieved in our country by the saintly armies of Iona, were far

---

* "Journey to the Western Islands of Scotland," by Dr. Samuel Johnson, p. 261. Edinburgh, 1798.

more beneficent and glorious than any that were ever gained on fields like that of Marathon; for the names of those who fought for these victories of the Gospel are inscribed — not in perishable records, but in the pages of the *Book of Life.*

"Who are these that fly as a cloud, and as the *Doves* to their windows? Surely the *Isles* shall wait for Me."

May we not be permitted to apply this prophetic language to them? The Hebrew word here used for Island is I, and is cognate with that by which Iona was first known. It was originally called Hii. The Hebrew word here used for *Dove* is *Yona.* And the name of St. Columba signifies Dove. Hence it was that the Island to which we now refer was called *I-ona,* or the *Island* of *St. Columba,* or of the *Dove.* And it was also, and is still, called by a word bearing the same sense, *I-Colm-Kill, i. e.,* the *Island* of *Columba,* the founder of *Churches ;* for Kill, it is well known, signifies *Church.* When, therefore, we bear in mind these circumstances; when we recollect that the Dove is the scriptural emblem of the Christian soul; and when we remember that Iona, in those days, was a central church, a sacred school of the West, a refuge for the weary soul, to which many flocked from afar— may we not say that it was like a Christian Columbarium, where the doves *found a house, and a nest where they might lay their young—even the altar of the Lord of Hosts?* And may we not here exclaim, " Who are these that fly as a cloud, and as the *Doves* to their windows? Surely the *Isles* shall wait for Me."

St. Columba, having founded the missionary Church of Iona, and having preached the Gospel in Scotland and the Isles, fell asleep in Christ, in a good old age, at the end of the sixth century (A.D. 597).

But he being dead yet speaketh.*

Before the middle of the following century—the seventh century (A.D. 635)—the King of Northumberland, Oswald, who had been educated in the Irish Church, sent to it for Christian teachers, that they might convert his subjects from Paganism. Accordingly, Aidan, an Irish bishop, and other Irish missionaries, went forth from the school of Columba, and were settled by the king in Lindisfarne, and preached the Gospel in Northumberland, and planted the Church there.

The happy effects of this mission from Iona were felt throughout England, from the river Humber to the Thames. Churches were built; the people

---

* Heb. xi. 4.

flocked with joy to hear the Word of God. The Heavenly Dove—the Holy Spirit of God—brooded invisibly over the heads of thousands baptized by these Irish missionaries in the faith of Christ in our own land. Multitudes, wearied by the storm, and finding no rest for the sole of their feet on the wilderness of the waters of this life, took refuge in the Ark of the Church.

BISHOP WORDSWORTH,
Occasional Sermons.

ELIZABETH'S REFORMATION IN IRELAND.

It now remains for us to notice the measures employed during the reign of Elizabeth to propagate the "reformed" religion in Ireland. One would naturally suppose that religion had been lost sight of amid all the slaughter, devastation, and hideous cruelty which characterized this reign. But no; the propagation of the Protestant religion was actually one of the pretences put forward by the English government for its "vigorous policy" toward the Irish! Protestantism and persecution went hand in hand; and while Grey, Carew, and Mountjoy were burning and devastating in Munster, Leinster, and Ulster, the zealous propagandists of the new religion were laboring to extend their creed by means of torture and cruelty. Many Catholic bishops and priests were put to death during Lord Grey's administration, for exercising their spiritual functions; some were hanged and quartered; others were beaten about the heads with stones, till their brains gushed out; others were murdered in cold blood, sometimes at the very altar; others had their bowels torn open, their nails and fingers torn off, and were thus painfully destroyed by slow torture, their remains being afterward treated with the most revolting indignity. The most common method, however, of executing the sentence of the law upon these Catholic recusants was as follows: They were first hanged up, and then cut down alive; they were next dismembered, ripped up, and had their bowels burned before their faces; after which, they were beheaded and quartered; the whole process lasting above half an hour, during which the unfortunate victims remained conscious and writhing under the agonies inflicted on them by their Protestant persecutors.

While the Catholic clergy were thus treated, the Protestants who had been created teachers of the State-religion by Act of Parliament, were notoriously profligate, lewd, simoniacal, slothful, and intemperate, even according to the testimony of English Protestant writers themselves. They were the refuse of the English Church—we had almost said, of England—of whom nothing else could be made but Irish parsons. They went to Ireland for gain, for tithes, for plunder; caring nothing for the souls of the flock, and watching over them rather with the care of the wolf than that of the shepherd. The Irish Church was, in fact, henceforward looked upon as a mere refuge for hungry adventurers from England, who, born within the atmosphere of gentility, were too idle to work; but were not beneath extracting from the hard earnings of the poor the means of profligate luxury and riotous extravagance. What was the consequence? That the great body of the Irish people, in whose eyes Protestantism had become identified with everything that was odious and intolerable, clung to their ancient faith, and to the native pastors who had been faithful to them for centuries.

Such was the reign of "good Queen Bess" in Ireland — one of the darkest and bloodiest passages to be found in history. In her time, almost the entire country was reduced to the condition of a desert, and at least half the entire population perished by famine or the sword. Nearly forty rebellions occurred during the half century that she occupied the throne—many of which rebellions were stirred up and fomented merely for the purpose of rapine, confiscation, and plunder. Famine and pestilence were then openly advocated as the only pacificators of Ireland, by one who is known in England as the most elegant and graceful of her early poets. In the Irish mind, however, Edmund Spenser is associated, not with the

Faery Queen, but with the royal vixen of England, of whose cruelty and ambition he was found the unscrupulous advocate. Sir Walter Raleigh, too, the chivalrous and polite, is known to Ireland only as the instrument of ruthless tyranny and barbarity. Elizabeth's entire reign, indeed, was a continued series of disgusting cruelties and crimes. Famine and devastation were the "good queen's" handmaidens; the rack, the gibbet, and the dungeon, her Protestant missionaries. And thus, at last, was Ireland "pacified"; and, after a contest of 440 years, brought under the dominion of the crown of England. The cost to Elizabeth was most serious. More than £3,000,000 sterling was expended on the conquest, with an incalculable number of her bravest soldiers. And after all, as the queen was assured by her own servants, "little was left in Ireland for her majesty to reign over but *carcasses* and *ashes*"!

The "Reformation from Popery" was also "completed" in Elizabeth's reign. The history of this movement in Ireland is, throughout, one of merciless persecution, of wholesale spoliation, and of murderous cruelty. The instruments by which it was accomplished were despotic monarchs, unprincipled ministers, a rapacious aristocracy, and venal and slavish parliaments. It sprung from brutal passion, was nurtured in selfish and corrupt policy, and was consummated in bloodshed and horrid crime. "The work," observes a contemporary, "which had been begun by Henry, the murderer of his wives, was continued by Somerset, the murderer of his brother, and completed by Elizabeth, the murderer of her guest." Such was the "Reformation," and such were its instruments; and the consequences which flowed from it, at least in Ireland, were of a kindred character for centuries to come.

SAMUEL SMILES,
History of Ireland and the Irish People, under the Government of England.

THE ACTS PASSED IN THE CATHOLIC PARLIAMENT OF JAMES II., AND THOSE PASSED BY THE PROTESTANT PARLIAMENT OF WILLIAM III.

As it has not unfrequently been alleged against the Catholics that, if they had the power, and possessed ascendency in the Irish Legislature, that the Protestants have done, they would use it for purposes of their own aggrandizement, and to the injury of other religious sects—it may not be uninteresting and uninstructive here to place in juxtaposition, the Acts passed in the Catholic Parliament of James and those passed by the Protestant Parliament of William, allowing the reader to judge for himself which of the two legislated most in the spirit of constitutional freedom, and for the true interests of Ireland:

Acts Passed in the Catholic Parliaments of James.	Acts Passed in the Protestant Parliaments of William and Mary.
An act declaring that the parliament of England can not bind Ireland; and against writs and appeals to be brought for removing judg-	An act, 3 William, recognized by the Irish parliament (thereby recognizing the supremacy of England), for ex-

ments, decrees, and sentences in Ireland to England.

An act for taking off all incapacities from the natives of this kingdom.

An act for *liberty of conscience*, and repealing such acts and clauses in any acts of Parliament which are inconsistent with the same.

An act for the encouragement of strangers and others to inhabit and plant in this kingdom of Ireland.

An act for vesting in his Majesty the goods of *absentees*.

An act for prohibiting the importation of English, Scotch, or Welsh wools into this kingdom.

An act for the advance and improvement of trade, and for the encouragement and increase of shipping and navigation, etc., etc.

cluding Catholics from parliament.—*Lords' Journal*, v. i., p. 496.

An act restraining foreign education.—7 *William*, c. 4.

An act for disarming Papists, containing a clause rendering their spoliation, robbery, etc., legal.—7 *Will.*, c. 5.

An act for banishing archbishops, priests, etc., for the purpose of extinguishing the Catholic religion.—9 *Will.*, c. 1.

An act for discouraging marriages between Catholics and Protestants.—9 *Will.*, c. 5.

An act confirming (*i. e.*, violating) the articles of Limerick.—9 *Will.*, c. 11.

The acts for discouraging the Woolen Trade of Ireland, passed in the English parliaments,—(1 *Will. and Mary*, c. 32; 4 *Will. and Mary*, c. 24; 7 *and* 8 *Will.*, c. 28; 9 *and* 10 *Will.*, c. 40), and recognized afterward by the Irish parliament, in the Bill passed 25th of March, 1699.

An act completing the ruin of the woollen manufactory, and imposed with all its violations of the trial by jury, etc., by the English parliament on Ireland. — 10 *and* 11 *Will. and Mary*, c. 10.

Such were the Protestant parliaments from the hands of which Ireland afterward received its destinies, and such the constitution to which the monopolists of the present day still wish that we should revert! Such men and such assemblies were much more fitting to entertain the petitions of coal-heavers for the exclusion of Papists from the trade, or to burn Molyneux's book by the public hangman, than to legislate for the rights and interest of a free nation.

SAMUEL SMILES,
History of Ireland and the Irish People, under the Government of England.

SAINT LOUIS.

In that long succession of eulogists on the Royal Saint, none have been more emphatic than Hume, and none more enthusiastic than Voltaire. Yet it was impossible, even to their subtle intellects, as it had been difficult to many students in a far nobler school than theirs, to trace the movements of that benignant Providence which planted and brought to a prolific maturity in the mind of Louis, as in a genial soil, the seeds of an habitual holiness, and of a wisdom which was at once elevated and profound. The more diligently his life is studied, the more distinctly will it, I think, appear, that his natural dispositions received from the associates and teachers of his youth the training which rendered them fruitful of so many virtues. Exquisitely alive to every domestic affection—often oppressed with a constitutional melancholy, which laid bare to him the illusions of life, yet occasionally animated with a constitutional gaiety, which enabled him for a while to cherish and play with those illusions—enamored of the beautiful, and revering the sublime — his temper, though thus sympathetic, pensive, and imaginative, was allied (it is no common alliance) to a courage which rose and exulted in the presence of danger, and to a fortitude which was unshaken in the lowest depths of calamity.

His mother, Blanche of Castile, watched over the royal boy (for he had not completed his thirteenth year when he ascended the throne of France) with all a mother's tenderness, united to a discipline more inflexible, and perhaps more stern, than most fathers have courage to exercise. In Isabella of France, his sister, who had preferred the cloister to the imperial crown, he had another kinswoman who bestowed on him all the thoughts, the time, and the affection which she ventured to divert from the object of her almost ceaseless worship. In his eighteenth year he married Marguerite of Provence, who after having been the idol of the Troubadours of her native land, herself became almost an idolater of him, cleaving to him with the same constancy of love in their quiet home at Poissy, and amid his disasters at Massourah and Damietta.

But the sagacity of Blanche foresaw that these filial, fraternal, and conjugal affections might enervate, even while they purified the spirit of her son, and she therefore selected for his tutor a man possessing, as she judged, the qualifications best adapted to counteract that danger. His name was Pacifico. He was an Italian gentleman, who, having been one of the first followers of St. Francis of Assisi, was animated by the profound and fervent devotion which characterized his master. He instructed his pupil in ancient and in more recent history, caused him to ride boldly in the chase, and required him to cultivate every martial exercise and courtly grace, which was then regarded as indispensable in a gentleman and a cavalier. Nor did the lowliness of the Franciscan institute prevent the friar from instilling into the soul of Louis the loftiest conceptions of his own royal dignity.

Other and far different associates contributed to form the character of the pupil of Pacifico. In the halls of the Louvre, then a fortress rather than a palace, veteran captains described to him the battles which they had fought with Saladin, and the victories which had expelled the English from Normandy. Beneath the same royal roof, gray-headed counsellors of Philippe Auguste explained to him the methods by which that prince had enlarged the domains and the powers of the kings of France; and there, also, civic bailiffs and provincial seneschals interpreted to their young sovereign the motives which had induced his ancestors to increase the number and to extend the franchises of the communes. Thus imbibing from aged men the hereditary maxims of his house, he learned to adopt them as the laws by which his future reign was to be directed.

But the yet higher laws by which his own personal conduct was to be governed, seem to have been derived from a far more eminent teacher than any of these. St. Thomas Aquinas, who had migrated from his native Italy into Northern France, was passing there a life which may be said to have been one of deep and unintermitted meditation; for the results of which he found utterance sometimes in acts of public or solitary worship, and at other times in interpreting to mankind the mysteries and the duties of their relations to the Deity and to each other. To the inquiry of Bonaventura as to the sources of his stupendous learning, he answered by pointing to the crucifix which stood upon his table; and, when seated at the table of the king, or introduced into his closet, he still directed to the same inexhaustible fountain of divine and human wisdom. From his intercourse with St. Thomas, Louis seems to have acquired his acquaintance with that science which the devout Pacifico could not have taught—the sacred science of Christian morality, in all the amplitude and in all the minuteness of its application to the offices of a legislator and a king.

St. Louis occupies in history a place apart from that of all the other moral heroes of our race. It is his peculiar praise to have combined in his own person the virtues which are apparently the most incompatible with each other, and with the state and trials of a king. Seated on the noblest of the thrones of Europe, and justly jealous of his high prerogatives, he was as meek and gentle as if he had been undistinguished from the meanest of his brethren of mankind. Endowed from his boyhood, by the lavish bounties of nature, with rank, wealth, power, health, and personal beauty, he was as compassionate as if sorrow had been his daily companion from his youth. An enthusiast in music, architecture, and polite learning, he applied himself to all the details of public business with the assiduity of one who had no other means of subsistence. Surpassed by no monarch in modern Europe in the munificence of his bounties or in the splendor of his public works, those purest and most sumptuous of the luxuries of royalty were in no single instance defrayed from any tributes levied from his people. Passionately attached to his kindred, he never enriched or exalted them at the public expense. The heir of conquests and territorial acquisitions of which the responsibility rested with his grandfather, the inestimable advantages with himself, he restored to his rivals and his adversaries every fief and province which, upon the strictest scrutiny by the most impartial umpires, appeared to have been added to the royal domain by unjust, or even by questionable means.

What, then, was the basis of this sacred harmony in the character of Louis? I answer, or rather every page of his history answers, that it flowed from his constant devotion to that holy canon, and to that divine model, in which every utterance and every action are harmonious. His eye was continually turned to that eternal fountain of light with all the docility of childhood. He had early attained to that maturity of moral stature in which the abdication of self-will to the supreme will becomes at once a habit and a delight. In the service of his Creator he found and enjoyed a perfect freedom. It was a service often rendered in pain, in toil, in sickness, and in danger, but ever rendered with a heart full of cheerfulness and confidence and hope.

SIR JAMES STEPHEN,
Lectures on the History of France.

JOAN OF ARC, THE MAID OF ORLEANS.

WHAT is to be thought of *her?* What is to be thought of the poor shepherd-girl from the hills and forests of Lorraine, that—like the Hebrew shepherd-boy from the hills and forests of Judea—rose suddenly out of the quiet, out of the safety, out of the religious inspiration, rooted in deep pastoral solicitudes, to a station in the van of armies, and to the more perilous station at the right hand of kings? The Hebrew boy inaugurated his patriotic mission by an *act,* by a victorious *act,* such as no man could deny. But so did the girl of Lorraine, if we read her story as it was read by those who saw her nearest. Adverse armies bore witness to the boy as no pretender; but so did they to the gentle girl. Judged by the voices of all who saw them *from a station of good-will,* both were found true and loyal to any promises involved in their first acts. Enemies it was that made the difference between their subsequent fortunes. The boy rose —to a splendor and a noonday prosperity, both personal and public, that rang through the records of his people, and became a by-word amongst his posterity for a thousand years, until the sceptre was departing from Judah. The poor, forsaken girl, on the contrary, drank not herself from that cup of rest which she had secured for France. She never sang together with them the songs that rose in her native Domrémy, as echoes to the departing steps of invaders. She mingled not in the festal dances at Vaucouleurs which celebrated in rapture the redemption of France. No! for her voice was then silent. No! for her feet were dust. Pure, innocent, noble-hearted girl! whom, from earliest youth, ever I believed in as full of truth and self-sacrifice, this was amongst the strongest pledges for *thy* side, that never once—no, not for a moment of weakness—didst thou revel in the vision of coronets and honors from men. Coronets for thee! Oh, no! Honors, if they come when all is over, are for those that share thy blood. Daughter of Domrémy, when the gratitude of thy king shall awaken, thou wilt be sleeping the sleep of the dead. Call her, king of France, but she will not hear thee! Cite her by thy apparitors to come and receive a robe of honor, but she will be found *en contumace*. When the thunders of universal France, as even yet may happen, shall proclaim the grandeur of the poor shepherd-girl that gave up all for her country—thy ear, young shepherd-girl, will have been deaf for five centuries. To suffer and to do, that was thy portion in this life; to *do*—never for thyself, always for others; to *suffer*—never in the persons of generous champions, always in thy own; that was thy destiny; and not for a moment was it hidden from thyself. "Life," thou saidst, "is short, and the sleep which is in the grave is long. Let me use that life, so transitory, for the glory of those heavenly dreams destined to comfort the sleep which is so long." This poor creature—pure from every suspicion of even a visionary self-interest, even as she was pure in senses more obvious— never once did this holy child, as regarded herself, relax from her belief in the darkness that was travelling to meet her. She might not prefigure the very manner of her death; she saw not in vision, perhaps, the aërial altitude of the fiery scaffold, the spectators without end on every road pouring into Rouen as to a coronation, the surging smoke, the volleying flames, the hostile faces all around, the pitying eye that lurked but here and there, until nature and imperishable truth broke loose from artificial restraints; these might not be apparent through the mists of the hurrying future. But the voice that called her to death, *that* she heard forever.

Great was the throne of France, even in those days, and great was he that sat upon it; but well Joanna knew that not the throne, nor he that sat upon it, was for *her;* but, on the contrary, that she was for *them;* not she by them, but they by her, should rise from the dust. Gorgeous were the lilies of France, and for centuries had the privilege to spread their beauty over land and sea, until, in another century, the wrath of God and man combined to wither them; but well Joanna knew, early at Domrémy she had read that bitter truth, that the lilies of France would decorate no garland for *her.* Flower nor bud, bell nor blossom, would ever bloom for *her.*

On the Wednesday after Trinity Sunday, in 1431, being then about nineteen years of age, the Maid of Arc underwent her martyrdom. She was conducted before midday, guarded by eight hundred spearmen, to a platform of prodigious height, constructed of wooden billets, supported by hollow spaces in every direction, for the creation of air-currents. "The pile struck terror," says M. Michelet, "by its height." .... There would be a certainty of calumny rising against her—some people would impute to her a willingness to recant. No innocence could escape *that.* Now, had she really testified this willingness on the scaffold it would have argued nothing at all but the weakness of a genial nature shrinking from the instant approach of torment. And those will often pity that weakness most who in their own person would yield to it least. Meantime there never was a calumny uttered that drew less support from the recorded circumstances. It rests upon no positive testimony, and it has a weight of contradicting testimony to stem..... What else but her meek, saintly demeanor won, from the enemies that till now had believed her a witch, tears of rapturous admiration? "Ten thousand men," says M. Michelet himself, "ten thousand men wept; and of those ten thousand the majority were political enemies." What else was it but her constancy, united with her angelic gentleness, that drove the fanatic English soldier—who had sworn to throw a faggot on her scaffold as *his* tribute of abhorrence that *did* so, that fulfilled his vow—suddenly to turn away a penitent for life, saying everywhere that he had seen a dove rising upon wings to heaven from the ashes where she had stood? What else drove the executioner to kneel at every shrine for pardon to *his* share in the tragedy? And if all this were insufficient, then I cite the closing act of her life as valid on her behalf, were all other testimonies against her. The executioner had been directed to apply the torch from below. He did so. The fiery smoke rose up in billowy columns. A Dominican monk was then standing almost at her side. Wrapped up in his sublime office, he saw not the danger, but still persisted in his prayers. Even then, when the last enemy was racing up the fiery stairs to seize her, even at that moment did this noblest of girls think only for *him*, the one friend that would not forsake her, and not for herself; bidding him with her last breath to care for his own preservation, but to leave *her* to God. That girl, whose latest breath descended in this sublime expression of self-oblivion, did not utter the word *recant*, either with her lips or in her heart. No, she did not, though one should rise from the dead to swear it.

THOMAS DE QUINCEY,
Miscellaneous Essays.

DEATH OF MARIE ANTOINETTE.

Is there a man's heart that thinks without pity of those long months and years and slow-wasting ignominy; of thy birth, self-cradled in imperial Schönbrunn, the winds of heaven not to visit thy face too roughly, thy foot to light on softness, thy eyes on splendor; and then of thy death, or hundred deaths, to which the guillotine, and Fouquier-Tinville's judgment bar was but the merciful end! Look *there*, O man born of woman! The blood of that fair face is wasted, the hair is gray with care; the brightness of those eyes is quenched, their lids hang drooping, the face is stony pale, as of one living in death. Mean weeds which her own hand has mended attire the queen of the world. The death hurdle where thou sittest pale, motionless, which only curses environ, has to stop; a people, drunk with vengeance, will drink it again in full draught, looking at thee there. Far as the eye reaches, a multitudinous sea of maniac heads, the air deaf with their triumph-yell! The living-dead must shudder with yet one other pang; her startled blood yet again suffuses with the hue of agony that pale face, which she hides with her hands. There is there *no* heart to say, God pity thee! Oh, think not of these; think of HIM whom thou worshippest, the Crucified—who also treading the wine-press *alone* fronted sorrow still deeper; and triumphed over it and made it holy, and built of it a "sanctuary of sorrow" for thee and all the wretched! Thy path of thorns is nigh ended, one long last look at the Tuilleries, where thy step was once so light—where thy children shall not dwell. The head is on the block; the axe rushes—dumb lies the world; that wild-yelling world, and all its madness, is behind thee.

THOMAS CARLYLE,
Critical and Miscellaneous Essays.

THE FRENCH REVOLUTION IN ITS RELATION WITH THE POPE.

It is not for his Holiness that we intend this consolatory declaration of our own weakness, and of the tyrannous temper of his grand enemy. That prince has known both the one and the other from the beginning. The artists of the French Revolution had given their very first essays and sketches of robbery and desolation against his territories, in a far more cruel "murdering piece" than had ever entered into the imagination of painter or poet. Without ceremony they tore from his cherishing arms the possessions which he had held for five hundred years, undisturbed by all the ambition of all the ambitious monarchs who during that period have reigned in France. Is it to him, in whose wrong we have in our late negotiation ceded his now unhappy countries near the Rhone, lately amongst the most flourishing (perhaps the most flourishing for their extent) of all the countries upon earth, that we are to prove the sincerity of our resolution to make peace with the Republic of Barbarism? That venerable potentate and Pontiff is sunk deep into the vale of years; he is half disarmed by his peaceful character; his dominions are more than half disarmed by a peace of two hundred years, defended as they were, not by force, but by reverence: yet, in all these straits, we see him display, against the recent ruins and the new defacements of his plundered capital, along with the mild and decorated piety of the modern, all the spirit and magnanimity of ancient Rome. Does he, who, though himself unable to defend them, nobly refuse to receive pecuniary compensation for the protection he owed to his people of Avignon, Carpentras, and the Venaissin,—does he want proofs of our good disposition to deliver over that people, without any security for them, or any compensation to their sovereign, to this cruel enemy? Does he want to be satisfied of the sincerity of our humiliation to France, who has seen his free, fertile, and happy city and State of Bologna, the cradle of regenerated law, the seat of sciences and of arts, so hideously metamorphosed, whilst he was crying to Great Britain for aid, and offering to purchase that aid at any price? Is it him who sees that chosen spot of plenty and delight converted into a Jacobin ferocious republic, dependent on the homicides of France,—is it him, who, from the miracles of his beneficent industry, has done a work which defied the power of the Roman Emperors, though with an enthralled world to labor for them,—is it him who has drained and cultivated the Pontine Marshes, that we are to satisfy of our cordial spirit of conciliation with those who, in their equity, are restoring Holland again to the seas, whose maxims poison more than the exhalations of the most deadly fens, and who turn all the fertilities of Nature and of Art into an howling desert? Is it to him we are to demonstrate the good faith of our submissions to the Cannibal Republic—to him, who is commanded to deliver up into their hands Ancona and Civita Vecchia, seats of commerce raised by the wise and liberal labors and expenses of the present and late Pontiffs, ports not more belonging to the Ecclesiastical State than to the commerce of Great Britain, thus wresting from his hands the power of the keys of the centre of Italy, as before they had taken possession of the keys of the northern part from the hands of the unhappy King of Sardinia, the natural ally of England? Is it to him we are to prove our good faith in the peace which we are soliciting to receive from the hands of his and our robbers, the enemies of all arts, all sciences, all civilization, and all commerce?

EDMUND BURKE,
Letter III., On a Regicide Peace.

THE IMPRISONMENT OF POPE PIUS VII.

THIS day of miracles, in which the human heart has been strung to its extremest point of energy, this day, to which posterity will look for instances of every crime and every virtue, holds not in its page of wonders a more sublime phenomenon than that calumniated Pontiff. Placed at the very pinnacle of human elevation, surrounded by the pomp of the Vatican and the splendors of the court, pouring forth the mandates of Christ from the throne of the Cæsars, nations were his subjects, kings were his companions, religion was his handmaid; he went forth gorgeous with the accumulated dignity of ages, every knee bending, and every eye blessing the prince of one world and the prophet of another. Have we not seen him, in one moment, his crown crumbled, his sceptre a reed, his throne a shadow, his home a dungeon! But if we have, Catholics, it was only to show how inestimable is human virtue compared with human grandeur; it was only to show those whose faith was failing, and whose fears were strengthening, that the simplicity of the patriarchs, the piety of the saints, and the patience of the martyrs, had not wholly vanished. Perhaps it was also ordained to show the bigot at home, as well as the tyrant abroad, that though the person might be chained, and the motive calumniated, Religion was still strong enough to support her sons, and to confound, if she could not reclaim, her enemies. No threats could awe, no promises could tempt, no suffering could appal him; mid the damps of his dungeon he dashed away the cup in which the pearl of his liberty was to be dissolved. Only reflect on the state of the world at that moment! All around him was convulsed, the very foundations of the earth seemed giving way, the comet was let loose that "from its fiery hair shook pestilence and death," the twilight was gathering, the tempest was roaring, the darkness was at hand; but he towered sublime, like the last mountain in the deluge—majestic, not less in his elevation than in his solitude, immutable amid change, magnificent amid ruin, the last remnant of earth's beauty, the last resting-place of heaven's light!

It is not unworthy of remark, that the last day of France's triumph, and the first of her decline, was that on which her insatiable chieftain smote the holy head of your religion. When the man now unborn shall trace the story of that eventful day, he will see the adopted child of fortune borne on the wings of victory from clime to clime, marking every movement with a triumph, and every pause with a crown, till time, space, seasons, nay, even nature herself, seeming to vanish before him, until in the blasphemy of his ambition he smote the apostle of his God, and dared to raise the everlasting Cross amid his perishable trophies!

CHARLES PHILLIPS,
Speeches.

CHATEAUBRIAND.

It was in the disastrous days of the French Revolution that Chateaubriand arose, and bent the force of his lofty mind to vindicate the persecuted but imperishable faith of his fathers. In early youth, he was at first carried away by the fashionable infidelity of his times; and in his "Essais Historiques," which was published in 1792, in London, while the principles of virtue and natural religion are unceasingly maintained, he seems to have doubted whether the Christian religion was not crumbling with the institutions of society. But misfortune, that great corrector of the vices of the world, soon changed these faulty views. In the days of exile and adversity, when, by the waters of Babylon, he sat down and wept, he reverted to the faith and belief of his fathers, and inhaled in the school of adversity those noble maxims of devotion and duty which have ever since regulated his conduct in life.

The great characteristic of the French author is the impassioned and enthusiastic turn of his mind. Master of immense information, thoroughly imbued at once with the learning of classical and catholic times ; gifted with a retentive memory, a poetical fancy, and a painter's eye, he brings to bear upon every subject the force of erudition, the images of poetry, the charms of varied scenery, and the eloquence of impassioned feeling. Hence his writings display a reach and variety of imagery, a depth of light and shadow, a vigor of thought, and an extent of illustration, to which there is nothing comparable in any other writer, ancient or modern, with whom we are acquainted. All that he has seen, or read, or heard seem present to his mind, whatever he does, or wherever he is. He illustrates the genius of Christianity by the beauties of classical learning, inhales the spirit of ancient prophecy on the shores of the Jordan, dreams on the banks of the Eurotas of the solitude and gloom of the American forests ; visits the Holy Sepulchre with a mind alternately devoted to the devotion of a pilgrim, the curiosity of an antiquary, and the enthusiasm of a crusader, and combines, in his romances, with the tender feelings of chivalrous love, the heroism of Roman virtue, and the sublimity of Christian martyrdom. His writings are less a faithful portrait of any particular age or country, than an assemblage of all that is grand, and generous, and elevated in human nature. He drinks deep of inspiration at all the fountains where it has ever been poured forth to mankind, and delights us less by the accuracy of any particular picture, than the traits of genius which he has combined from every quarter where its footsteps have trod. His style seems formed on the lofty strains of Isaiah, or the beautiful images of the Book of Job, more than all the classical or modern literature with which his mind is so amply stored. He is admitted by all Frenchmen, of whatever party, to be the most perfect living master of their language, and to have gained for it beauties unknown to the age of Bossuet and Fenelon. Less polished in his periods, less sonorous in his diction, less melodious in his rhythm, than these illustrious writers, he is incomparably more varied, rapid, and energetic; his ideas flow in quicker succession, his words flow in more striking antithesis; the past, the present, and the future rise up at once before us; and we see how strongly the stream of genius, instead of gliding down the smooth current of ordinary life, has been broken and agitated by the cataract of revolution.

Sir Archibald Alison,
Miscellaneous Essays.

ISABELLA OF CASTILE.

THE acquisition of an important kingdom in the heart of Europe, and of the New World beyond the waters, which promised to pour into her lap all the fabled treasures of the Indies, was rapidly raising Spain to the first rank of European powers. But, in the noontide of her success, she was to experience a fatal shock in the loss of that illustrious personage, who had so long and so gloriously presided over her destinies. We have had occasion to notice more than once the declining state of the queen's health for the last few years. Her constitution had been greatly impaired by incessant personal fatigue and exposure, and by the unremitting activity of her mind. It had suffered far more severely, however, from a series of heavy domestic calamities, which had fallen on her with little intermission since the death of her mother in 1496. The next year, she followed to the grave the remains of her only son, the heir and hope of the monarchy, just entering on his prime; and in the succeeding, was called on to render the same sad offices to the best beloved of her daughters, the amiable queen of Portugal.

The severe illness occasioned by this last blow terminated in a dejection of spirits, from which she never entirely recovered. Her surviving children were removed far from her into distant lands; with the occasional exception, indeed, of Joanna, who caused a still deeper pang to her mother's affectionate heart, by exhibiting infirmities, which justified the most melancholy presages for the future.

Far from abandoning herself to weak and useless repining, however, Isabella sought consolation, where it was best to be found, in the exercises of piety, and in the discharge of the duties attached to her exalted station. Accordingly, we find her attentive as ever to the minutest interest of her subjects; supporting her great minister Ximenes in his schemes of reform, quickening the zeal for discovery in the west, and, at the close of the year 1503, on the alarm of the French invasion, rousing her dying energies, to kindle a spirit of resistance in her people. These strong mental exertions, however, only accelerated the decay of her bodily strength, which was gradually sinking under that sickness of heart which admits of no cure, and scarcely of consolation.

Ferdinand soon after fell ill of a fever, and the queen was seized with the same disorder, accompanied with more alarming symptoms. Her illness was exasperated by anxiety for her husband, and she refused to credit the favorable reports of his physicians, while he was detained from her presence. His vigorous constitution, however, threw off the malady, while hers gradually failed under it. Her tender heart was more keenly sensible than his to the unhappy condition of their child, and to the gloomy prospects which awaited her beloved Castile.

Her faithful follower, Martyr, was with the court at this time in Medina del Campo. In a letter to the Count of Tendilla, dated October 7th, he states, that the most serious apprehensions were entertained by the physicians for the queen's fate. "Her whole system," he says, "is pervaded by a consuming fever. She loathes food of every kind, and is tormented with incessant thirst, while the disorder has all the appearance of terminating in a dropsy."

In the meanwhile Isabella lost nothing of her solicitude for the welfare of her people, and the great concerns of government. While reclining, as she was obliged to do a great part of the day, on her couch, she listened to the recital or reading of whatever occurred of interest at home or abroad. She gave audience to distinguished foreigners, especially such Italians as could acquaint her with particulars of the late war, and above all in regard to Gonsalvo de Cordova, in whose fortunes she had always taken the liveliest concern. She received with pleasure, too, such intelligent travellers as her renown had attracted to the Castilian Court. She drew forth their stores of various information, and dismissed them, says a writer of the age, penetrated with the deepest admiration of that strength of mind which sustained her so nobly under the weight of a mortal malady.

This malady was now rapidly gaining ground. On the 15th of October we have another epistle of Martyr, of the following melancholy tenor: "You ask me respecting the state of the queen's health. We sit sorrowful in the palace all day long, tremblingly waiting the hour when religion and virtue shall quit the earth with her. Let us pray that we may be permitted to follow hereafter where she is soon to go. She so far transcends all human excellence, that there is scarcely anything of mortality about her. She can hardly be said to die, but to pass into a nobler existence, which should rather excite our envy than our sorrow. She leaves the world filled with her renown, and she goes to enjoy life eternal with her God in heaven. I write this," he concludes, "between hope and fear, while the breath is still fluttering within her."

The deepest gloom now overspread the nation. Even Isabella's long illness had failed to prepare the minds of her faithful people for the sad catastrophe. Isabella in the meantime was deluded with no false hopes. She felt too surely the decay of her bodily strength, and she resolved to perform what temporal duties yet remained for her, while her faculties were yet unclouded.

On the 12th of October she executed that celebrated testament, which reflects so clearly the peculiar qualities of her mind and character. She begins with prescribing the arrangements for her burial. She orders her remains to be transported to Granada, to the Franciscan monastery of Santa Isabella in the Alhambra, and there deposited in a low and humble sepulchre, without other memorial than a plain inscription on it. "But," she continues, "should the king my lord, prefer a sepulchre in some other place, then my will is that my body be there transported, and laid by his side; that the union we have enjoyed in this world, and, through the mercy of God, may hope again for our souls in heaven, may be represented by our bodies in the earth." Then, desirous of correcting by her example, in this last act of her life, the wasteful pomp of funeral obsequies to which the Castilians were addicted, she commanded that her own should be performed in the plainest and most unostentatious manner, and that the sum saved by this economy should be distributed in alms among the poor.

Concluding in the same beautiful strain of conjugal tenderness in which she began, she says, " I beseech the king, my lord, that he will accept all my jewels, or such as he shall select, so that, seeing them, he may be reminded of the singular love I bore him while living, and that I am now waiting for him in a better world; by which remembrance he may be encouraged to live more justly and holily in this."

She had now adjusted all her worldly concerns, and she prepared to devote herself, during the brief space which remained, to those of a higher nature. It was but the last act of a life of preparation. She had the misfortune, common to persons of her rank, to be separated in her last moments from those whose filial tenderness might have done so much to soften the bitterness of death. But she had the good fortune, most rare to have secured for this trying hour the solace of disinterested friendship; for she beheld around her the friends of her childhood, formed and proved in the dark season of adversity.

As she saw them bathed in tears around her bed, she calmly said, "Do not weep for me, nor waste your time in fruitless prayers for my recovery, but pray rather for the salvation of my soul." At length, having received the sacraments, and performed all the offices of a sincere and devout Christian, she gently expired a little before noon, on Wednesday, November 26, 1504, in the fifty-fourth year of her age, and thirtieth of her reign.

"My hand," says Peter Martyr, in a letter written on the same day to the archbishop of Granada, "falls powerless by my side, for very sorrow. The world has lost its noblest ornament; a loss to be deplored not only by Spain, which she has so long carried forward in the career of glory, but by every nation in Christendom; for she was the mirror of every virtue, the shield of the innocent, and an avenging sword to the wicked. I know of none of her sex, in ancient or modern times, who in my judgment is at all worthy to be named with this incomparable woman."

Isabella was of the middle height, and well proportioned. She had a clear, fresh complexion, with light blue eyes and auburn hair—a style of beauty exceedingly rare in Spain. Her features were regular, and universally allowed to be uncommonly handsome. The illusion which attaches to rank, more especially when united with engaging manners, might lead us to suspect some exaggeration in the encomiums so liberally lavished on her. But they would seem to be in a great measure justified by the portraits that remain of her, which combine a faultless symmetry of features with singular sweetness and intelligence of expression.

Her manners were most gracious and pleasing. They were marked by natural dignity and modest reserve, tempered by an affability which flowed from the kindliness of her disposition. She was the last person to be approached with undue familiarity; yet the respect which she imposed was mingled with the strongest feelings of devotion and love.

Among her moral qualities, the most conspicuous, perhaps, was her magnanimity. She betrayed nothing little or selfish, in thought or action. Her schemes were vast, and executed in the same noble spirit in which they were conceived. She scorned to avail herself of advantages offered by the perfidy of others. Where she had once given her confidence, she gave her hearty and steady support; and she was scrupulous to redeem any pledge she had made to those who had ventured in her cause. She sustained Ximenes in all his salutary reforms. She seconded Columbus in the prosecution of his arduous enterprise, and shielded him from the calumny of his enemies. She did the same good service to her favorite, Gonsalvo de Cordova; and the day of her death was, and, as it proved, truly for both, as the last of their good fortune. Artifice and duplicity were abhorrent to her character. She was incapable of harboring any petty distrust or latent malice; and although stern in the execution and exaction of public justice, she made the most generous allowance, and even sometimes advances, to those who had personally injured her.

But the principle which gave a peculiar coloring to every feature of Isabella's mind, was her piety. It shone forth from the very depths of her soul with a heavenly radiance which illuminated her whole character. Fortunately, her earliest years had been passed in the rugged school of adversity, under the eye of a mother who implanted in her serious mind such strong principles of religion as nothing in after-life had power to shake.

WILLIAM H. PRESCOTT,
History of the Reign of Ferdinand and Isabella the Catholic.

THE JESUITS.

The party which had now the undisputed ascendant were denominated "Jesuits," as a term of reproach, by the enemies of that famous society in the Church of Rome, as well as by those among the Protestant communions. A short account of their origin and character may facilitate a faint conception of the admiration, jealousy, fear, and hatred,—the profound submission or fierce resistance,—which that formidable name once inspired. Their institution originated in pure zeal for religion, glowing in the breast of Loyola, a Spanish soldier,—a man full of imagination and sensibility,—in a country where wars, rather civil than foreign, waged against unbelievers for ages, had rendered a passion for spreading the Catholic faith a national point of honor, and blended it with the pursuit of glory as well as with the memory of past renown. The legislative forethought of his successors gave form and order to the product of enthusiasm, and bestowed laws and institutions on their society, which were admirably fitted to its various ends. Having arisen in the age of the Reformation they naturally became the champions of the Church against her enemies. They cultivated polite literature with splendid success; they were the earliest and perhaps the most extensive reformers of European education, which in their schools made a larger stride than it has done at any succeeding moment;* and by the just reputation of their learning, as well as by the weapons with which it armed them, they were enabled to carry on a vigorous contest against the most learned impugners of the authority of the Church.

While the nations of the Peninsula hastened to spread religion in the newly explored regions of the East and West, the Jesuits, the missionaries of that age, either repaired or atoned for the evils caused by their countrymen. In India they suffered martyrdom with heroic constancy. They penetrated through the barrier which Chinese

---

* "For education," says Bacon, within fifty years of the institution of the Order, "consult the schools of the Jesuits. Nothing hitherto tried in practice surpasses them" (De Augment. Scient., lib. vi., cap. 4.) "Education, that excellent part of ancient discipline, has been, in some sorts, revived of late times in the colleges of the Jesuits, of whom in regard of this and of some other points of human learning and moral matters I may say 'Talis cum sis utinam noster esses'" (Advancement of Learning).

policy opposed to the entrance of strangers,—cultivating the most difficult of languages with such success as to compose hundreds of volumes in it; and, by the public utility of their scientific acquirements, obtained toleration, patronage, and personal honors, from that jealous government. The natives of America, who generally felt the comparative superiority of the European race only in a more rapid or a more gradual destruction, and to whom even the Quakers dealt out little more than penurious justice, were, under the paternal rule of the Jesuits, reclaimed from savage manners, and instructed in the arts and duties of civilized life. At the opposite point of society, they were fitted by their release from conventual life, and their allowed intercourse with the world, for the perilous office of secretly guiding the conscience of princes. They maintained the highest station as a religious body in the literature of Catholic countries. No other association ever sent forth so many disciples who reached such eminence in departments so various and unlike. While some of their number ruled the royal penitents at Versailles or the Escurial, others were teaching the use of the spade and the shuttle to the naked savages of Paraguay; a third body daily endangered their lives in an attempt to convert the Hindus to Christianity; a fourth carried on the controversy against the Reformers; a portion were at liberty to cultivate polite literature; while the greater part continued to be employed either in carrying on the education of Catholic Europe, or in the government of their society, and in ascertaining the ability and disposition of the junior members, so that well-qualified men might be selected for the extraordinary variety of offices in their immense commonwealth. The most famous Constitutionalists, the most skilful casuists, the ablest schoolmasters, the most celebrated professors, the best teachers of the humblest mechanical arts, the missionaries who could most bravely encounter martyrdom, or who with the most patient skill could infuse the rudiments of religion into the minds of ignorant tribes or prejudiced nations, were the growth of their fertile schools.

SIR JAS. MACKINTOSH,
Review of the Causes of Revolution. 1688.

RESIGNATION OF CHARLES V.

This great Emperor, in the plenitude of his power, and in possession of all the honors which can flatter the heart of man, took the extraordinary resolution to resign his kingdoms; and to withdraw entirely from any concern in business or the affairs of this world, in order that he might spend the remainder of his days in retirement and solitude.

Though it requires neither deep reflection, nor extraordinary discernment, to discover that the state of royalty is not exempt from cares and disappointments; though most of those who are exalted to a throne, find solicitude, and satiety, and disgust, to be their perpetual attendants, in that envied pre-eminence; yet, to descend voluntarily from the supreme to a subordinate station, and to relinquish the possession of power in order to attain the enjoyment of happiness, seems to be an effort too great for the human mind.

Several instances, indeed, occur in history, of monarchs who have quitted a throne, and have ended their days in retirement. But they were either weak princes, who took this resolution rashly, and repented of it as soon as it was taken; or unfortunate princes, from whose hands some strong rival had wrested their sceptre, and compelled them to descend with reluctance into a private station.

Diocletian is, perhaps, the only prince capable of holding the reins of government, who ever resigned them from deliberate choice; and who continued, during many years, to enjoy the tranquillity of retirement, without fetching one penitent sigh, or casting back one look of desire toward the power or dignity which he had abandoned.

No wonder, then, that Charles' resignation should fill all Europe with astonishment, and give rise, both among his contemporaries and among the historians of that period, to various conjectures concerning the motives which determined a prince, whose ruling passion had been uniformly the love of power, at the age of fifty-six, when objects of ambition operate with full force on the mind, and are pursued with the greatest ardor, to take a resolution so singular and unexpected.

The Emperor, in pursuance of his determination, having assembled the States of the Low Countries at Brussels, seated himself, for the last time, in the chair of state; on one side of which was placed his son, and on the other his sister, the queen of Hungary, regent of the Netherlands, with a splendid retinue of the grandees of Spain, and princes of the empire standing behind him.

The president of the council of Flanders, by his command, explained in a few words his intention in calling this extraordinary meeting of the state. He then read the instrument of resignation by which Charles surrendered to his son Philip all his territories, jurisdiction, and authority in the Low Countries; absolving his subjects there from their oath of allegiance to him, which he required them to transfer to Philip, his lawful heir; and to serve him with the same loyalty and zeal that they had manifested during so long a course of years, in support of his government.

Charles then rose from his seat, and leaning on the shoulder of the Prince of Orange, because he was unable to stand without support, he addressed himself to the audience; and, from a paper which he held in his hand, in order to assist his memory, he recounted with dignity, but without ostentation, all the great things which he had undertaken and performed since the commencement of his administration.

He observed, that from the seventeenth year of

his age, he had dedicated all his thoughts and attention to public objects, reserving no portion of his time for the indulgence of his ease, and very little for the enjoyment of private pleasures; that either in a pacific or hostile manner, he had visited Germany nine times, Spain six times, France four times, Italy seven times, and the Low Countries ten times, England twice, Africa as often, and had made eleven voyages by sea.

That while his health permitted him to discharge his duty, and the vigor of his constitution was equal in any degree to the arduous office of governing dominions so extensive, he had never shunned labor nor repined under fatigue; that now when his health was broken, and his vigor exhausted by the rage of an incurable distemper his growing infirmities admonished him to retire.

Nor was he so fond of reigning, as to retain the sceptre in an impotent hand which was no longer able to protect his subjects, or to render them happy; that instead of a sovereign worn out with diseases, and scarcely half alive, he gave them one in the prime of life, accustomed already to govern, and who added to the vigor of youth all the attention and sagacity of maturer years.

That if during the course of a long administration, he had committed any material error in government; or if under the pressure of so many and great affairs, and amid the attention which he had been obliged to give to them he had either neglected or injured any of his subjects, he now implored their forgiveness.

That for his part, he should ever retain a grateful sense of their fidelity and attachment, and would carry the remembrance of it along with him to the place of his retreat, as his sweetest consolation, as well as the best reward for all his services; and in his last prayers to Almighty God would pour forth his ardent wishes for their welfare.

Then turning toward Philip, who fell on his knees and kissed his father's hand, "If," said he, "I had left you by my death this rich inheritance to which I had made such large additions, some regard would have been justly due to my memory on that account; but now, when I voluntarily resign to you what I might have still retained, I may well expect the warmest expression of thanks on your part.

"With these, however, I dispense, and shall consider your concern for the welfare of your subjects and your love of them, as the best and most acceptable testimony of your gratitude to me. It is in your power, by a wise and virtuous administration, to justify the extraordinary proof which I give this day of my paternal affection, and to demonstrate that you are worthy of the confidence which I repose in you.

"Preserve an inviolable regard for religion; maintain the Catholic faith in its purity; let the laws of your country be sacred in your eyes; encroach not on the rights and privileges of your people; and if the time shall ever come when you shall wish to enjoy the tranquillity of private life, may you have a son endowed with such qualities that you can resign your sceptre to him with as much satisfaction as I give up mine to you."

As soon as Charles had finished this long address to his subjects, and to their new sovereign, he sunk into the chair exhausted and ready to faint with the fatigue of so extraordinary an effort. During his discourse, the whole audience melted into tears; some from admiration of his magnanimity; others softened by the expressions of tenderness toward his son, and of love to his people; and all were affected with the deepest sorrow at losing a sovereign who had distinguished the Netherlands, his native country, with particular marks of his regard and attachment.

A few weeks after the resignation of the Netherlands, Charles, in an assembly no less splendid, and with a ceremonial equally pompous, resigned to his son the crowns of Spain, with all the territories depending on them, both in the old and in the new world. Of all these vast possessions, he reserved nothing for himself but an annual pension of a hundred thousand crowns, to defray the charges of his family and to afford him a small sum for acts of beneficence and charity.

Nothing now remained to detain him from that retreat for which he languished. Everything having been prepared some time for his voyage, he set out for Zuitberg in Zealand, where the fleet had orders to rendezvous.

In his way thither, he passed through Ghent; and after stopping there a few days, to indulge that tender and pleasing melancholy, which arises in the mind of every man in the decline of life, on visiting the place of his nativity, and viewing the scenes and objects familiar to him in his early youth, he pursued his journey, accompanied by his son Philip, his daughter the archduchess, his sisters the dowager queens of France and Hungary, Maximilian his son-in-law, and a numerous retinue of the Flemish nobility.

Before he went on board, he dismissed them, with marks of his attention or regard; and taking leave of Philip with all the tenderness of a father who embraced his son for the last time, he set sail under convoy of a large fleet of Spanish, Flemish, and English ships.

His voyage was prosperous, and agreeable; and he arrived at Laredo in Biscay, on the eleventh day after he left Zealand. As soon as he landed, he fell prostrate on the ground; and considering himself now as dead to the world, he kissed the earth, and said, "Naked came I out of my mother's womb, and naked I now return to thee, thou common mother of mankind."

From Laredo he proceeded to Valladolid. There he took a last and tender leave of his two sisters; whom he would not permit to accompany him to his solitude, though they entreated it with tears; not only that they might have the consolation of contributing, by their attendance and care, to mitigate or to soothe his sufferings, but that they might reap instruction and benefit, by joining with him in those pious exercises to which he had consecrated the remainder of his days.

From Valladolid, he continued his journey to Plazencia in Estremadura. He had passed through that city a great many years before; and having been struck at that time with the delightful situation of the monastery of St. Justus, belonging to the order of St. Jerome, not many miles distant from that place, he had then observed to some of his attendants, that this was a spot to which Diocletian might have retired with pleasure.

The impression had remained so strong on his mind, that he pitched upon it as the place of his retreat. It was seated in a vale of no great extent, watered by a small brook, and surrounded by rising grounds, covered with lofty trees. From the nature of the soil, as well as the temperature of the climate, it was esteemed the most healthful and delicious situation in Spain.

Some months before his resignation, he had sent an architect thither, to add a new apartment to the monastery, for his accommodation; but he gave strict orders that the style of the building should be such as suited his present station, rather than his former dignity. It consisted only of six rooms, four of them in the form of friars' cells, with naked walls; the other two, each twenty feet square, were hung with brown cloth, and furnished in the most simple manner.

They were on a level with the ground, with a door on one side into a garden, of which Charles himself had given the plan, and had filled it with various plants, which he purposed to cultivate with his own hands. On the other side, they communicated with the chapel of the monastery, in which he was to perform his devotions.

Into this humble retreat, hardly sufficient for the comfortable accommodation of a private gentleman, did Charles enter, with twelve domestics only. He buried there, in solitude and silence, his grandeur, his ambition, together with all those vast projects which, during half a century, had alarmed and agitated Europe; filling every kingdom in it, by turns, with the terror of his arms, and the dread of being subjected to his power.

In this retirement, Charles formed such a plan of life for himself as would have suited the condition of a private person of a moderate fortune. His table was neat but plain; his domestics few; his intercourse with them familiar; all the cumbersome and ceremonious forms of attendance on his person were entirely abolished, as destructive of that social ease and tranquillity which he courted, in order to soothe the remainder of his days.

As the mildness of the climate, together with his deliverance from the burdens and cares of government, procured him, at first, a considerable remission from the acute pains with which he had been long tormented, he enjoyed, perhaps, more complete satisfaction in this humble solitude than all his grandeur had ever yielded him.

The ambitious thoughts and projects which had so long engrossed and disquieted him, were quite effaced from his mind. Far from taking any part in the political transactions of the princes of Europe, he restrained his curiosity even from any inquiry concerning them; and he seemed to view the busy scene which he had abandoned, with all the contempt and indifference arising from his thorough experience of its vanity, as well as from the pleasing reflection of having disentangled himself from its cares.

WILLIAM ROBERTSON,
History of the Reign of the Emperor Charles the Fifth.

THE NECESSITY OF AN INFALLIBLE GUIDE.

THE characteristic I speak of is an absolute infallibility. Any supernatural religion that renounces its claim to this, it is clear can profess to be a semi-revelation only. It is a hybrid thing, partly natural and partly supernatural, and it thus practically has all the qualities of a religion that is wholly natural. In so far as it professes to be revealed, it of course professes to be infallible; but if the revealed part be in the first place hard to distinguish, and in the second place hard to understand—if it may mean many things, and many of those contradictory—it might just as well have been never made at all. To make it in any sense an infallible revelation, or in other words a revelation at all, *to us*, we need a power to interpret the testament that shall have equal authority with that testament itself.

Simple as this truth seems, mankind have been a long time in learning it. Indeed, it is only in the present day that its practical meaning has come generally to be recognized. But now at this moment, upon all sides of us, history is teaching it to us by an example, so clearly that we can no longer mistake it.

That example is Protestant Christianity, and the condition to which, after three centuries, it is now visibly bringing itself. It is at last beginning to exhibit to us the true results of the denial of infallibility to a religion that professes to be supernatural. It is fast evaporating into a mere natural theism, and is thus showing us what, as a governing power, natural theism is. Let us look at England, Europe, and America, and consider the condition of the entire Protestant world. Religion, it is true, we shall find in it; but it is religion from which not only the supernatural element is disappearing, but in which the natural element is fast becoming nebulous. It is indeed growing, as Mr. Leslie Stephen says it is, into a religion of dreams. All its doctrines are growing vague as dreams, and like dreams their outlines are forever changing. There is hardly any conceivable aberration of moral license that has not, in some quarter or other, embodied itself into a rule of life, and claimed to be the proper outcome of Protestant Christianity.

Now considering the way in which I have just

spoken of Protestantism, it may seem to many that I have dismissed this question already. With the '*enlightened*' English thinker such certainly will be the first impression. But there is one point that such thinkers all forget: Protestant Christianity is not the only form of it. They have still the form to deal with, which is the oldest, the most legitimate, and the most coherent—the Church of Rome. They surely can not forget the existence of this Church or her magnitude. To suppose this, would be to attribute to them too insular, or rather too provincial, an ignorance. The cause, however, certainly is ignorance, and an ignorance which, though less surprising, is far deeper. In this country the popular conception of Rome has been so distorted by our familiarity with Protestantism, that the true conception of her is something quite strange to us. Our divines have exhibited her to us as though she were a lapsed Protestant sect, and they have attacked her for being false to doctrines that were never really hers. They have failed to see that the first and essential difference which separates her from them lies, primarily, not in any special dogma, but in the authority on which all her dogmas rest. Protestants, basing their religion on the Bible solely, have conceived that Catholics of course profess to do likewise; and have covered them with invective for being traitors to their supposed profession. But the Church's primary doctrine is her own perpetual infallibility. She is inspired, she declares, by the same Spirit that inspired the Bible; and her voice is, equally with the Bible, the voice of God.

Her doctrines, as she one by one unfolds them, emerge upon us like the petals of a half-closed bud. They are not added arbitrarily from without; but are developed from within. When she formulates in these days something that has not been formulated before, she is no more enunciating a new truth than was Newton when he enunciated the theory of gravitation. Whatever truths, hitherto hidden, she may in the course of time grow conscious of, she holds that these were always implied in her teaching.

But the picture of the Church thus far is only half drawn. She is all this, but she is something more than this. She is not only the parliament of spiritual man, but she is such a parliament guided by the Spirit of God. The work of that Spirit may be secret, and to the natural eye untraceable, as the work of the human will is in the human brain. But none the less it is there.

Totam infusa per artus
Mens agitat molem, et magno se corpore miscet.

If we would obtain a true view of Catholicism, we must begin by making a clean sweep of all the views that, as outsiders, we had been taught to entertain about her. We must, in the first place, learn to conceive her as a living, spiritual body, as infallible and as authoritative now, as she ever was, with her eyes undimmed and her strength not abated, continuing to grow still as she has continued to grow hitherto: and the growth of the new dogmas that she may from time to time enunciate, we must learn to see are, from her standpoint, signs of life and not signs of corruption. And further, when we come to look into her more closely, we must separate carefully the diverse elements we find in her — her discipline, her pious opinions, her theology, and her religion.

Let honest inquirers do this to the best of their power, and their views will undergo an unlooked-for change.

WILLIAM HURRELL MALLOCK,
Is Life Worth Living?

THE PRESENT STATE OF PROTESTANTISM.

The Protestant religion, the union of its several Churches having been shaken, and indeed entirely dissolved, by the multiplicity of confessions and sects which were formed during, and after, the Reformation, does not, like the Catholic Church, present an appearance of external unity, but a motley variety of forms. And we freely acknowledge that, as in outward appearance, our Church is split into numberless divisions and subdivisions, so also in her religious principles and opinions she is internally divided and disunited. The Lutheran Society resembles, in its separate Churches and spiritual power, a worm cut up into the most minute portions, each one of which continues to move as long as it retains power; but at last, by degrees, loses at once the life and the power of motion which it retained. Were Luther to rise up from his grave, he could not possibly recognize as his own, or as members of the society which he founded, those teachers who in our Church would fain, nowadays, be considered as his successors.

The dissolution of the Protestant Church is inevitable: her frame is so thoroughly rotten that no farther patching will avail. The whole structure of evangelical religion is shattered and few look with sympathy on its tottering or its fall.

Within the compass of a square mile you may hear four, five, six different gospels. The people, believe me, mark it well; they speak most contemptuously of their teachers, whom they hold either for blockheads or knaves, in teaching these opposite doctrines; because in their simplicity they believe that *truth is but one*, and can not conceive how each of these gentlemen can have a separate one of his own. Growing immorality, a *consequence* of contempt for religion, in many places concurs also as a *cause* to its deeper downfall. The multitude cut the knot which galls them, march boldly forward, and fling themselves into the arms of Atheism in thought and deed. Oh, Protestantism, has it then, at last, come to this with thee, that thy disciples *protest against all religion?* Facts, which are before the eyes of the whole world, declare aloud, that this signification of thy name is no idle play upon words; though I know that the confession will excite a flame of indignation against myself.

WILHELM MARTIN LEBERECHT DE WETTE.

SACRIFICE OF THE MASS.

IN every sacrifice there is the person who offers, the thing which is offered, and the cause of offering. Now in this Sacrament of the Altar, the offerer is the Priest; and indeed the sovereign Priest is Christ himself, who not only offered Himself on the cross when He was suffering for us, but also exercises His priestly office forever to the consummation of ages, and now also offers Himself for us to God the Father through the ministry of the Priest. It is therefore He is called in Scripture, "*a priest forever according to the order of Melchisedec*"; in which offering of bread (as nothing can be more manifest) the Eucharistic sacrifice is allegorically prefigured in the Scripture itself. The thing offered, or the Victim or Host, is Christ himself, whose Body and Blood are subject to immolation and libation, under the appearance of the elements. Nor do I see what is wanting here to the nature of a true sacrifice. For why may not that be offered to God which is present under the symbols, since the sensible species of bread and wine are meet matter to be offered, and in them did the oblation of Melchisedec consist; and since that which is contained in the Eucharist is the most precious of all things, and the most worthy to be offered to God? Thus, by this most beautiful provision has the Divine mercy enabled our poverty to present an offering which God may not disdain; whereas He himself is infinite, and nothing would otherwise proceed from us bearing any proportion to His infinite perfection, no libation could be found capable of propitiating God, but one which itself should be of infinite perfection. For, by a mysterious disposition, it occurs that, as often as the consecration takes place, Christ, always giving Himself to us anew, may always again be offered to God, and thus represents and seals the perpetual efficacy of His first oblation on the Cross. For no new efficacy is superadded to the efficacy of the Passion, from this propitiatory Sacrifice, repeated for the remission of sins; but its entire efficacy consists in the representation and application of that first bloody Sacrifice, the fruit of which is the Divine Grace bestowed on all those who, being present at this tremendous Sacrifice, worthily celebrate the oblation in unison with the Priest. And since, in addition to the remission of eternal punishment and the gift of the merits of Christ for the hope of eternal life, we further ask of God, for ourselves and others, both living and dead, many other salutary gifts (and among those, the chief is the mitigation of that paternal chastisement which is due to every sin, even though the penitent be restored to favor); it is therefore clearly manifest, that there is nothing in our entire worship more precious than the Sacrifice of this Divine Sacrament, in which the Body of our Lord itself is present.

GOTTFRIED WILHELM VON LEIBNITZ,
Systema Theologicum.

THE ADORATION OF THE BLESSED SACRAMENT.

It is difficult to supply to a Christian a greater occasion than is presented in this Divine Sacrament, wherein God himself renders present to us the Body which He has assumed. For although He is equally present at all times, and in all places, as well by His substance as by His aid, yet, as it is impossible for us, at all times, and in all places, to direct our mind expressly to Him, and to render Him perpetual signs of honor, prudence will point out the propriety, in ordering the details of divine worship, of making of certain times, places, causes, and occasions. And God himself, in assuming a human body into the unity of His Person, has given us a peculiar and most signal occasion of adoring Him; for no one will doubt the justice and congruity of adoring God while He appears in the visible form of Christ; and the same must be admitted wherever it is certain that Christ is corporeally present (for the Divinity is present in all places and times), even though it be after an invisible manner; *now it is perfectly certain that this condition is fulfilled in the most holy Sacrament.* Hence, if there be any case in which the practice of adoring may congruously be introduced, it is in the case of this Sacrament. And thus it has been justly ordained that the highest solemnity of external Christian worship should be devoted to the Sacrament of the Eucharist; because the object proposed by our Saviour in its institution, was to enkindle the love of God, which is the highest act of external Christian worship, and to testify and nourish charity. For when our Lord, at the Last Supper, delivered the supreme commands of His last will, He wished that we should remember Him (like all who love and are beloved in turn), and that we should love one another as members of His one Body, whereof He has made us all partakers. And hence the Church has always employed the Eucharist as the test of unity, and has been careful not to admit to its mysteries, which may be regarded as the inmost recesses of Christianity, any except the proven and purified. To no others, indeed, was it permitted to be even present at the mysteries. It is certain, moreover, that the ancients also adored the Eucharist; and indeed Ambrose and Augustine expressly apply to the adoration of Christ's Body in the mysteries the words of the Psalm, "*Adore ye His footstool.*"

And in the end, since the necessity has ceased for deferring to Pagan prejudices, either by concealing the mysteries, or by abstaining from certain external signs, which might offend the weak, or wear the semblance of Paganism, it has gradually come to pass that the most exquisite rites of our external worship have been devoted to this venerable Sacrament; especially in the West, where there has not been any necessity to consult for the prejudices of the Saracens. Hence it has been ordained, not only that the people prostrate themselves at the elevation of the Sacrament after consecration; but also, that when borne to the sick, or otherwise carried in procession, it shall be attended with every demonstration of honor; that from time to time, whether on occasions of public necessity, or from some other cause, it shall be exposed for adoration; and that as the pledge of God's presence on earth, it shall be celebrated yearly by a special festival, with the utmost joy, and, as it were, triumph of the Church.

GOTTFRIED WILHELM VON LEIBNITZ,
Systema Theologicum.

A PROCESSION OF THE BLESSED SACRAMENT IN THE CATHEDRAL OF AMIENS.

I CAN almost fancy that I see it now, as I saw it for the first time on such an evening as this. The stupendous height of the vaulted roof; the rich foliage of the piers; the tall lancet arches throwing themselves upward; the interlacings of the decorated window-tracery; the richness of the stained glass; the glow of the sunlight on the southern chapels; the knotted intricacies of the vaulting ribs; the flowers and wreaths and holy symbols, that hung self-poised over the head; the graceful shafts of triforium; the carved angels, that with outstretched wings keep guard over the sacred building; the low, yet delicately carved choir-stalls; the gorgeous altar, faintly seen beyond them; the sublime apse, with its inimitably slim lancets, carrying the eye up higher and higher, through the dark cloister-gallery, through the blaze of the crimson clere-story to the marble grandeur of the fretted roof; lights and carving and jewels, and gold, and the sunny brightness of the nave, and the solemn grayness of the choir; these are all but accessories to the scene. The huge nave-piers rise from the midst of a mighty multitude; the high-born lady; the peasant mother, with her infant; the gray-headed laborer; the gay bourgeoisie; the child that knows only the sanctity of the place; the strong man and the cripple; the wise and the unlearned; the great and the small; the rich and the poor; all meet as equals. The sweet music floats along from the choir; the amen bursts from the congregation. Now the organ, at the west-end, takes up the strain, sweetly and solemnly, like the music of far-off angels, and as the holy doors open, pours forth the hymn, "The banners of the King come forth." White-robed boys strew the way with rose-leaves; there is the gleaming and the perfume of silver censers; there are the rich silver crosses and the pastoral staff; there is the sumptuous pall that covers the Host; there is an endless train of priests with copes and vestments bright as the hues of a summer sunset, gemmed with jewels of many lands, lustrous with gold, and chased with flowers, and wreaths, and devices of pearl; but each and all bearing, though in different forms, that one symbol, the cross. Right and left the crowd part as the train passes, and as the pall is borne by, every knee is bent, every head bowed. And now the soft breathings of the organ die away; voice, and clarionet, and flute take up the hymn. "The banners of the King" move statelily down the nave; and in every pause of the strain, not a sound is to be heard save the silver chime of the falling censer chains. Now they enter the north aisle; now they bear up again towards the choir; now they wind among its chapels; fainter and fainter arises the holy hymn as they recede eastward; now with faint mellowed sweetness it steals from the distant shrine of our Lady; now it is silent, and the organ takes up the note of praise.

REV. J. M. NEALE,
Hierologus; or, the Church Tourists.

JACQUELINE.

> Death lies on her, like an untimely frost
> Upon the sweetest flower of all the field.
> SHAKESPEARE.

"DEAR mother, is it not the bell I hear?"

"Yes, my child; the bell for morning prayers. It is Sunday to-day."

"I had forgotten it. But now all days are alike to me. Hark! it sounds again,—louder,—louder. Open the window, for I love the sound. The sunshine and the fresh morning air revive me. And the church bell,—O mother,—it reminds me of the holy Sunday mornings by the Loire,—so calm, so hushed, so beautiful! Now give me my prayer-book, and draw the curtain back, that I may see the green trees and the church-spire. I feel better to-day, dear mother."

It was a bright, cloudless morning in August. The dew still glistened on the trees; and a slight breeze wafted to the sick-chamber of Jacqueline the song of the birds, the rustle of the leaves, and the solemn chime of the church-bells. She had been raised up in bed, and, reclining upon the pillow, was gazing wistfully upon the quiet scene without. Her mother gave her the prayer-book, and then turned away to hide a tear that stole down her cheek.

At length the bells ceased. Jacqueline crossed herself, kissed a pearl crucifix that hung around her neck, and opened the silver clasps of her missal. For a time she seemed wholly absorbed in her devotions. Her lips moved, but no sound was audible. At intervals the solemn voice of the priest was heard at a distance, and then the confused responses of the congregation, dying away in inarticulate murmurs. Ere long the thrilling chant of the Catholic service broke upon the ear. At first it was low, solemn, and indistinct; then it became more earnest and entreating, as if interceding and imploring pardon for sin; and then arose louder and louder, full, harmonious, majestic, as it wafted the song of praise to heaven—and suddenly ceased. Then the sweet tones of the organ were heard,—trembling, thrilling, and rising higher and higher, and filling the whole air with their rich, melodious music. What exquisite accords!—what noble harmonies!—what touching pathos! The soul of the sick girl seemed to kindle into more ardent devotion, and to be wrapt away to heaven in the full, harmonious chorus, as it swelled onward, doubling and redoubling, and rolling upward in a full burst of rapturous devotion! Then all was hushed again. Once more the low sound of the bell smote the air, and announced the elevation of the Host. The invalid seemed entranced in prayer. Her book had fallen beside her,—her hands were clasped,—her eyes closed,—her soul retired within its secret chambers. Then a more triumphant peal of bells arose. The tears gushed from her closed and swollen lids; her cheek was flushed; she opened her dark eyes, and fixed them with an expression of deep adoration and penitence upon an image of the Saviour on the cross, which hung at the foot of her bed, and her lips again moved in prayer. Her countenance expressed the deepest resignation. She seemed to ask only that she might die in peace, and go to the bosom of her Redeemer.

The mother was kneeling by the window, with her face concealed in the folds of the curtain. She arose, and, going to the bedside of her child, threw her arms around her and burst into tears.

"My dear mother, I shall not live long; I feel it here. This piercing pain,—at times it seizes me, and I can not—can not breathe."

"My child, you will be better soon."

"Yes, mother, I shall be better soon. All tears, and pain, and sorrow will be over. The hymn of adoration and entreaty I have just heard, I shall never hear again on earth. Next Sunday, mother, kneel again by that window as to-day. I shall not be here, upon this bed of pain and sickness; but when you hear the solemn hymn of worship, and the beseeching tones that wing the spirit up to God, think, mother, that I am there, with my sweet sister who has gone before us,—kneeling at our Saviour's feet, and happy,—O, how happy!"

The afflicted mother made no reply,—her heart was too full to speak.

"You remember, mother, how calmly Amie died. She was so young and beautiful! I always pray that I may die as she did. I do not fear death, as I did before she was taken from us. But, O,—this pain,—this cruel pain!—it seems to draw my mind back from heaven. When it leaves me, I shall die in peace."

"My poor child! God's holy will be done!"

The invalid soon sank into a quiet slumber. The excitement was over, and exhausted nature sought relief in sleep.

The persons between whom this scene passed were a widow and her sick daughter, from the neighborhood of Tours. They had left the banks of the Loire to consult the more experienced physicians of the metropolis, and had been directed to the *Maison de santé* at Auteuil for the benefit of the pure air. But all in vain. The health of the uncomplaining patient grew worse and worse, and it soon became evident that the closing scene was drawing near.

Of this Jacqueline herself seemed conscious; and toward evening she expressed a wish to receive the last sacraments of the church. A priest was sent for; and ere long the tinkling of a little bell in the street announced his approach. He bore in his hand a silver chalice containing the consecrated Host, and a small vessel filled with the holy oil of the extreme unction hung from his neck. Before him walked a boy carrying a little bell, whose sound announced the passing of these symbols of the Catholic faith. In the rear, a few of the villagers, bearing lighted wax tapers, formed a short and melancholy procession. They soon entered the sick-chamber, and the glimmer of the tapers mingled with the red light of the setting sun that shot his farewell rays through the open window. The vessel of oil and the silver chalice were placed upon the table in front of a crucifix that hung upon the wall, and all present, excepting the priest, threw themselves upon their knees. The priest then approached the bed of the dying girl, and said, in a slow and solemn tone,—

"The King of kings and Lord of lords has passed thy threshold. Is thy spirit ready to receive him?"

"It is, father."

"Hast thou confessed thy sins?"

"Holy father, no."

"Confess thyself, then, that thy sins may be forgiven, and thy name recorded in the book of life."

And, turning to the kneeling crowd around, he waved his hand for them to retire, and was left alone with the sick girl. He seated himself beside her pillow, and the subdued whisper of the confession mingled with the murmur of the evening air, which lifted the heavy folds of the curtains, and stole in upon the holy scene. Poor Jacqueline had few sins to confess,—a secret thought or two toward the pleasures and delights of the world,— a wish to live, unuttered, but which, to the eye of her self-accusing spirit, seemed to resist the wise providence of God;—no more. The confession of a meek and lowly heart is soon made. The door again opened; the attendants entered, and The around the bed, and the priest proceeded,— were a d now prepare thyself to receive with con- neighbor rt the body of our blessed Lord and Redeemer. Dost thou believe that our Lord Jesus Christ was conceived by the Holy Spirit, and born of the Virgin Mary?"

"I believe."

And all present joined in the solemn response,—
"I believe."

"Dost thou believe that the Father is God, that the Son is God, and that the Holy Spirit is God,— three persons and one God?"

"I believe."

"Dost thou believe that the Son is seated on the right hand of the Majesty on high, whence he shall come to judge the quick and the dead?"

"I believe."

"Dost thou believe that by the holy sacraments of the church thy sins are forgiven thee, and that thus thou art made worthy of eternal life?"

"I believe."

"Dost thou pardon, with all thy heart, all who have offended thee in thought, word, or deed?"

"I pardon them."

"And dost thou ask pardon of God and thy neighbor for all offences thou hast committed against them, either in thought, word, or deed?"

"I do!"

"Then repeat after me,—O Lord Jesus, I am not worthy, nor do I merit, that thy divine majesty should enter this poor tenement of clay; but, according to thy holy promises, be my sins forgiven, and my soul washed white from all transgression."

Then, taking a consecrated Host from the vase, he placed it between the lips of the dying girl, and, while the assistant sounded the little silver bell, said,—

"*Corpus Domini nostri Jesu Christi custodiat animam tuam in vitam eternam.*"

And the kneeling crowd smote their breasts and responded in one solemn voice,—

"Amen!"

The priest then anointed the invalid. When these ceremonies were completed, the priest and his attendants retired, leaving the mother alone with her dying child, who, from the exhaustion caused by the preceding scene, sank into a deathlike sleep.

> "Between two worlds life hovered like a star,
> 'Twixt night and morn, upon the horizon's verge."

The long twilight of the summer evening stole on; the shadows deepened without, and the night-lamp glimmered feebly in the sick-chamber; but still she slept. She was lying with her hands clasped upon her breast,—her pallid cheek resting upon the pillow, and her bloodless lips apart, but motionless and silent as the sleep of death. Not a breath interrupted the silence of her slumber. Not a movement of the heavy and sunken eyelid, not a trembling of the lip, not a shadow on the marble brow, told when the spirit took its flight. It passed to a better world than this:—

> "There's a perpetual spring,—perpetual youth;
> No joint-benumbing cold, nor scorching heat,
> Famine, nor age, have any being there."

H. W. LONGFELLOW,
Outre-Mer.

PENANCE.

There is another circumstance connected with the institutions of the Church, which has not, in general, been so much noticed as it deserves. I allude to its penitentiary system, which is the more interesting in the present day, because, so far as the principles and applications of moral law are concerned, it is almost completely in unison with the notions of modern philosophy. If we look closely into the nature of the punishments inflicted by the Church at public penance, which was its principal mode of punishing, we shall find that their object was, above all other things, to excite repentance in the soul of the guilty; and in that of the lookers-on, the moral terror of example. But there is another idea which mixes itself up with this—the idea of expiation. I know not, generally speaking, whether it be possible to separate the idea of punishment from that of expiation; and whether there be not in all punishment, independently of the desire to awaken the guilty to repentance, and to deter those from vice who might be under temptation, a secret and imperious desire to expiate the wrong committed. Putting this question, however, aside, it is sufficiently evident that repentance and example were the objects proposed by the Church in every part of its system of penance. And is not the attainment of these very objects the end of every truly philosophical legislation? Is it not for the sake of these very principles that the most enlightened lawyers have clamored for reform in the penal legislation of Europe? Open their books—those of Jeremy Bentham for example—and you will be astonished at the numerous resemblances which you will everywhere find between their plans of punishment and those adopted by the Church.

F. GUIZOT,
History of Civilization.

CONFESSION.

THE remission of sins, which takes place in the sacrament of Baptism, and that in Confession, are both equally gratuitous; both are equally founded on the faith of Christ; both equally require penitence in the adults;—but there is this difference, that, in the former, nothing is especially prescribed by God beyond the rite of ablution; but, in the latter, it is commanded, that he who would be made clean, shall show himself to the priest, and confess his sins; and that, afterward, he shall, at the sentence of the priest, subject himself to some punishment, which may serve as an admonition for the future. And, whereas God appointed His priests to be the physicians of the soul, He willed that the malady of the patient should be made known to them, and his conscience bared before their eyes: whence the penitent Theodosius is related to have said wisely to Ambrose, "'Tis thine to prescribe and compound the medicines: 'tis mine to receive them." Now the medicines are the laws which the priest imposes on the penitent, as well that he may feel the evil that is past, as that he may avoid it for the time to come; and they are called by the name, "Satisfaction," because this obedience of the penitent, in voluntarily chastising himself, is agreeable to God, and mitigates or removes the temporal punishment which should otherwise be expected at the hands of God.

This whole institution, it can not be denied, is worthy of Divine wisdom; and if, in the Christian religion, there be any ordinance singularly excellent, and worthy of admiration, it is this, which even the Chinese and Japanese admired; for the necessity of confessing at once deters many, especially those who are not yet obdurate, from sinning and administers great comfort to the fallen; insomuch that I believe a pious, grave, and prudent confessor to be a powerful instrument in the hands of God for the salvation of souls; for his counsel is of great avail in assisting us to govern our passions; to discover our vices; avoid occasions of sin; to make restitution and reparation for injury; to dissipate doubts; to raise up the broken spirit; and, in one word, to remove, or mitigate, all the evils of the soul. And if, in human things, there is scarce anything better than a faithful friend, what must it be, when that friend is bound, by the inviolable religious obligation of a Divine sacrament, to hold faith with us, and assist us in difficulties? And although of old when the fervor of piety was more warm, public confession and penance were in use among Christians, nevertheless, in order to consult our weakness, it hath pleased God to declare by the Church, that private confession to a priest is sufficient for the faithful; an obligation of silence being further attached, in order that the confession may be more thoroughly freed from the influence of human respect.

GOTTFRIED WILHELM VON LEIBNITZ,
Systema Theologicum.

THE INVOCATION OF THE SAINTS.

It is certain that angel-guardians are assigned to us by God. Now the Scripture compares the saints to angels, and calls them "equal to angels." That the saints have some concern in human affairs appears to be conveyed by the "talking of Moses and Elias with Christ"; and that even particular events come to the knowledge of the saints and angels, (whether it be in the mirror of the divine vision, or by the natural clearness and wide-ranging powers of vision, possessed by the glorified minds,) is insinuated in Christ's declaration, that there is "joy in heaven upon one sinner that doth penance." Further, that God, in consideration of the saints, even after their death, grants favors to men, (although it is only through Christ that the saints, whether of the Old or of the New Testament, possess their dignity,) is indicated by the prayers found in the Scripture: "Remember, O Lord, Abraham, Isaac, and Jacob, thy servants": a form not very different from that which the Church commonly employs: "Grant, O Lord, that we may be assisted by the merits and intercession of Thy saints"; that is, "Regard their labors, which by Thy gift they have borne for Thy name; hear their prayers, to which Thine only-begotten Son hath given efficacy and value."

Seeing, therefore, that the blessed souls, in their present state, are much more intimately present in all our affairs, and see all things more nearly than while they lived on earth, (for men are only acquainted with the few which occur in their sight, or are reported to them by others,) seeing that their charity, or desire for aiding us is more ardent; seeing, in fine, that their prayers are more efficacious than those which they offered formerly in this life, that it is certain that God has granted many favors even to the intercession of the living, and that we look for great advantages from the union of the prayers of our brethren with our own; I do not perceive how it can be made a crime to invoke a blessed soul, or a holy angel, and to beg his intercession or his assistance, according as the life and history of the martyr, or other circumstances appear to suggest; especially if this worship is considered but as a slender accessory of that supreme worship which is immediately directed to God alone; and if, whatever may be its character, it is offered for the sake of testifying our reverence and humility toward God, and our affection for God's servants, and springs from that pious solicitude which prompts us in proportion to the lowly sense we entertain of our own unworthiness to desire to unite the prayers of other pious persons, and, above all those of the Blessed, with our own. And thus when it is analyzed, this very accessory of worship terminates with God himself; to whose gifts alone the saints are indebted for all that they are or can do, and to whom is due a sovereign honor and love incomparably transcending all other love.

GOTTFRIED WILHELM VON LEIBNITZ,
Systema Theologicum.

THE SYMBOLISM OF RITUAL.

Very few, comparatively, are sufficiently instructed in the significance of Catholic worship thoroughly to appreciate and enjoy it. If the Ceremonial of the Church be generally considered beautiful and imposing, even by those who understand but the material part, what effect ought it not to produce on such as really understand its spirit? "If, instead of condemning from the elevation of their ignorance," says the Abbé Martinet, "the numerous ceremonies of the Catholic worship, the objectors would take the pains to penetrate the deep significance of them, and study their vast and beautiful symbolism, they would see that everything is perfectly connected in this beautiful system, that every part has its reason, and also its effect, and that the skill with which the Church has introduced so great a variety into the very limited plan of its Liturgy can not be sufficiently admired. What do we find in this series of mysterious pictures which it presents to our eye in the course of a year?

Nothing less than the history of the world, from the Word which created Heaven and earth, to the Word which is to produce a new Heaven and a new earth; the history of the Redeemer, from the day He was promised to guilty man, to the day when He will receive into His glory, the last in time, of the elect; the history of the Christian Church, from the period when it was sighing in the Catacombs, to the final period, when, pursued into the depths of the deserts by triumphant impiety, it will see the banner of the spouse unfurled in heaven, and will entone an eternal Hosannah."

The order and arrangement of the whole external system of the Church is so contrived as plainly to symbolize her office toward her people, and to exhibit her life and energies side by side with the energies and life of the world, sanctifying and exalting, by the power of the hidden life with *God*, the entire circle of our daily life in communion with our fellow-men. The whole year is, as it were, thus taken up, and sanctified by Religion; and we see that, during its course, there is not a truth which the Church does not preach, not a virtue or grace which she does not put forth for our imitation, not a chord of the human heart which she does not strive to touch, so that "one is led," says the Abbé Gaume, "to feel of each several solemnity that which one is forced to say of every Christian verity, '*Si elle n'existit pas, il faudrait l'inventer.*'"

Rev. Charles James Le Geyt,
The Church and the World: Essays on Questions of the Day. By Various Writers.

RELIGIOUS MEMORIALS.

THE rosary, which you see suspended around my neck, is a memorial of sympathy and respect for an illustrious man. I was passing through France, in the reign of Napoleon, by the peculiar privilege granted to a *savant,* on my road to Italy. I had just returned from the Holy Land and had in my possession two or three of the rosaries which are sold to pilgrims at Jerusalem, as having been suspended in the Holy Sepulchre. Pius VII. was then in imprisonment at Fontainebleau. By a special favor, on the plea of my return from the Holy Land, I obtained permission to see this venerable and illustrious pontiff. I carried with me one of my rosaries.

He received me with great kindness. I tendered my services to execute any commissions, not political ones, he might think fit to intrust me with, in Italy, informing him that I was an Englishman; he expressed his thanks, but declined troubling me. I told him that I was just returned from the Holy Land; and, bowing with great humility, offered him my rosary from the Holy Sepulchre.

He received it with a smile, touched it with his lips, gave his benediction over it, and returned it into my hands, supposing, of course, that I was a Roman Catholic. I had meant to present it to his Holiness; but the blessing he had bestowed upon it, and the touch of his lips, made it a precious relic to me; and I restored it to my neck, round which it has ever since been suspended. . . . . "We shall meet again; adieu": and he gave me his paternal blessing.

It was eighteen months after this interview, that I went out, with almost the whole population of Rome, to witness and welcome the triumphal entry of this illustrious father of the Church into his capital. He was borne on the shoulders of the most distinguished artists, headed by Canova; and never shall I forget the enthusiasm with which he was received; it is impossible to describe the shouts of triumph and of rapture sent up to heaven by every voice. And when he gave his benediction to the people, there was a universal prostration, a sobbing, and marks of emotion and joy, almost like the bursting of the heart. I heard everywhere around me cries of "The holy father! the most holy father! His restoration is the work of God!"

I saw tears streaming from the eyes of almost

all the women about me, many of whom were sobbing hysterically, and old men were weeping as if they were children. I pressed my rosary to my breast on this occasion, and repeatedly touched with my lips that part of it which had received the kiss of the most venerable pontiff. I preserve it with a kind of hallowed feeling, as the memorial of a man whose sanctity, firmness, meekness, and benevolence are an honor to his Church and to human nature: and it has not only been useful to me, by its influence upon my own mind, but it has enabled me to give pleasure to others; and has, I believe, been sometimes beneficial in insuring my personal safety.

I have often gratified the peasants of Apulia and Calabria, by presenting them to kiss a rosary from the Holy Sepulchre, which had been hallowed by the touch of the lips and benediction of the Pope: and it has even been respected by, and procured me a safe passage through, a party of brigands, who once stopped me in the passes of the Apennines.

SIR HUMPHRY DAVY,
Consolation in Travel, or the Last Days of a Philosopher.

THE BEAUTIES OF THE CATHOLIC WORSHIP.

There is something extremely touching in the maternal, accessible, and poetical character of Catholicism: and the soul finds a constant asylum in her quiet chapels, before the Christmas candles, in the soft purifying atmosphere of incense, in the outstretched arms of the heavenly mother, while it sinks down before her in humility, filial meekness, and contemplation of the Saviour's love. The Catholic churches, with their ever-opened portals, their ever-burning lamps, the ever-resounding voices of their thanksgiving, with their masses, their ever-recurring festivals and days of commemoration, declare with touching truth, that here the arms of a mother are ever open, ready to refresh every one who is troubled and heavy laden; that here the sweet repast of love is prepared for all, and a refuge by day and by night. When we consider this constant occupation of priests, this carrying in and out of the Holy of Holies, the fulness of emblems, the ornaments, varying every day, like the changing leaves of the flower, the Catholic Church will appear like a deep, copious well in the midst of a city, which collects around it all the inhabitants, and whose waters, perpetually cool, refresh, bless, and pervade all around.

Count Isidore von Löben.

CHARLES CARROLL OF CARROLLTON.

We do a thing of very pernicious tendency if we confine the records of history to the most eminent personages who bear a part in the events which it commemorates. There are often others whose sacrifices are much greater, whose perils are more extreme, and whose services are nearly as valuable as those of the more prominent actors, and who yet have, from chance or by the modesty of a retiring and unpretending nature, never stood forward to fill the foremost places, or occupy the larger spaces in the eyes of the world. To forget such men is as inexpedient for the public service as it is unjust toward the individuals. But the error is the far greater of those who, in recording the annals of revolution, confine their ideas of public merit to the feats of leaders against established tyranny, or the triumphs of orators in behalf of freedom. Many a man in the ranks has done more by his zeal and self-devotion than any chief to break the chains of a nation, and among such men Charles Carroll, the last survivor of the Patriarchs of the American Revolution, is entitled to the first place.

His family was settled in Maryland ever since the reign of James II., and had during that period been possessed of the same ample property, the largest in the Union. It stood, therefore, at the head of the aristocracy of the country; was naturally in alliance with the Government; could gain nothing while it risked everything by a change of dynasty; and therefore, according to all the rules and the prejudices and the frailties which are commonly found guiding the conduct of men in a crisis of affairs, Charles Carroll might have been expected to take part against the revolt, certainly never to join in promoting it. Such, however, was not this patriotic person. He was among the foremost to sign the celebrated Declaration of Independence. All who did so were believed to have devoted themselves and their families to the Furies. As he set his hand to the instrument, the whisper ran round the Hall of Congress, "There goes millions of property!" And there being many of the same name, when he heard it said, "Nobody will know what Carroll it is," as no one signed more than his name, and one at his elbow addressing him remarked, "You'll get clear—there are several of the name—they will never know which to take." "Not so," he replied, and instantly added his residence, "of Carrollton."

He was not only a man of firm mind, and steadily-fixed principles; he was also a person of great accomplishments and excellent abilities. Educated in the study of the civil law at one of the French colleges, he had resided long enough in Europe to perfect his learning in all the ordinary branches of knowledge. On his return to America, he sided with the people against the mother country, and was soon known and esteemed as among the ablest writers of the Independent party. The confidence reposed in him soon after was so great, that he was joined with Franklin in the commission of three sent to obtain the concurrence of the Canadians in the revolt. He was a Member of Congress for the first two trying years, when the body was only fourteen in number, and might rather be deemed a cabinet council for action than anything like a deliberative senate. He then belonged, during the rest of the war, to the legislature of his native State, Maryland, until 1788, when he was elected one of the United States' Senate, and continued to act for three years in this capacity. The rest of his time, until he retired from public life in 1804, was passed as a Senator of Maryland. In all these capacities he has left behind him a high reputation for integrity, eloquence, and judgment.

It is usual with Americans to compare the last

thirty years of his life to the Indian summer—sweet as it is tranquil, and partaking neither of the fierce heats of the earlier, nor the chilling frosts of the later season. His days were both crowned with happiness, and lengthened far beyond the usual period of human existence. He lived to see the people whom he had once known 900,000 in number pass twelve millions; a handful of dependent colonists become a nation of freemen; a dependent settlement assume its place among the first-rate powers of the world; and he had the delight of feeling that to this consummation he had contributed his ample share. As no one had run so large a risk by joining the revolt, so no one had adhered to the standard of freedom more firmly, in all its fortunes, whether waving in triumph or over disaster and defeat. He never had despaired of the commonwealth, nor ever had lent his ear to factious councils; never had shrunk from any sacrifice, nor ever had pressed himself forward to the exclusion of men better fitted to serve the common cause. Thus it happened to him that no man was more universally respected and beloved; none had fewer enemies; and notwithstanding the ample share in which the gifts of fortune were showered upon his house, no one grudged its prosperity.

It would, however, be a very erroneous view of

his merits and of the place which he filled in the eye of his country, which should represent him as only respected for his patriotism and his virtues. He had talents and acquirements which enabled him effectually to help the cause he espoused. His knowledge was various; and his eloquence was of a high order. It was, like his character, mild and pleasing: like his deportment, correct and faultless. Flowing smoothly, and executing far more than it seemed to aim at, every one was charmed by it, and many were persuaded. His taste was peculiarly chaste, for he was a scholar of extraordinary accomplishments; and few, if any, of the speakers in the New World came nearer the model of the more refined oratory practiced in the parent state. Nature and ease, want of effort, gentleness united with sufficient strength, are noted as its enviable characteristics; and as it thus approached the tone of conversation, so, long after he ceased to appear in public, his private society is represented as displaying much of his rhetorical powers, and has been compared not unhappily, by a late writer, to the words of Nestor, which fell like vernal snows as he spake to the people. In commotions, whether of the Senate or the multitude, such a speaker, by his calmness and firmness joined, might well hope to have the weight, and to exert the control and mediatory authority of him, *pietate gravis et meritis*, who

—— regit dictis animos et pectora mulcet.

In 1825, on the anniversary of the Half Century after the Declaration of Independence was signed, the day was kept over the whole Union as a grand festival, and observed with extraordinary solemnity. As the clock struck the hour when that mighty instrument had been signed, another bell was also heard to toll. It was the passing bell of John Adams, one of the two surviving Presidents who had signed the Declaration. The other was Jefferson; and it was soon after learned that at this same hour he too had expired in a remote quarter of the country.

There now remained only Carroll to survive his fellows; and he had already reached extreme old age; but he lived yet seven years longer, and, in 1832, at the age of 95, the venerable patriarch was gathered to his fathers.

The Congress went into mourning on his account for three months, as they had done for Washington, and for him alone.

HENRY, LORD BROUGHAM,
Historical Sketches of Statesmen.

THE SUBVERSION OF LIBERTY IN NORTHERN EUROPE.

It is one of the most remarkable circumstances in modern history, that about the middle of the seventeenth century, when all other countries were advancing toward constitutional arrangement of some kind or other, for the security of civil and religious liberty, Denmark, by a formal act of the States or Diet, abrogated even that shadow of a constitution, and invested her sovereigns with full despotic power to make and execute law without check or control on their absolute authority. Lord Molesworth, who wrote an account of Denmark in 1692, thirty-two years after this singular transaction, makes the curious observation : "That in the Roman Catholic religion, there is a resisting principle to absolute civil power from the division of authority with the head of the Church of Rome; but in the north, the Lutheran Church is entirely subservient to the civil power, and the whole of the northern people of Protestant countries have lost their liberties ever since they changed their religion." "The blind obedience which is destructive of national liberty is, he conceives, more firmly established in the northern kingdoms, by the entire and sole dependence of the clergy on the prince, without the interference of any spiritual superior as that of the Pope among the Catholics, than in the countries which remained Catholic."

SAMUEL LAING,
A Tour in Sweden.

THE RELIGIOUS ORDERS OF THE ROMAN CATHOLIC CHURCH.

Since the glory of God and the happiness of our fellow-creatures may be promoted by various means, by command or by example, according to the condition and disposition of each, the advantages of that institution are manifest, by which besides those who are engaged in active and every-day life, there are also found in the Church ascetic and contemplative men, who, abandoning the cares of life and trampling its pleasures underfoot, devote their whole being to the contemplation of the Deity, and the admiration of His works; or who, freed from personal concerns, apply themselves exclusively to watch and relieve the necessities of others, some by instructing the ignorant or erring; some by assisting the needy and afflicted. Nor is it the least among those marks which commend to us that Church, which alone has preserved the name and the badges of Catholicity, that we see her alone produce and cherish these illustrious examples of the eminent virtues and of the ascetic life.

Wherefore, I confess, that I have ardently admired the religious orders, and the pious confraternities, and the other similar admirable institutions; for they are a sort of celestial soldiery upon earth, provided they are governed according to the institutes of the founders, and regulated by the Supreme Pontiff for the use of the universal Church. For what can be more glorious than to carry the light of truth to distant nations, through seas and fires and swords—to traffic in the salvation of souls alone—to forego the allurements of pleasure, and even the enjoyment of conversation and of social intercourse, in order to pursue, undisturbed, the contemplation of abstruse truths and divine meditation—to dedicate oneself to the education of youth in science and in virtue—to assist and console the wretched, the despairing, the lost, the captive, the condemned, the sick—in squalor, in chains, in distant lands—undeterred even by the fear of pestilence from the lavish exercise of these heavenly offices of charity! The man who knows not, or despises these things, has but a vulgar and plebeian conception of virtue; he foolishly measures the obligations of men toward their God by the perfunctory discharge of ordinary duties, and by that frozen habit of life, devoid of zeal, and even of soul, which prevails commonly among men. For it is not a counsel, as some persuade themselves, but a strict precept, to labor with every power of soul and body, no matter in what condition of life we may be, for the attainment of Christian perfection, with which neither wedlock, nor children, nor public office, are incompatible (although they throw difficulties in the way), but it is only a counsel to select that state of life which is more free from earthly obstacles, upon which selection our Lord congratulated Magdalen.

GOTTFRIED WILHELM VON LEIBNITZ,
Systema Theologicum.

VOWS.

THE general principles and sacred obligation of Vows are plainly revealed in Holy Scripture. Not that their institution is recorded. The Law did not introduce them; but they are incidentally spoken of. Jacob's vow is recorded in the annals of the earliest ages, as a religious ordinance in ordinary use, and in the Book of Job, which is identified with the most universal traditions of primeval revelation, vows are classed among the simplest acts of personal religion: "Thou shalt make thy prayer unto Him, and He shall hear thee, and thou shalt pay thy vows." They are to be regarded, therefore, as one of the many religious practices of patriarchal times, which being subsequently embodied in the Law, and regulated by its enactments, were thus invested with a fresh and more binding authority.

Two classes of vows were recognized in the Mosaic Law,—vows of devotion and of abstinence. They were also distinguished as vows affirmative and negative—the one as implying some offering made to *God*, the other some restraint laid on the natural desires, or the use of certain things in themselves lawful.

There was no limit to the objects which a vow might embrace. Persons, lands, cattle, houses, and property of any sort, are either expressly or by implication included in the possible category of votive offerings. The only exceptions were the first-born of man or beast, and the property of priests. But these were excepted only as being already devoted to *God*. They were His by a special covenant, the first-born as the representatives of the race which He had redeemed, the sacerdotal possessions as consecrated to His service. These exceptions, therefore, only the more strikingly proved, that the subject-matter of vows was coextensive with every human personality or possession.

The Nazarite vow was of all others the most important, on account both of its own special provisions and their symbolic significance. It is generally believed that the custom prevailed before the Mosaic period. Only its peculiar regulations were provided for in the Law. The external obligations incurred by this vow were, to let the hair grow, to abstain from wine, vinegar, or any produce of the grape, even from grapes themselves, and to avoid all approach to a dead body, even that of the nearest relation.

It has been observed, and the point is of deep interest, as strikingly exhibiting the inner meaning of this remarkable self-consecration, that there is a close resemblance, as to their outward provisions, between the obligations of the Nazarite and those of the High-Priest. The rule of avoiding all contact with the dead, and that of abstinence from wine, applied to both. There is even ground for supposing that the Nazarite was permitted to enter the sanctuary, as bearing something of the priestly character, at least of the sanctity specially belonging to the sacred office. Moreover, Jewish writers generally were of opinion that some deep spiritual import was involved in the Nazarite rule, though they differ as to its interpretation. Philo viewed it as expressive of spotless inward purity and entire devotion of the person and his possessions. Some even regarded it as symbolizing the operation of the Divine Nature in man. That it embraced the whole life, and implied an entire consecration, was thought to be denoted by the provision, that at the completion of the vow, or renewal in case of being broken, the three chief sacrifices of the Law, the burnt-offering, the sin-offering, and the peace-offering, which together consecrated the whole man, were required. A Nazarite was understood to identify himself with each of these several acts of oblation. The shorn hair laid and burnt in the fire of the altar, was also, according to this deeper view, supposed to indicate that person was offered to *God*,—the Divine Law not permitting the offering of human blood, and the hair, as a portion of the person, being understood to represent the whole. That the idea implied is that of the setting apart of the life, a self-sacrifice to *God*, is in accordance with the Scriptural terms denoting the state : " The Lord spake unto Moses, saying, Speak unto the children of Israel and say unto them, When either man or woman shall *separate* themselves to vow the vow of a Nazarite, to *separate themselves unto the Lord,*" etc. It was apparently the typical anticipation of the regenerate soul offering the "living sacrifice, holy, acceptable unto the *Lord.*"

Some writers of note have even supposed that the Nazarite rule was ordained as a quasi-sacramental representation of man before the fall; nor is it improbable that *God* would preserve on earth some visible signs of man's original creation, a state which knew not death, and which implied the restraint of the appetites in subjection to the will, in harmony with the Divine law, when, as a priest, man lived before *God*, consecrating himself and all his possessions as the highest offering of nature to its Creator.

The Nazarite rule embraced women as well as men. It was, moreover, applicable equally to limited periods of days or years, or to the whole life. The former case constituted the "Nazarite of days." Most commonly the vow was limited to a definite period,—thirty, sixty, or a hundred days being the ordinary terms. Of Nazarites for life, the notable instances mentioned in Scripture, are Samson, Samuel, and St. John the Baptist, and in each case with the additional element of obedience to a superior will in the choice of a rule, the devotee accepting his consecration as an act of his parents, who were, we can not question, moved by *God* to make this dedication of their child. That there was a tendency in the Jewish mind to such acts of self-devotion, in order to win the favor of *God*, or deprecate His wrath, or for the cultivation of greater strictness of life, is evident from many tokens in their history. Beside the Nazarite rule, which had the highest possible sanction in the Revelations of *God*, other forms of self-consecration had grown up of themselves. The Institutes of Rechabites and Essenes arose out of this tendency. Josephus records, that in his day there were many, particularly persons oppressed by sickness, or adverse fortune, who vowed to abstain from wine, and go with the head shaven—their rule thus being distinguished from that of the Nazarite—and to spend a prolonged time in prayer during thirty days previously to their offering up the promised sacrifice.

Such vows, especially if undertaken only for short periods, would ordinarily pass almost unnoticed. "But the Nazarite for life must have been, with his flowing hair and persistent refusal of strong drink, a marked man. He may have had some privileges (as we have seen) which gave him something of a priestly character, and (as it has been conjectured) he may have given much of his time to sacred studies. Though not necessarily cut off from social life, yet when the turn of his mind was devotional, consciousness of his peculiar dedication must have influenced his habits and manner, and in some cases probably led him to retire from the world."

Voluntariness was always considered to be an essential characteristic of a vow; and its subject-matter some devotion left free to the conscience. It was the willing adoption of a rule of life not enjoined by the Law, but revealed as pleasing to *God*, and expressive of some high truth by which the soul might aspire to greater nearness to Him. That a parent could dedicate his child, is not at variance with this principle; because it was assumed that the child, when capable of a choice, would willingly concur in the dedication. But though wholly voluntary before the choice was made, it became, when made and uttered "before the *Lord*," solemnly binding. The expressions of Holy Scripture on both these points are strong and unmistakable. "When thou shalt vow a vow unto the *Lord* thy *God*, thou shalt not be slack to pay it: for the *Lord* thy *God* will surely require it of thee." And again, "*That which is gone out of thy lips* thou shalt keep and perform; even a *free-will offering*, according as thou hast vowed unto the *Lord* thy *God*, which thou hast promised with thy mouth."

The term "before the *Lord*" had a deep significance in the faith of Israel. He was believed in, and dealt with as with a personal God with whom definite relations could be formed, by which His own dealings also would be influenced. The idea involved in the vow was that of a definite contract or covenant, entailing a whole series of after consequences depending on the condition of being fulfilled; a promise and an acceptance mutually sealed by which both parties in the covenant were affected. A momentous reality attached to the uttered word beyond what the thought of the heart could express. The utterance gave it a palpable shape and being, and thus constituted it a reality of existence, sealing its truth beyond recall. The instinct which to human consciousness invests a word with a power and a life beyond the unspoken thought, is evidently an indication of some profound truth in the spiritual world, and is assumed in the revelations of *God* as the turning-point of the obligations incurred by a vow. It lives "before the *Lord*," when spoken, as it did not live before, an image, as it were, of the outward form of the life of *God*, impressed on the mind of man, and projected forth, uniting him with God. Even as God comes forth out of Himself to make a covenant with His creature, and confirms it by an oath, thus establishing it "by two immutable things, in which it is impossible for God to lie," so man may go forth from himself and bind himself, sealing the covenant by his promise. As he speaks the purpose of his heart, it assumes a substantial existence in Heaven, which stands before *God* as a witness for or against the soul which has uttered the word, and thus committed itself to all its consequences.

It is sometimes urged that a continual self-devotion, ever renewed by ever-repeated acts, while the soul is still free to withdraw, is a more generous and self-denying sacrifice than an act which allows no recall, which is done once and forever. There is no doubt a seeming attractiveness in the thought; but it is difficult to understand what is meant. In regard to a material offering, external to oneself, such a course would be simply impossible. We can not give while we yet retain. To retain the power of continually giving, we must be really still holding it in our possession. We have not given it from the very fact that we have still the power of giving it. Can there be a difference in the case of giving oneself? If we continually offer ourselves, we have at all times the power of withdrawing the offering; and this very freedom, which is supposed to be deliberately retained, really makes it no gift. While it is still in our power it is still our own. We may give, or not give, the very next hour. It is not that the vow constitutes the gift, but the conscious acceptance of the call of God necessarily, if it be true, involves the future equally with the present. It is of *God*, and partakes of His eternity. There ought, indeed, to be the utmost caution, forethought, and deliberation, embracing both inward dispositions and outward duties, a spirit of self-distrust and fear, in the lowliest dependence on the leadings of grace and the providence of God; and all this, moreover, accompanied with such assistance as can be attained through the guidance of those to whom the care of the soul is rightfully entrusted. But these considerations, though they greatly affect the wisdom and rectitude of the decision, are but conditions of its character, not the constituent elements of its life. It is the following of *Jesus*, and the being united with His life in the form which He wills to impress on the soul, which constitutes its reality; and to leave any reserve of self-choosing in the future, is but to "keep back part of the price."

Rev. T. Thellusson Carter,
The Church and the World: Essays on Questions of the Day. By Various Writers.

CELIBACY.

Ever since the beginning of Christianity there hath been two orders or ranks of people among good Christians.

The *one* that feared and served God in the common offices and business of a secular worldly life; the *other*, renouncing the common business and common enjoyments of life, as riches, marriage, honors, and pleasures, devoted themselves to voluntary poverty, virginity, devotion, and retirement; that by this means they might live wholly unto God in the daily exercise of a divine and heavenly life.

This testimony I have from the famous ecclesiastical historian Eusebius, who lived at the time of the first general council, when the Church was in its greatest glory, when its bishops were so many holy fathers and eminent saints. "Therefore," saith he, "there hath been instituted in the Church of Christ two ways or manners of living. The *one*, raised above the ordinary state of nature and common ways of living, rejects wedlocks, possessions and worldly goods, and being wholly separate and removed from the ordinary conversations of common life, is appropriated and devoted solely to the worship and service of God, through an exceeding degree of heavenly love.

"They who are of this order of people seem dead to the life of this world, and having their bodies only upon earth, are in their minds and contemplations dwelling in heaven, from whence, like so many heavenly inhabitants, they look down upon human life, making intercessions and oblations to Almighty God for the whole race of mankind; and this not with the blood of beasts, but the highest exercises of true piety, with cleansed and purified hearts, and with a whole form of life strictly devoted to virtue.

"Christianity receives this as a perfect manner of life. The *other* is of lower form, and suiting itself more to the conditions of human nature, admits chaste wedlock, care of children and family, of trade and business, and goes through all the employments of life, under a sense of piety and fear of God."

If Truth itself hath assured us that *there is but one thing needful*, what wonder is it that there should be some among Christians so full of faith as to believe this in the highest sense of the words, and to desire such a separation from the world that their care and attention to the one thing needful may not be interrupted?

If the chosen vessel St. Paul hath said, "*He that is unmarried careth for the things that belong to the Lord, how he may please the Lord*"; and that "*there is this difference also between a wife and a virgin: the unmarried woman careth for the things of the Lord, that she may be holy, both in body and in spirit*"; what wonder is it if the purity and perfection of the virgin state hath been the praise and glory of the Church in its first and purest ages?—that there hath been always some, so desirous of pleasing God, so zealous after every degree of purity and perfection, so glad of every means of improving their virtue, that they have renounced the comforts and enjoyments of wedlock, to trim their lamps, to purify their souls and wait upon God in a state of perpetual virginity?

And if in these our days we want examples of these several degrees of perfection; if neither clergy nor laity have enough of this spirit; if we are so far departed from it, that a man seems like St. Paul at Athens, *a setter forth of strange doctrines*, when he recommendeth self-denial, renunciation of the world, regular devotion, retirement, virginity, and voluntary poverty, it is because we are fallen into an age when the love not only of the many, but of most, has waxen cold. These rules of holy living are found in the sublimest counsels of Christ and His Apostles, suitable to the high expectations of another life, proper instances of a heavenly love, and all followed by the greatest saints of the Church.

WILLIAM LAW,
Serious Call to a Devout and Holy Life.

THE ANCIENT MONK.

The great antique heart: how like a child's in its simplicity, like a man's in its earnest solemnity and depth! Heaven lies over him wheresoever he goes or stands on the Earth; making all the Earth a mystic Temple to him, the Earth's business all a kind of worship. Glimpses of bright creatures flash in the common sunlight; angels yet hover doing God's messages among men: that rainbow was set in the clouds by the hand of God. Wonder, miracle encompass the man; he lives in an element of miracle: Heaven's splendor over his head, Hell's darkness under his feet. A great Law of Duty, high as these two Infinities, dwarfing all else, annihilating all else—making royal Richard as small as peasant Samson, smaller if need be! The "imaginative faculties"? "Rude poetic ages?" The "primeval poetic element"? O for God's sake, good readers, talk no more of all that! It was not a Dilettantism this of Abbot Samson.

It was a Reality, and it is one. The garment only of it is dead: the essence of it lives through all Time and all Eternity!

THOMAS CARLYLE,
Past and Present.

ST. IGNATIUS LOYOLA AND HIS COMPANIONS.

On the dawn of the day on which, in the year 1534, the Church of Rome celebrated the feast of the Assumption of Our Blessed Lady, a little company of men, whose vestments bespoke their religious character, emerged in solemn procession from the deep shadows cast by the towers of Notre Dame over the silent city below them. In a silence not less profound, except when broken by the chant of the matins appropriate to that sacred season, they climbed the Hill of Martyrs, and descended into the Crypt, which then ascertained the spot where the Apostle of France had won the crown of martyrdom. With a stately though halting gait, as one accustomed to military command, marched at their head a man of swarthy complexion, baldheaded, and of middle stature, who had passed the meridian of life; his deep-set eyes glowing as with a perennial fire from beneath brows which, had phrenology then been born, she might have portrayed in her loftiest style, but which without her aid, announced a commission from on high to subjugate and to rule mankind. So majestic, indeed, was the aspect of Ignatius Loyola, that during the sixteenth century few if any of the books of his order appeared without the impress of that imperial countenance. Beside him in the chapel of St. Denys knelt another worshipper, whose manly bearing, buoyant step, clear blue eye, and finely-chiselled features, contrasted strangely with the solemnities in which he was engaged. Then in early manhood, Francis Xavier united in his person the dignity befitting his birth as a grandee of Spain, and the grace which should adorn a page of the Queen of Castile and Arragon. Not less incongruous with the scene in which they bore their parts, were the slight forms of the boy Alphonso Salmeron, and of his bosom friend, Jago Laynez, the destined successor of Ignatius in his spiritual dynasty. With them Nicholas Alphonso Bobadilla, and Simon Rodriguez—the first a teacher, the second a student of philosophy—prostrated themselves before the altar, where ministered Peter Faber, once a shepherd in the mountains of Savoy, but now a priest in holy orders. By his hands was distributed to his associates the *seeming* bread, over which he had uttered words of more than miraculous efficacy; and then were lifted up their united voices, uttering, in low but distinct articulation, a vow, at the deep significance of which the nations might have well rejoiced. Never did human lips pronounce a vow more religiously observed, or pregnant with results more momentous.

Descended from an illustrious family, Ignatius had in his youth been a courtier and a cavalier, and if not a poet, at least a cultivator of poetry. At the siege of Pampeluna his leg was broken. Books of knight-errantry relieved the lassitude of sickness, and when these were exhausted, he betook himself to pious books. In the lives of the Saints the disabled soldier discovered a new field of emulation and of glory. Compared with their self-conquest and their high rewards, the achievements and the renown of Roland and of Amadis waxed dim. Compared with the peerless damsels for whose smiles Paladins had fought and died, how transcendently glorious the image of feminine loveliness and angelic purity which had irradiated the hermit's cell and the path of the wayworn pilgrims! Far as the heavens are above the earth would be the plighted fealty of the knight of the Virgin Mother beyond the noblest devotion of mere human chivalry. Nor were these vows unheeded by her to whom they were addressed. Environed in light, and clasping her infant to her bosom, she revealed herself to the adoring gaze of her champion. He rose, suspended at her shrine his secular weapons, performed there his nocturnal vigils, and with returning day retired to consecrate his future life to the glory of the *Virgo Deipara.*

Standing on the steps of a Dominican church, he recited the office of Our Lady, when suddenly heaven itself was laid open to the eye of the worshipper. That ineffable mystery, which the author of the Athanasian creed has so beautifully enunciated in words, was disclosed to him as an object not of faith but of actual sight. The past ages of the world were rolled back in his presence, and he beheld the material fabric of things rising into being, and perceived the motives which had prompted the exercise of the creative energy. To his spiritualized sense was disclosed the actual process by which the Host is transubstantiated; and the other Christian verities which it is permitted to common men to receive but as exercises of their belief, now became to him the objects of immediate inspection and of direct consciousness. For eight successive days his body reposed in an unbroken trance, while his spirit thus imbibed disclosures for which the tongues of men have no appropriate language.

On his restoration to human society, Ignatius reappeared in the garb, and addressed himself to the occupations of other religious men. The first fruit of his labors was the book of "Spiritual Exercises." It was originally written in Spanish, and appeared in a Latin version. By the order of the present Pope, Loyola's manuscript, still remaining in the Vatican, has been again translated. In this new form the book is commended to the devout study of the faithful by a bull of Pope Paul III., and by an Encyclical Epistle from the present General of the Order of Jesus.

From the publication of the "Spiritual Exercises" to the vow of Montmartre, nine years elapsed. They wore away in pilgrimages, in the working of miracles, and in escapes all but miraculous, from dangers which the martial spirit of the saint, no less than his piety, impelled him to incur. In the caverns of Manresa he had vowed to scale the heights of "*perfection*," and it therefore behooved him thus to climb that obstinate eminence, in the path already trodden by all the canonized and beatified heroes of the Church. But he had also vowed to conduct his fellow-pilgrims from the city of destruction to the land of Beulah. In prison and in shipwreck, fainting with hunger or wasted with disease, his inflexible spirit still meditated over that bright, though as yet shapeless vision; until at length it assumed a coherent form as he knelt on the Mount of Olives, and traced the last indelible foot-print of the ascending Redeemer of mankind. At that hallowed spot had ended the weary way of Him who had bowed the heavens, and came down to execute on earth a mission of unutterable and matchless self-denial; and there was revealed to the prophetic gaze of the future founder of the Order of Jesus, the long line of missionaries who, animated by his example and guided by his instructions, should proclaim that holy Name from the rising to the setting sun. At the mature age of thirty, possessing no language but his own, no science but that of the camp, and no literature beyond the biographies of Saints, he became the self-destined teacher of the future teachers of the world. Hoping against hope, he returned to Barcelona, and there, as the class-fellow of little children, commenced the study of the first rudiments of the Latin tongue.

Of the seven decades of human life, the brightest and the best, in which other men achieve or contend for distinction, was devoted by Ignatius to the studies preparatory to his great undertaking. Grave professors examined him on their prælections, and, when these were over, he sought the means of subsistence by traversing the Netherlands and Italy as a beggar. Unheeded and despised as he sat at the feet of the learned, or solicited alms of the rich, he was still maturing in the recesses of his bosom designs more.lofty than the highest to which the monarchs of the houses of Valois or of Tudor had ever dared to aspire. In the University of Paris he at length found the means of carrying into effect the cherished purposes of so many years. It was the heroic age of Spain, and the countrymen of Gonsalvo and Cortez lent a willing ear to counsels of daring on any field of adventure, whether secular or spiritual. His companions in study thus became his disciples in religion. Nor were his the commonplace methods of making converts. To the contemplative and the timid, he enjoined hardy exercises of active virtue. To the gay and ardent, he appeared in a spirit still more buoyant than their own. To a debauchee, whom nothing else could move, he presented himself neck-deep in a pool of frozen water, to teach the more impressively the duty of subduing the carnal appetites. Nay, he even engaged at billiards with a joyous lover of the game, on condition that the defeated player should serve his antagonist for a month ; and the victorious saint enforced the penalty by consigning his adversary to a month of secluded devotion. Others yielded at once and without a struggle to the united influence of his sanctity and genius; and it is remarkable that, from these more docile converts, he selected, with but two exceptions, the original members of his infant order. Having performed the initiatory rite of the "Spiritual Exercises," they all made a vow on the consecrated Host in the Crypt of St. Denys, to accompany their spiritual father on a mission to Palestine; or, if that should be impracticable, to submit themselves to the Vicar of Christ, to be disposed of as missionaries at his pleasure.

It was in the year 1506 that Francis Xavier, the youngest child of a numerous family, was born in the castle of his ancestors, in the Pyrenees. Robust and active, of a gay humor and ardent spirit, the young mountaineer listened with a throbbing heart to the military legends of his house, and to the inward voice which spoke of days to come, when his illustrious lineage should derive new splendor from his own achievements. But the hearts of his parents yearned over the son of their old age; and the enthusiasm which would have borne him to the pursuit of glory in the camp, was diverted by their counsels to the less hazardous contest for literary eminence at the University of Paris. From the embrace of Aristotle and his commentators, he would, however, have been prematurely withdrawn by the failure of his resources (for the Lords of

Xavier were not wealthy), if a domestic prophetess, his elder sister, had not been inspired to reveal his marvellous career and immortal recompense. For a child destined to have altars raised to his name throughout the Catholic Church, and Masses chanted in his honor till time should be no longer, every sacrifice was wisely made; and he was thus enabled to struggle on at the College of St. Barbara, till he had become qualified to earn his own maintenance as a public teacher of philosophy. His chair was crowded by the studious, and his society courted by the gay, the noble, and the rich. It was courted, also, by one who stood aloof from the thronging multitude; among them, but not of them. Miserable in dress, but of lofty bearing, at once unimpassioned and intensely earnest, abstemious of speech, yet occasionally uttering, in deep and most melodious tones, words of strange significance, Ignatius Loyola was gradually working over the mind of his young companion a spell which no difference of tastes, of habits, or of age, was of power to subdue. Potent as it was, the charm was long resisted. Hilarity was the native and indispensable element of Francis Xavier, and in his grave monitor he found an exhaustless topic of mirth and raillery. Armed with satire, which was not always playful, the light heart of youth contended, as best it might, against the solemn impressions which he could neither welcome nor avoid. Whether he partook of the frivolities in which he delighted, or in the disquisitions in which he excelled, or traced the windings of the Seine through the forest which then lined its banks, Ignatius was still at hand to discuss with him the charms of society, of learning, or of nature; but, whatever had been the theme, it was still closed by the same awful inquiry, "What shall it profit a man if he gain the whole world and lose his own soul?" The world which Xavier had sought to gain, was indeed already exhibiting to him its accustomed treachery. It had given him amusements and applause; but with his self-government had stolen from him his pupils and his emoluments. Ignatius recruited both. He became the eulogist of the genius and the eloquence of his friend, and, as he presented to him the scholars attracted by these panegyrics, would repeat them in the presence of the delighted teacher; and then, as his kindling eye attested the sense of conscious and acknowledged merit, would check the rising exultation by the ever-recurring question, "What shall it profit?" Nothing could damp the zeal of Ignatius. There he was, though himself the poorest of the poor, ministering to the wants of Xavier, from a purse filled by the alms he had solicited; but there was also the same unvarying demand, urged in the same rich though solemn cadence, "What shall it profit?" In the unrelaxing grasp of the strong man—at once forgiven and assisted, rebuked and beloved by his stern associate—Xavier gradually yielded to the fascination. He became, like his master, impassive to all sublunary pains and pleasures; and having performed the initiatory rite of the Spiritual Exercises, excelled all his brethren of the Society of Jesus in the fervor of his devotion and the austerity of his self-discipline.

John III. of Portugal, resolving to plant the Christian faith on the Indian territories which had become subject to the dominion or influence of his crown, petitioned the Pope to select some fit leader in this peaceful crusade. On the advice of Ignatius, the choice of the Holy Father fell on Francis Xavier. A happier selection could not have been made, nor was a summons to toil, to suffering, and to death, ever so joyously received.

As the vessel in which Xavier embarked for India fell down the Tagus and shook out her reefs to the wind, many an eye was dimmed with unwonted tears; for she bore a regiment of a thousand men to reinforce the garrison of Goa; nor could the bravest of that gallant host gaze on the receding land without foreboding that he might never see again those dark chestnut forests and rich orange groves, with the peaceful convents and the long-loved homes reposing in their bosom. The countenance of Xavier alone beamed with delight. He knew that he should never tread his native mountains more; but he was not an exile. He was to depend for food and raiment on the bounty of his fellow-passengers; but no thought for the morrow troubled him. He was going to convert nations, of which he knew neither the language nor even the names; but he felt no misgivings. Worn by incessant sea-sickness, with the refuse food of the lowest seamen for his diet, and the cordage of the ship for his couch, he rendered to the diseased services too revolting to be described; and lived among the dying and the profligate the unwearied minister of consolation and of peace. In the midst of that floating throng, he knew how to create for himself a sacred solitude, and how to mix in all their pursuits in the free spirit of a man of the world, a gentleman, and a scholar. With the viceroy and his officers he talked, as pleased them best, of war or trade, of politics or navigation; and to restrain the common soldiers from gambling, would invent for their amusement less dangerous pastimes, or even hold the stakes for which they played, that by his presence and his gay discourse he might at least check the excesses which he could not prevent.

Five weary months (weary to all but him) brought the ship to Mozambique, where an endemic fever threatened a premature grave to the Apostle of the Indies. But his was no spirit to be quenched or allayed by the fiercest paroxysms of disease. At each remission of his malady, he crawled to the beds of his fellow-sufferers to soothe their terrors or assuage their pains. To the eye of any casual observer the most wretched of mankind, in the esteem of his companions the happiest and the most holy, he reached Goa just thirteen months after his departure from Lisbon.

At Goa, Xavier was shocked, and had fear been an element in his nature, would have been dismayed, by the almost universal depravity of the inhabitants. It exhibited itself in those offensive forms which characterize the crimes of civilized men when settled among a feebler race, and released from even the conventional decencies of civilization. Swinging in his hand a large bell, he traversed the streets of the city, and implored the astonished crowd to send their children to him, to be instructed in the religion which they still at least professed. Though he had never been addressed by the soul-stirring name of father, he knew that in the hardest and the most dissolute heart which had once felt the parental instinct, there is one chord which can never be wholly out of tune. A crowd of little ones were quickly placed under his charge. He lived among them as the most laborious of teachers, and the gentlest and the gayest of friends; and then returned them to their homes, that by their more hallowed example they might there impart, with all the unconscious eloquence of filial love, the lessons of wisdom and of piety they had been taught. No cry of human misery reached him in vain. He became an inmate of the hospitals, selecting that of the lepers as the object of his peculiar care. Even in the haunts of debauchery, and at the tables of the profligate, he was to be seen, an honored and a welcome guest; delighting that most unmeet audience with the vivacity of his discourse, and sparing neither pungent jests to render vice ridiculous, nor sportive flatteries to allure the fallen back to the still distasteful paths of soberness and virtue. Strong in purity of purpose, and stronger still in one sacred remembrance, he was content to be called the friend of publicans and sinners. He had in truth long since deserted the standard of prudence, the offspring of forethought, for the banners of wisdom, the child of love, and followed them through perils not to be hazarded under any less triumphant leader.

Rugged were the ways along which he was thus conducted. In those times, as in our own, there was on the Malabar coast a pearl fishery, and then, as now, the pearl-divers formed a separate and a degraded caste. It was not till after a residence of twelve months at Goa, that Xavier heard of these people. He heard that they were ignorant and miserable, and he inquired no farther. On that burning shore his bell once more rang out an invitation of mercy, and again were gathered around him troops of inquisitive and docile children. For fifteen months he lived among these abject fishermen, his only food their rice and water, reposing in their huts, and allowing himself but three hours' sleep in the four-and-twenty. He became at once their physician, the arbiter in their disputes, and their advocate for the remission of their annual tribute with the government of Goa. The bishop of that city had assisted him with two interpreters, but his impassioned spirit struggled, and not in vain, for some more direct intercourse with the objects of his care. Committing to memory translations, at the time unintelligible to himself, of the creeds and other symbols of his faith, he recited them with tones and gestures, which spoke at once to the senses and to the hearts of his disciples. All obstacles yielded to his restless zeal. He soon learned to converse, to preach, and to write in their language. Many an humble cottage was surmounted by a crucifix, the mark of its consecration; and many a rude countenance reflected the sorrows and the hopes which they had been taught to associate with that sacred emblem. "I have nothing to add," (the quotation is from one of the letters which at this same time he wrote to Loyola,) "but that they who come forth to labor for the salvation of idolaters, receive from on high such consolations, that if there be on earth such a thing as happiness, it is theirs."

If there be such a thing, it is but as the checkered sunshine of a vernal day. A hostile inroad from Madura overwhelmed the poor fishermen who had learned to call Xavier their father, threw down their simple chapels, and drove them for refuge to the barren rocks and sand-banks which line the western shores of the strait of Manar. But their father was at hand to share their affliction, to procure for them from the viceroy at Goa relief and food, and to direct their confidence to a still more powerful Father whose presence and goodness they might adore even amidst the wreck of all their earthly treasures.

It was a lesson not unmeet for those on whom such treasures had been bestowed in the most ample abundance; and Xavier advanced to Travancore, to teach it there to the Rajah and his courtiers. No facts resting on remote human testimony can be more exempt from doubt than the general outline of the tale which follows. A solitary, poor, and unprotected stranger, he burst through the barriers which separate men of different tongues and races: and with an ease little less than miraculous, established for himself the means of interchanging thoughts with the people of the East. They may have ill-gathered his meaning, but by some mysterious force of sympathy they soon caught his ardor. Idol temples fell by the hands of their former worshippers. Christian churches rose at his bidding; and the kingdom of Travancore was agitated with new ideas and unwonted controversies. The Brahmins argued—as the Church by law established has not seldom argued—with fire and sword, and the interdict of earth and water, to the enemies of their repose.

On the Coromandel coast, near the city of Meliapor, might be seen in those times the oratory and the tomb of St. Thomas, the first teacher of Christianity in India. It was in a cool and sequestered grotto that the apostle had been wont to pray; and there yet appeared on the living rock, in bold relief, the cross at which he knelt, with a crystal fountain of medicinal waters gushing from the base of it. On the neighboring height, a church with a marble altar, stained, after the lapse of fifteen centuries, with the blood of the martyr, ascertained the sacred spot at which his bones had been committed to the dust. To this venerable shrine Xavier retired, to learn the will of Heaven concerning him. He maintained, on this occasion, for seven successive days an unbroken fast and silence—no unfit preparation for his approaching conflicts.

Thirty years before the arrival of Xavier, Malacca had been conquered by Alphonso Albuquerque. It was a place abandoned to every form of sensual and enervating indulgence. Through her crowded streets a strange and solemn visitor passed along, pealing his faithful bell, and earnestly imploring the prayers of the faithful for that guilty people. Curiosity and alarm soon gave way to ridicule; but Xavier's panoply was complete. The messenger of divine wrath judged this an unfit occasion for courting aversion or contempt. He became the gayest of the gay, and, in address at least, the very model of an accomplished cavalier. Foiled at their own weapons, his dissolute countrymen acknowledged the irresistible authority of a self-devotion so awful, relieved and embellished as it was by every social grace. Thus the work of reformation prospered, or seemed to prosper. Altars rose in the open streets, the confessional was thronged by penitents, translations of devout books were multiplied; and the saint, foremost in every toil, applied himself with all the activity of his spirit to study the structure and the graceful pronunciation of the Malayar tongue. But the plague was not thus to be stayed. A relapse into all their former habits filled up the measure of their crimes. With prophetic voice Xavier announced the impending chastisements of Heaven; and shaking off from his feet the dust of the obdurate city, pursued his indefatigable way to Amboyna.

That island, then a part of the vast dominions of Portugal in the East, had scarcely witnessed the commencement of Xavier's exertions, when a fleet of Spanish vessels appeared in hostile array on the shores. They were invaders, and even corsairs; for their expedition had been disavowed by Charles V. Pestilence, however, was raging among them; and Xavier was equally ready to hazard his life in the cause of Portugal, or in the service of her afflicted enemies. Day and night he lived in the infected ships, soothing every spiritual distress, and exerting all the magical influence of his name to procure for the sick whatever might contribute to their recovery or soothe their pains. The coals of fire thus heaped on the heads of the pirates, melted hearts otherwise steeled to pity; and to Xavier belonged the rare, perhaps the unrivalled, glory of repelling an invasion by no weapons but those of self-denial and love.

But glory, the praise of men, or their gratitude, what were these to him? As the Spaniards retired peacefully from Amboyna, he, too, quitted the half-adoring multitude, whom he had rescued from the horrors of a pirate's war, and spurning all the timid councils which would have stayed his course, proceeded, as the herald of good tidings, to the half barbarous islands of the neighboring Archipelago. "If those lands," such was his indignant exclamation, "had scented woods and mines of gold, Christians would find courage to go there; nor would all the perils of the world prevent them. They are dastardly and alarmed, because there is nothing to be gained there but the souls of men, and shall love be less hardy and less generous than avarice? They will destroy me, you say, by poison.

It is an honor to which such a sinner as I am may not aspire; but this I dare to say, that whatever form of torture or of death awaits me, I am ready to suffer it ten thousand times for the salvation of a single soul." Nor was this the language of a man insensible to the sorrows of life, or really unaffected by the dangers he had to incur. "Believe me, my beloved brethren" (we quote from a letter written by him at this time to the Society at Rome), "it is in general easy to understand the evangelical maxim, that he who will lose his life shall find it. But when the moment of action has come, and when the sacrifice of life for God is to be really made, oh, then, clear as at other times the meaning is, it becomes deeply obscure! so dark, indeed, that he alone can comprehend it, to whom, in His mercy, God himself interprets it. Then it is we know how weak and frail we are."

Weak and frail he may have been; but from the days of St. Paul to our own, the annals of mankind exhibit no higher example of a soul borne onward so triumphantly through distress and danger, in all their most appalling aspects. He battled with hunger, and thirst, and nakedness, and assassination, and pursued his mission of love, with even increasing ardor, amidst the wildest war of the contending elements. At the island of Moro (one of the group of the Moluccas) he took his stand at the foot of a volcano; and as the pillar of fire threw up its wreaths to heaven, and the earth tottered beneath him, and the firmament was rent by falling rocks and peals of unintermitting thunder, he pointed to the fierce lightnings, and the river of molten lava, and called on the agitated crowd which clung to him for safety, to repent, and to obey the truth. Repairing for the celebration of Mass to some edifice which he had consecrated for the purpose, an earthquake shook the building to its base. The terrified worshippers fled; but Xavier standing in meek composure before the rocking altar, deliberately completed that mysterious Sacrifice.

The history of Xavier now reaches an unwelcome pause. He pined for solitude and silence. He had been too long in constant intercourse with man, and found that, however high and holy may be the ends for which social life is cultivated, the habit, if unbroken, will impair that inward sense through which alone the soul can gather any true intimations of her nature and her destiny. He retired to commune with himself in a seclusion where the works of God alone were to be seen, and where no voices could be heard but those which, in each varying cadence, raise an unconscious anthem of praise and adoration to their Creator. There for a while reposing from labors such as few or any other of the sons of men have undergone, he consumed days and weeks in meditating prospects beyond the reach of any vision unenlarged by the habitual exercise of beneficence and piety.

Scarcely four years had elapsed from the first discovery of Japan by the Portuguese, when Xavier, attended by Auger and his two servants, sailed from Goa to convert the islanders to the Christian faith. Much good advice had been, as usual, wasted on him by his friends. To Loyola alone he confided the secret of his confidence. " I can not express to you" (such are his words) " the joy with which I undertake this long voyage ; for it is full of extreme perils, and we consider a fleet sailing to Japan as eminently prosperous in which one ship out of four is saved. Though the risk far exceeds any which I have hitherto encountered, I shall not decline it." Xavier left behind him a code of instructions for his brother missionaries, illuminated in almost every page by that profound sagacity which results from the union of extensive knowledge with acute observation, mellowed by the intuitive wisdom of a compassionate and lowly heart. The science of self-conquest, with a view to conquer the stubborn will of others, the act of winning admission for painful truth, and the duties of fidelity and reverence in the attempt to heal the diseases of the human spirit, were never taught by uninspired men with an eloquence more gentle, or an authority more impressive. A long voyage, pursued through every disaster which the malevolence of man and demons could oppose to his progress (for he was constrained to sail in a piratical ship, with idols on her deck and whirlwinds in her path), brought him, in the year 1549, to Japan, there to practice his own lessons, and to give a new example of heroic perseverance.

Carrying on his back his only property, the vessels requisite for performing the Sacrifice of the Mass, he advanced to Firando, at once the seaport and the capital of the kingdom of that name. Some Portuguese ships riding at anchor there, announced his arrival in all the forms of nautical triumph—flags of every hue floating from the masts, seamen clustering on the yards, cannon roaring from beneath, and trumpets braying from above. Firando was agitated with debate and wonder; all asked, but none could afford, an explanation of the homage rendered by the wealthy traders to the meanest of their countrymen. It was given by the humble pilgrim himself, surrounded in the royal presence by all the pomp which the Europeans could display in his honor. Great was the effect of these auxiliaries to the work of an evangelist; and the modern, like the ancient Apostle, ready to become all things to all men, would no longer decline the abasement of assuming for a moment the world's grandeur, when he found that such puerile acts might allure the children of the world to listen to the voice of wisdom. At Meaco, then the seat of empire in Japan, the discovery might be reduced to practice with still more important success, and thitherwards his steps were promptly directed.

At Amanguchi, the capital of Nagoto, he found the hearts of men hardened by sensuality; and his exhortations to repentance were repaid by showers of stones and insults. They drove him forth half naked, with no provision but a bag of parched rice, and accompanied only by three of his converts, prepared to share his danger and his reproach.

It was in the depth of winter; dense forests, steep mountains, half-frozen streams, and wastes of untrodden snow, lay in his path to Meaco. An entire month was consumed in traversing the wilderness, and the cruelty and scorn of man not seldom adding bitterness to the rigors of nature. On one occasion the wanderers were overtaken in a thick jungle by a horseman bearing a heavy package. Xavier offered to carry the load, if the rider would requite the service by pointing out his way. The offer was accepted, but hour after hour the horse was urged on at such a pace, and so rapidly sped the panting missionary after him, that his tortured feet and excoriated body sank in seeming death under the protracted effort. In the extremity of his distress no repining word was ever heard to fall from him. He performed this dreadful pilgrimage in silent communion with Him for whom he rejoiced to suffer the loss of all things; or spoke only to sustain the hope and courage of his associates. At length the walls of Meaco were seen, promising a repose not ungrateful even to his adamantine frame and fiery spirit. But repose was no more to visit him. He found the city in all the tumult and horror of a siege. It was impossible to gain attention to his doctrines amidst the din of arms. Chanting from the Psalmist—When Israel went out of Egypt and the house of Jacob from a strange people—the Saint again plunged into the desert, and retraced his steps to Amanguchi.

Xavier describes the Japanese very much as a Roman might have depicted the Greeks in the age of Augustus, as at once intellectual and sensual voluptuaries; on the best possible terms with themselves, a good-humored but faithless race, equally acute and frivolous, talkative and disputatious—" their inquisitiveness," he says, "is incredible, especially in their intercourse with strangers, for whom they have not the slightest respect, but make incessant sport of them." Surrounded at Amanguchi by a crowd of these babblers, he was plied with innumerable questions about the immortality of the soul, the movements of the planets, eclipses, the rainbow—sin, grace, paradise, and hell. He heard and answered. A single response solved all these problems. Astronomers, meteorologists, metaphysicians, and divines, all heard the same sound, but to each it came with a different and an appropriate meaning. So wrote from the very spot Father Anthony Quadros four years after the event, and so the fact may be read in the process of Xavier's canonization.

In such controversies, and in doing the work of an evangelist in every other form, Xavier saw the third year of his residence at Japan gliding away, when tidings of perplexities at the mother church of Goa recalled him thither; across seas so wide and stormy, that even the lust of gold hardly braved them in that infancy of the art of navigation. As his ship drove before the monsoon, dragging after her a smaller bark which she had taken in tow, the connecting ropes were suddenly burst asunder, and in a few minutes the two vessels were no longer in sight. Thrice the sun rose and set on their dark course, the unchained elements roaring as in mad revelry around them, and the ocean seething like a caldron. Xavier's shipmates wept over the loss of friends and kindred in the foundered bark, and shuddered at their own approaching doom. He also wept; but his were grateful tears. As the screaming whirlwind swept over the abyss, the present Deity was revealed to His faithful worshipper, shedding tranquillity, and peace, and joy over the sanctuary of a devout and confiding heart. "Mourn not, my friend," was his gay address to Edward de Gama, as he lamented the loss of his brother in the bark; "before three days the daughter will have returned to her mother." They were weary and anxious days; but, as the third drew toward a close, a sail appeared on the horizon. Defying the adverse winds, she made straight toward them, and at last dropped alongside as calmly as the sea-bird ends her flight, and furls her ruffled plumage on the swelling surge. The cry of miracle burst from every lip; and well it might. There was the lost bark, and not the bark only, but Xavier himself on board of her! What though he had ridden out the tempest in the larger vessel, the stay of their drooping spirits, he had at the same time been in the smaller ship, performing there also the same charitable office; and yet, when the two hailed and spoke to each other, there was but one Francis Xavier, and he composedly standing by the side of Edward de Gama on the deck of the *Holy Cross.* Such was the name of the Commodore's vessel. For her services on this occasion, she obtained a sacred charter of immunity from risks of every kind; and as long as her timbers continued sound, bounded merrily across seas in which no other craft could have lived.

During this wondrous voyage her deck had often been paced in deep conference by Xavier and Jago de Pereyra, her commander. The great object which expanded the thoughts of Pereyra was the conversion of the Chinese empire. Before the *Holy Cross* had reached Goa, Pereyra had pledged his whole fortune, Xavier his influence and his life, to this gigantic adventure. In the spring of the following year, the apostle and Pereyra sailed from Goa in the *Holy Cross*, for the then unexplored coasts of China. As they passed Malacca, tidings came to Xavier of the tardy though true fulfilment of one of his predictions. Pestilence, the minister of Divine vengeance, was laying waste that stiff-necked and luxurious people; but the woe he had foretold he was the foremost to alleviate. Heedless of his own safety, he raised the sick in his arms and bore them to the hospitals. He esteemed no time, or place, or office too sacred to give way to this work of mercy. Ships, colleges, churches, all at his bidding became so many lazarettos. Night and day he lived among the diseased and the dying, or quitted them only to beg food or medicine, from door to door, for their relief. For the moment even China was forgotten; nor would he advance a step though it were to convert to Christianity a third part of the human race, so long as one victim of the plague demanded his sympathy, or could be directed to an ever-present and still more compassionate Comforter. The career of Xavier was now drawing to a close; and with him the time was ripe for practicing those deeper lessons of wisdom which he had imbibed from his long and arduous discipline.

Again the *Holy Cross* prepared for sea; and the apostle of the Indies, followed by a grateful and admiring people, passed through the gates of Malacca to the beach. Falling on his face to the earth, he poured forth a passionate though silent prayer. His body heaved and shook with the throes of that agonizing hour. What might be the fearful portent none might divine, and none presumed to ask. A contagious terror passed from eye to eye, but every voice was hushed. It was as the calm preceding the first thunder peal which is to rend the firmament. Xavier arose, his countenance no longer beaming with its accustomed grace and tenderness, but glowing with a sacred indignation, like that of Isaiah when breathing forth his inspired menaces against the king of Babylon. Standing on a rock amidst the waters, he loosed his shoes from off his feet, smote them against each other with vehement action, and then casting them from him, as still tainted with the dust of that devoted city, he leaped barefooted into the bark, which bore him away forever from a place from which he had so long and vainly labored to avert her impending doom.

She bore him, as he had projected, to the island of Sancian. It was a mere commercial factory; and the merchants who passed the trading season there, vehemently opposed his design of penetrating farther into China. True he had ventured into the forest, against the tigers which infested it, with no other weapon than a vase of holy water; and the savage beasts, sprinkled with that sacred element, had forever fled the place: but the mandarins were fiercer still than they, and would avenge the preaching of the saint on the inmates of the factory.

Long years had now passed away since the voice of Loyola had been heard on the banks of the Seine urging the solemn inquiry, "What shall it profit?" But the words still rung on the ear of Xavier, and were still repeated, though in vain, to his worldly associates at Sancian. They sailed away with their cargoes, leaving behind them only the *Holy Cross* in charge of the officers of Alvaro, and depriving Xavier of all means of crossing the channel to Macao. They left him destitute of shelter and of food, but not of hope. He had heard that the King of Siam meditated an embassy to China for the following year; and to Siam he resolved to return in Alvaro's vessel, to join himself, if possible, to the Siamese envoys, and so at length to force his way into the empire.

But his earthly toils and projects were now to cease forever. The angel of death appeared with a summons, for which, since death first entered our world, no man was ever more triumphantly prepared. It found him on board the vessel on the point of departing for Siam. At his own request he was removed to the shore, that he might meet his end with the greater composure. Stretched on the naked beach, with the cold blasts of a Chinese winter aggravating his pains, he contended alone with the agonies of the fever which wasted his vital power. It was a solitude and an agony for which the happiest of the sons of men might well have exchanged the dearest society and the purest of the joys of life. It was an agony in which his still uplifted crucifix reminded him of a far more awful woe endured for his deliverance; and a solitude thronged by blessed ministers of peace and consolation, visible in all their bright and lovely aspects to the now unclouded eye of faith; and audible to the dying martyr through the yielding bars of his mortal prison-house, in strains of exulting joy till then unheard and unimagined. Tears burst from his fading eyes, tears of an emotion too big for utterance. In the cold collapse of death his features were for a few brief moments irradiated as with the first beams of approaching glory. He raised himself on his crucifix, and exclaiming, *In te Domine, speravi—non confundar in æternum!* he bowed his head and died.

SIR JAMES STEPHEN,
Essays on Ecclesiastical Biography.

MISSIONARY CONTRAST.

This great success of the Catholics in these islands, reminds us of the more glorious results attendant on the mission of the priests than on that of the Puritans in North America. While the former, through the benign influence of genuine religion, and a reasonable conformance to the outward life, simple habits, and natural instincts of the Indian, possessed themselves of the door of human nature, *the heart*, and by kindness, sympathy, persuasion, and rational appeal, passed through it to the inner seat of his convictions; the cold, unbending, unpitying, and uncompromising disciple of Puritanism, sought to attain the same end by dictatorial harangues on *election*, *justification*, and *sanctification*, unintelligible to themselves and incomprehensible to their hearers; and by harsh decrees, fierce denunciations, and finally by the practical enforcement of death and damnation. The result of these two systems of proselytism are matters of record. The former, introduced by the French Franciscans, on the rocky shores of Maine, was subsequently borne thence along the great valley of the St. Lawrence and the lakes, even to that of the Father of Waters, by the Jesuits; winning the confidence and love of the untamed savage, guiding him to the peaceful contemplation of truth, and along the path that leads to eternal life. While the latter wrote in blood the record of aboriginal repugnance, and of their own persecutions, oppression, and final extermination of a race whom they professed to seek with the Gospel of Peace, but in fact destroyed with the weapons of war; and when at a later day they seized the happier fields of Catholic missions along the St. Lawrence and the lakes, there too they blasted the fair face of a benignant Christianity, by the terrors of uncompromising heartlessness, intolerance, cruelty, and selfishness. As a New England historian has asked in regard to the contrasted spirit of the missions of that day, equally applicable to the missions of which we have been speaking in the Hawaiian Islands—"Can we wonder that Rome succeeded and that Geneva failed? Is it strange that the tawny pagan fled from the icy embrace of Puritanism, and took refuge in the arms of the priest and Jesuit?"

H. WILLIS BAXLEY,
West Coast of South and North America, and the Hawaiian Islands.

HOSPITALS AND SISTERHOODS.

It would take far too much time were I to go over the history of the early ages of Christendom, and show you that women, associated under the ruling civil and ecclesiastical powers, were then officially, but voluntarily, employed in works of social good. That these women should have been early associated with the Church, and held their duties by ecclesiastical appointment, was natural and necessary, because all moral sway, and all moral influence, and all education, and every peaceful and elevating pursuit, belonged for many centuries to the ecclesiastical order only. The singular and beneficent power exercised by the religious and charitable women in those times is remarked by all writers. The whole of the early history of Christianity is full of examples. I will give you one which, on looking over these authorities, struck me vividly.

Paula, a noble Roman lady, a lineal descendant of the Scipios and the Gracchi, is mentioned among the first Christian women remarkable for their active benevolence. In the year 385 she quitted Rome, then a Pagan city; with the remains of a large fortune, which had been expended in aiding and instructing a wretched and demoralized people, and accompanied by her daughter, she sailed for Palestine, and took up her residence in Bethlehem of Judea. There, as the story relates, she assembled around her a community of women. In the old English translation of her life there is a picture of this charitable lady which I can not refrain from quoting: "She was marvellous debonair, and piteous to them that were sick, and comforted them, and served them right humbly; and gave them largely to eat such as they asked; but to herself she was hard in her sickness and scarce, for she refused to eat flesh how well she gave it to others, and also to drink wine. She was oft by them that were sick, and she laid the pillows aright and in point; and she rubbed their feet, and boiled water to wash them; and it seemed to her that the less she did to the sick in service, so much the less service did she to God, and deserved the less mercy; therefore she was to them piteous and nothing to herself."

This picture, drawn fifteen hundred years ago, so quaintly graphic, and yet so touching in its simplicity, will, perhaps, bring before the mind's eye of those who listen to me, scenes of the same kind, where female ministry has been called upon to do like offices of mercy; to wash the wounds and smooth the couch, and "lay the pillows aright," of the maimed, the war-broken, the plague-stricken soldier. But we must for a while turn back to the past. It is in the seventh century that we find the communities of charitable women first mentioned under a particular appellation. We read in history that when Landry, Bishop of Paris, about the year 650, founded an hospital, since known as the Hôtel Dieu, as a general refuge for disease and misery, he placed it under the direction of the *Hospitalières*, or nursing-sisters of the time,—women whose services are understood to have been voluntary, and undertaken from motives of piety. Innocent IV., who would not allow of any outlaying religious societies, collected and united those hospital-sisters under the rule of the Augustine Order, making them amenable to the government and discipline of the Church.

The novitiate or training of a *Sœur Hospitalière* was of twelve years' duration, after which she was allowed to make her profession. At that time, and even earlier, we find many hospitals expressly founded for the reception of the sick pilgrims and wounded soldiers returning from the East, and bringing with them strange and hitherto unknown forms of disease and suffering. Some of the largest hospitals in France and the Netherlands originated in this purpose, and were all served by the Hospitalières; and to this day the Hôtel Dieu, with its one thousand beds, and the hospital of St. Louis, with its seven hundred beds, and that of *La Pitié*, with its six hundred beds, are served by the same sisterhood under whose care they were originally placed centuries ago.

For about five hundred years the institution of the *Dames* or *Sœur Hospitalières* remained the only one of its kind. During this period it had greatly increased its numbers, and extended all through Western Christendom.

The thirteenth century saw the rise of another community of compassionate women. These were the *Sœurs Grises*, or Grey Sisters, so called at first from the original color of their dress. Their origin was this: the Franciscans (and other regular orders) admitted into their community a third or secular class, who did not seclude themselves in cloisters, who took no vows of celibacy, but were simply bound to submit to certain rules and regulations, and united together in works of charity, devoting themselves to visiting the sick in the hospitals or at their own homes, and doing good wherever and whenever called upon.

Women of all classes were enrolled in this sisterhood,—queens, princesses, ladies of rank, wives of burghers, as well as poor widows and maidens. The higher class and the married women occasionally served; the widows and unmarried devoted themselves almost entirely to the duties of nursing the sick in the hospitals.

Gradually it became a vocation apart, and a novitiate or training of from one to three years was required to fit them for their profession.

When at Florence, in 1857, I found the noble hospital of S. Maria-Nuova, the Hôtel Dieu of Florence, served by this Franciscan sisterhood, to whom it really belonged, though all responsibility with regard to the management had long been taken from them and placed in the hands of government officials. In former times there were at least thirty-three hospitals, each of the guilds or companies having its own, supported by its own members and managed by religious sisterhoods and confraternities. All these small hospitals became gradually merged in the large one; this rendered the whole establishment more convenient as a medical school, and as an assemblage of professorships, but the patients probably suffered from being crowded under one roof. At the time I visited it there were nearly 3,000 sick.

The Béguines, so well known in Flanders, seem to have existed as hospital-sisters in the seventh century, and to have been settled in communities at Liege and elsewhere in 1173. They wear a particular dress (the black gown and white hood), but take no vows, and may leave the community at any time—a thing which rarely happens.

No one who has travelled in Flanders, visited Ghent, Bruges, Brussels, or indeed any of the Netherlandish towns, will forget the singular appearance of these, sometimes young and handsome, but always staid, respectable-looking women, walking about protected by the universal reverence of the people, and busied in their compassionate vocation.

In their few moments of leisure, the Béguines are allowed to make lace and cultivate flowers, and they act under a strict self-constituted government, maintained by strict traditional forms. All the hospitals in Flanders are served by these Béguines. They have, besides, attached to their own houses, hospitals of their own, with a medical staff of physicians and surgeons, under whose directions, in all cases of difficulty, the sisters administer relief; and of the humility, skill, and tenderness with which they do administer it, I have heard but one opinion;* nor did I ever meet with any one who had travelled in those countries who did not wish that some system of the kind could be transferred to England.

In Germany, the Sisters of Charity are styled "Sisters of St. Elizabeth," in honor of Elizabeth of Hungary. At Vienna, a few years ago, I had the opportunity, through the kindness of a distinguished physician, of visiting one of the houses of these Elizabethan Sisters. There was an hospital attached to it of fifty beds, which had received about 450 patients during the year. Nothing could exceed the propriety, order, and cleanliness of the whole establishment. On the ground-floor was an extensive "Pharmaci," a sort of apothecaries' hall; part of this was divided off by a long table or counter, and surrounded by shelves filled with drugs, much like an apothecary's shop; behind the counter two Sisters, with their sleeves tucked up, were busy weighing and compounding medicines, with

---

* A recent traveller mentions their hospital of St. John at Bruges as one of the best conducted he had ever met with. "Its attendants, in their religious costume and with their nuns' head-dresses, moving about with a quiet tenderness and solicitude, worthy their name as 'Sisters of Charity'; and the lofty wards, with the white linen of the beds, present in every particular an example of the most accurate neatness and cleanliness."

such a delicacy, neatness, and exactitude as women use in these matters. A physician and surgeon, appointed by the Government, visited this hospital, and were resorted to in cases of difficulty or where operations were necessary. Howard, in describing the principal hospital at Lyons, which he praises for its excellent and kindly management, as being "so clean and so quiet," tells us that at that time (1776) he found it attended by nine physicians and surgeons, and managed by twelve Sisters of Charity. "There were Sisters who made up as well as administered all the medicines prescribed; for which purpose there was a laboratory and an apothecary's shop, the neatest and most elegantly fitted up that can be conceived." *

Louise de Marillac—better known as Madame Legras,—when left a widow in the prime of life, could find no better refuge from sorrow than in active duties, undertaken "for the love of God." The famous Vincent de Paul, who had been occupied for years with a scheme to reform thoroughly the prisons and hospitals of France, found in

---

* Howard also mentions the hospitals belonging to the order of Charity, in all countries, as the best regulated, the cleanest, the most tenderly served and managed of all he had met with. He mentions the introduction of iron bedsteads into one of their hospitals as something new to him.—(In 1776).

Madame Legras a most efficient coadjutor. They constituted on an improved basis the order Hospitalières, since known as the Sisterhood of Charity.

Within twenty years this new community had two hundred houses and hospitals; in a few years more it had spread over all Europe. Madame Legras died in 1660. Already, before her death, the women prepared and trained under her instructions, and under the direction of Vincent de Paul, had proved their efficiency, on some extraordinary occasions. In the campaigns of 1652 and 1658, they were sent to the field of battle, in groups of two and four together, to assist the wounded. They were invited into the besieged towns to take charge of the military hospitals.

They were particularly conspicuous at the siege of Dunkirk, and in the military hospitals established by Anne of Austria, at Fontainebleau. When the plague broke out in Poland, in 1672, they were sent to direct the hospitals at Warsaw, and to take charge of the orphans, and were thus introduced into Eastern Europe; and, stranger than all! they were even sent to the prison-infirmaries, where the branded *forçats*, and condemned felons lay cursing and writhing in their fetters.

It is not, I believe, generally known in this country that the same experiment has been lately tried, and with success, in the prisons of Piedmont, where the Sisters were first employed to nurse the wretched criminals perishing with disease and despair; afterward, and during convalescence, to read to them, to teach them to read and to knit, and in some cases to sing. The hardest of these wretches had probably some remembrance of a mother's voice and look thus recalled, or he could at least feel gratitude for sympathy from purer, higher nature. As an element of reformation, I might almost say of regeneration, this use of the feminine influence has been found efficient where all other means had failed.

At the commencement of the French Revolution the Sisterhood of Charity had 426 houses in France, and many more in other countries; the whole number of women then actively employed was about 6,000. During the Reign of Terror, the Superior (Madame Duleau), who had become a Sister of Charity at the age of nineteen, and was now sixty, endeavored to keep the society together, although suppressed by the Government, and in the midst of the horrors of that time, it appears that the feeling of the people protected these women from injury. As soon as the Consular government was established, the indispensable Sisterhood was recalled by a decree of the Minister of the Interior.

I can not resist giving you a few passages from the preamble to this edict—certainly very striking and significant—as I find it quoted in a little book now before me.

It begins thus:

"Seeing that the services rendered to the sick can only be properly administered by those whose vocation it is, and who do it in the spirit of love;

"Seeing, farther, that among the hospitals of the Republic, those are in all ways best served wherein the female attendants have adhered to the noble example of their predecessors, whose only object was to practice a boundless love and charity;

"Seeing that the members still existing of this society are now growing old, so that there is reason to fear that an order which is a glory to the country may shortly become extinct;

"It is decreed that the Citoyenne Duleau, formerly Superior of the Sisters of Charity, is authorized to educate girls for the care of the hospitals," etc.

I confess I should like to see an Act of our Parliament beginning with such a preamble!

In all the Sisters of Charity I have known, I

have found a mingled bravery and tenderness, if not by nature, by habit; and a certain tranquil self-complacency, arising not from self-applause, but out of the very abnegation of self, which had been adopted as the rule of life.

I have now given you a rapid and most imperfect sketch of what has been done by an organized system of charity in the Roman Catholic Church.

MRS. JAMESON,
Sisters of Charity.

THE PROFESSION OF A NUN.

THE places allotted to us as being strangers, whom the Italians never fail to distinguish by the most courteous manners, were such as not only to enable us to view the whole ceremony, but to contemplate the features and expression of this interesting being.

All awaited the moment of her entrance with anxious impatience, and on her appearance every eye was directed toward her with an expression of the deepest interest. Splendidly adorned, and attended by a female friend of high rank, she slowly advanced to the seat assigned her near the altar. Her fine form rose above the middle stature, a gentle bend marked her contour; her deep blue eyes, which were occasionally in pious awe raised to Heaven, and her long, dark eyelashes, gave life to a beautiful countenance.

She was the only child of doating parents; but while their afflicted spirit found vent in tears which coursed over cheeks chilled by sorrow, they yet beheld their treasure about to be separated from them, with that resignation which piety inspires, while yielding to a sacrifice made to Heaven. The ceremony now began, the priest pronounced a discourse, and the other observances proceeded in the usual order.

At length the solemn moment approached which was to bind her vows to Heaven. She arose and stood for a few moments before the altar; when suddenly, yet with noiseless action, she sank extended on the marble floor. A momentary pause ensued: when the deep silence was broken, by the low tones of the organ, accompanied by soft and beautiful female voices. The sound gently swelled in the air, and as the harmonious volume became more powerful, the deep church-bell at intervals sounded with a loud clamor, exciting a mixed feeling of agitation and grandeur.

This solemn music continued long, and still fell mournfully on the ear; and yet seraphic as in softened tones, and as it were receding in the distance, it gently sank into silence. The young novice was then raised, and advancing toward the priest, she bent down, kneeling at his feet, while he cut a lock of her hair, as a type of the ceremony that was to deprive her of this, to her no longer valued, ornament. Her attendant then despoiled her of the rich jewels with which she was adorned;

her splendid upper vesture was thrown off, and replaced by a monastic garment; her long tresses bound up, her temples covered with fair linen; the white crown, emblem of innocence, fixed on her head, and the crucifix placed in her hands.

Then kneeling low once more before the altar, she uttered her last vow to Heaven; at which moment the organ and choristers burst forth in loud shouts of triumph.

The ceremony finished, she arose and attended in procession, proceeding toward a wide gate, dividing the church from the convent, which, opening wide, displayed a small chapel beautifully illuminated; a thousand lights shed a brilliant lustre, whose lengthened gleams seemed sinking into darkness, as they shot through the long perspective of the distant aisle. In the foreground, in a blazing focus of light, stood an altar, from which, in a divided line, the nuns of the community were seen, each holding a large burning wax taper. They seemed to be disposed in order of seniority, and the two youngest were still adorned with the white crown, as being in the first week of their novitiate.

Both seemed in early youth, and their cheeks, yet unpaled by vigils, bloomed with a brightened tint, while their eyes sparkled, and a smile seemed struggling with the solemnity of the moment, in expression of their innocent delight in beholding the approach of her who had that day offered up her vows, and become one of the community.

The others stood in succession, with looks more subdued, pale, mild, collected, the head gently bending toward the earth in contemplation. The procession stopped at the threshold of the church, when the young nun was received and embraced by the Lady-Superior, who, leading her onward, was followed in procession by the nuns, each bearing her lighted torch.

JOHN BELL,
Observations on Italy.

DIVORCE.

The civil-contract theory of marriage is strictly in place in any system which banishes God from the world and human life. It is in order in rationalized communities, in societies which have ceased to be Christian. Some of us are reproached for not being in accord with the spirit of the age; how can we be, if the spirit of the age and its movements are practically atheistic? To induce men to ignore God's word and reject His law, to show men how to do without God, is the avowed aim of the advanced thinker of the day; and the view of marriage, as a civil contract only, falls in with the rest of his programme.

Unfortunately we can not stop at that. The truth must be told, however painfully it may strike the unaccustomed ear. This is not only a sign of an infidel society, it is also an outgrowth from the principles which form the evil side of Protestantism. There can be no doubt as to the genesis of this abomination. I quote the language of the Bishop of Maine: "Laxity of opinion and teachings on the sacredness of the marriage bond and on the question of divorce originated among the Protestants of Continental Europe in the sixteenth century. It soon began to appear in the legislation of Protestant States on that continent, and nearly at the same time to affect the laws of New England. And from that time to the present it has proceeded from one degree to another in this country until, especially in New England and in States most directly affected by New England opinions and usages, the Christian conception of the nature and obligations of the marriage bond finds scarcely any recognition in legislation, or, as must thence be inferred, in the prevailing sentiment of the community."* This is a heresy, born and bred of free thought as applied to religion; it is the outcome of the habit of interpreting the Bible according to man's private judgment, rejecting ecclesiastical authority and Catholic tradition.

REV. MORGAN DIX,
Lectures on the Calling of a Christian Woman.

---

* It is hardly necessary to remind the reader of the obsequiousness of Cranmer; the matter of the divorces of Henry VIII., of the conduct of Luther and Melancthon in the case of the Landgrave of Hesse; of the abortive "*Reformatio Legum Ecclesiasticarum*" in the reign of Edward VI., and of John Milton's tractate addressed to Parliament on the "*Doctrine and Discipline of Divorce.*"

THE ROMAN CATHOLIC CHURCH.

The history of that Church joins together the two great ages of human civilization. No other institution is left standing which carries the mind back to the times when the smoke of sacrifice rose from the Pantheon, and when camelopards and tigers bounded in the Flavian amphitheatre. The proudest royal-houses are but of yesterday, when compared with the line of the Supreme Pontiffs. That line we trace back in an unbroken series, from the Pope who crowned Napoleon in the nineteenth century, to the Pope who crowned Pepin in the eighth; and far beyond the time of Pepin the august dynasty extends. The republic of Venice came next in antiquity. But the republic of Venice was modern when compared with the Papacy, and the republic of Venice is gone, and the Papacy remains. The Papacy remains, not in decay, not a mere antique, but full of life and youthful vigor. The Catholic Church is still sending forth to the farthest ends of the world missionaries as zealous as those who landed in Kent with Augustine, and still confronting hostile kings with the same spirit with which she confronted Attila. The number of her children is greater than in any former age. Her acquisitions in the New World have more than compensated for what she has lost in the Old. Her spiritual ascendency extends over the vast countries which lie between the plains of the Missouri and Cape Horn, countries which, a century hence, may not improbably contain a population as large as that which now inhabits Europe. The members of her communion are certainly not fewer than one hundred and fifty millions,* and it will be difficult to show that all other Christian sects united amount to a hundred and twenty millions. Nor do we see any sign which indicates that the term of her long dominion is approaching. She saw the commencement of all the governments and of all the ecclesiastical establishments that now exist in the world; and we feel no assurance that she is not destined to see the end of them all. She was great and respected before the Saxon had set foot on Britain, before the Frank had passed the Rhine, when Grecian eloquence still flourished at Antioch, when idols were still worshipped in the temple of Mecca. And she may still exist in un-

---

* Estimated now at two hundred and twenty-five millions.

diminished vigor when some traveller from New Zealand shall, in the midst of a vast solitude, take his stand on a broken arch of London Bridge to sketch the ruins of St. Paul's.

We often hear it said, that the world is constantly becoming more and more enlightened; and that this enlightening must be favorable to Protestantism, and unfavorable to Catholicism. We wish that we could think so. But we see great reason to doubt whether this be a well-founded expectation. We see that during the last two hundred and fifty years, the human mind has been in the highest degree active—that it has made great advances in every branch of natural philosophy—that it has produced innumerable inventions tending to promote the convenience of life—that medicine, surgery, chemistry, engineering, have been very greatly improved—that government, police, and law have been improved, though not quite to the same extent. Yet we see that during these two hundred and fifty years, Protestantism has made no conquests worth speaking of. Nay, we believe that as far as there has been a change, that change has been in favor of the Church of Rome.

LORD MACAULAY,
Essays, Critical and Miscellaneous.

THE POPULATION, WEALTH, POWER, FREEDOM, AND PLENTY OF ENGLAND AND IRELAND BEFORE THE REFORMATION.

Kensington, 31*st March*, 1826.

My Friends :—This Letter is to conclude my task, which task was to make good this assertion, that the event called the "Reformation" had *impoverished* and *degraded* the main body of the people of England and Ireland. In paragraph 4, I told you, that a fair and honest inquiry would teach us, that the word "Reformation" had, in this case, been misapplied; that there was a change, but a change greatly *for the worse ;* that the thing, called the Reformation, was engendered in beastly lust, brought forth in hypocrisy and perfidy, and cherished and fed by plunder, devastation, and by rivers of innocent English and Irish blood; and that, as to its more remote consequences, they are, some of them, now before us, in that misery, that beggary, that nakedness, that hunger, that everlasting wrangling and spite, which now stare us in the face and stun our ears at every turn, and which the "Reformation" has given us in exchange for the ease and happiness and harmony and Christian charity, enjoyed so abundantly, and for so many ages, by our Catholic forefathers.

All this has been amply proved in the fifteen foregoing Letters, except that I have not yet shown, in detail, how our Catholic forefathers lived, what sort and what quantity of food and raiment they had, compared with those which we have. This I am now about to do. I have made good my charge of beastly lust, hypocrisy, perfidy, plunder, devastation, and bloodshed; the charge of misery, of beggary, of nakedness, and of hunger, remains to be fully established.

But I choose to be better rather than worse than my word; I did not pledge myself to prove anything as to the population, wealth, power, and freedom of the nation; but I will now show not only that the people were better off, but better fed and clad, before the "Reformation" than they ever have been since; but, that the nation was more populous, wealthy, powerful, and free before, than it ever has been since that event. Read modern romancers, called historians, every one of whom has written for place or pension; read the statements about the superiority of the present over former times; about our prodigious increase in population, wealth, power, and, above all things, our superior freedom; read the monstrous lies of Hume, who (vol. 5, p. 502) unblushingly asserts "that one good county of England is now capable of making a greater effort than the whole kingdom was in the reign of Henry V., when to maintain the garrison of the small town of Calais required more than a third of the ordinary revenues"; this is the way in which every Scotchman reasons. He always estimates the wealth of a nation by the money the government squeezes out of it. He forgets that "a poor government makes a rich people." According to this criterion of Hume, America must now be a wretchedly poor country. This same Henry V. could conquer, really conquer, France, and that, too, without beggaring England by hiring a million of Prussians, Austrians, Cossacks, and all sorts of hirelings. But writers have, for ages, been so dependent on the government and the aristocracy, and the people have read and believed so much of what they have said, and especially in praise of the "Reformation," and its effects, that it is no wonder that they should think that, in Catholic times, England was a poor, beggarly spot, having a very few people on it; and that the "Reformation," and the House of Brunswick and the Whigs, have given us all we possess of wealth, of power, of freedom, and have almost created us, or, at least, if not actually begotten us, caused nine-tenths of us to be born. These are all monstrous lies; but they have succeeded for ages. Few men dared to attempt to refute them; and, if any one made the attempt, he obtained few hearers, and ruin, in some shape or other, was pretty sure to be the reward of his virtuous efforts. Now, however, when we are smarting under the lash of calamity; now, when every one says, that no state of things ever was so bad as this; now men may listen to the truth, and, therefore, I will lay it before them.

PopuLOUSNESS is a thing not to be proved by positive facts, because there are no records of the numbers of the people in former times; and because those which we have in our own day are notoriously false; if they be not, the English nation has added a third to its population during the last twenty years! In short, our modern records I have, over and over again, proved to be false, particularly in my Register, No. 2, of Volume 46. That England was more populous in Catholic times than it is now we must believe, when we know, that in the three first Protestant reigns, thousands of parish churches were pulled down, that parishes were united, in more than two thousand instances, and when we know from the returns now before Parliament, that, out of 11,761 parishes, in England and Wales, there are upwards of a thousand which do not contain a hundred persons each, men, women, and children. Then again, the size of the churches. They were manifestly built, in general, to hold three, four, five, or ten times the number of their present parishioners, including all the sectarians. What should men have built such large churches for? We are told of their "piety and zeal"; yes, but there must have been men to raise the buildings. The Lord might favor the work; but there must have been hands as well as prayers. And, what motive could there have been for putting together such large quantities of stone and mortar, and to make walls four feet thick, and towers and steeple, if there had not been people to fill the buildings? And how could the labor have been performed? There must have been men to perform the labor; and, can any one believe, that this labor would have been performed, if there had not been a necessity for it? We now see large and most costly ancient churches, and these in great numbers too, with only a few mud-huts to hold the thirty or a hundred of parishioners. Our forefathers built forever, little thinking of the devastation that we were to behold! Next come the lands, which they cultivated, and which we do not, amounting to millions of acres. This any one may verify, who will go into Sussex, Hampshire, Dorsetshire, Devonshire, and Cornwall. They grew corn on the sides of hills, which we now never attempt to stir. They made the hill into the form of steps of a stairs, in order to plough and sow the flat parts. These flats, or steps, still remain, and are, in some cases, still cultivated; but, in nine cases out of ten, they are not. Why should they have performed this prodigious labor, if they had not had mouths to eat the corn? And how could they have performed such labor without numerous hands? On the high lands of Hampshire and Dorsetshire, there are spots of a thousand acres together, which still bear the ineffaceable marks of the plough, and which now never feel that implement. The modern writings on the subject of ancient population are mere romances; or they have been put forth with a view of paying court to the government of the day. George Chalmers, a placeman, a pensioner, and a Scotchman, has been one of the most conspicuous in this species of deception. He, in what he calls an "Estimate," states the population of England and Wales, in 1377, at 2,092,978. The half of these were, of course, females. The males, then, were 1,046,486. The children, the aged, the infirm, the sick, made a half of these; so that there were 523,243 left of able-bodied men in this whole kingdom! Now, the churches and the religious houses amounted, at that time, to upwards of 16,000 in number. There was one Priest to every church, and these Priests, together with the Monks and Friars, must have amounted to about 40,000 able men, leaving 483,243 able men. So that, as there were more than 14,000 parish churches, there were not quite twelve able-bodied men to each! Hume says, vol. iii., p. 9, that Wat Tyler had, in 1381 (four years after Chalmers' date), "a hundred thousand men assembled on Blackheath"; so that, to say nothing of the numerous bodies of insurgents, assembled, at the same time, "in Hertford, Essex, Suffolk, Norfolk, and Lincoln"; 'to say nothing of the King's army of 40,000 (Hume, vol. iii., p. 8); and, to say nothing of all the nobility, gentry, and rich people, here Wat Tyler had got together, on Blackheath, more than one-fifth of all the able-bodied men in England and Wales! And he had, too, collected them together in the space of about six days. Do we want, can we want, anything more than this, in answer, in refutation of these writers on the ancient population of the country? Let it be observed, that, in these days there were, as Hume himself relates, and his authorities relate also, frequently 100,000 pilgrims at a time assembled at Canterbury, to do penance, or make offerings at the shrine of Thomas à Becket. There must, then, have been 50,000 men here at once; so that, if we were to believe this pensioned Scotch writer, we must believe that more than a tenth of all the able-bodied men of England and Wales were frequently assembled, at one and the same time, in one city, in an extreme corner of the island, to kneel at the tomb of one single saint. Monstrous lie! And yet it has been sucked down by "enlightened Protestants," as if it had been a part of the Gospel. But, if Canterbury could give entertainment to 100,000 strangers at a time, what must Canterbury itself have been? A grand, a noble, a renowned city it was, venerated, and even visited, by no small part of the Kings, Princes, and Nobles of all Europe. It is now a beggarly, gloomy-looking town, with about 12,000 inhabitants, and, as the public accounts say, with 3,000 of those inhabitants paupers, and with a part of the site of its ancient and splendid churches, convents, and streets, covered with barracks, the Cathedral only remaining, for the purpose, as it were, of keeping the people in mind of the height from which they have fallen. The best criterion of the population is, however, to be found in the number and size of the churches, and that of the religious houses. There was one parish church to every four square miles, throughout the kingdom; and one religious house (including all the kinds) to every thirty square miles. That is to say, one parish church to every piece of land two miles each way; and one religious house to every piece of land five miles long and six miles wide. These are facts that nobody can deny. The geography tells us the number of square miles in the country, and as to the number of parishes and religious houses, it is too well known to admit of dispute, being recorded in books without number. Well, then, if the father of lies himself were to come, and endeavor to persuade us that England was not more populous before the "Reformation" than it is now, he must fail with all but downright idiots. The same may be said with regard to Ireland, where there were, according to Archdall, 742 religious houses in the reign of Henry VIII.; and, of course, one of these to every piece of land six miles each way; and where there was a parish church to every piece of land a little more than two miles and a half each way. Why these churches? What were they built for? By whom were they built? And how were all these religious houses maintained? Alas! Ireland was, in those days, a fine, a populous, and a rich country. Her people were not then half naked and half starved. There were then no projects for relieving the Irish by sending them out of their native land!

THE WEALTH of the country is a question easily decided. In the reign of Henry VIII., just before the "Reformation," the whole of the lands in England and Wales had, according to Hume, been rated, and the annual rental was found to be three millions; and as to this, Hume (vol. iv., p. 197) quotes undoubted authorities. Now, in order to know what these three millions were worth in our money, we must look at the Act of Parliament, 24th year of Henry VIII., chap. 3, which says, that "no person shall take for beef or pork above a halfpenny, and for mutton or veal above three farthings a pound, avoirdupois weight, and less in those places where they be now sold for less." This is by retail, mind. It is sale in the butchers' shops. So that in order to compare the then with the present amount of the rental of the country, we must first see what the annual rental of England and Wales now is, and then we must see what the price of meat now is. I wish to speak here of nothing that I have not unquestionable authority for, and I have no such authority with regard to the amount of the rental as it is just at this moment; but I have that authority for what the rental was in the year 1804. A return, printed by order of the House of Commons, and dated 10th July, 1804, states that "the returns to the Tax office [property tax], prove the rack-rental of England and Wales to be thirty-eight millions a year." Here, then, we have the rental to a certainty; for what was there that could escape the all-searching, taxing eye of Pitt and his understrappers? Old Harry's inexperience must have made him a poor hand, compared with Pitt, at finding out what people got for their land. Pitt's return included the rent of mines, canals, and of every species of real property; and the rental, the rack-rental, of the whole amounted to thirty-eight millions. This, observe, was in time of bank restrictions; in time of high prices; in time of monstrously high rents; in time of high price of meat. That very year I gave 18*s*. a score for fat hogs, taking head, feet, and all together; and, for many years, before and after, and including 1804, beef, pork, mutton, and veal were, taken on the average, more than tenpence a pound by retail. Now, as Old Harry's Act orders the meat to be sold in some places for less than the halfpenny and the three farthings, we may, I think, fairly presume that the general price was a halfpenny. So that a halfpenny of Old Harry's money was equal in value to tenpence of Pitt's money; and, therefore, the three millions of rental in the time of Harry, ought to have become sixty millions in 1804; and it was, as we have seen, only thirty-eight millions. In 1822 Mr. Curwen said the rental had fallen to twenty millions. But then meat had also fallen in price. It is safer to take 1804, where we have undoubted authority to go on. This proof is of a nature to bid defiance to cavil. No man can dispute any of the facts, and they are conclusive as to the point that the nation was more wealthy before the "Reformation" than it is now. But there are two other Acts of Parliament to which I will refer as corroborating in a very striking manner this fact of the superior general opulence of Catholic times. The Act, 18th year of Henry VI., Chap. XI., after setting forth the cause for the enactment, provides that no man shall, under a heavy penalty, act as a justice of the peace who has not lands and tenements of the clear yearly value of twenty pounds. This was in 1439, about a hundred years before the above-mentioned act about meat of Henry VIII. The money was of still higher value in the reign of Henry VI. However, taking it as before, at twenty times the value of our money, the justice of the peace must then have had four hundred pounds a year of our money; and we all know that we have justices of the peace of one hundred a year. This Act of Henry VI. shows that the country abounded in gentlemen of good estate; and, indeed, the Act itself says that the people are not contented with having "men of small behavior set over them." A thousand fellows calling themselves historians would never overset such a proof of the superior general opulence and ease and happiness of the country. The other of the acts to which I have alluded is the first year of Richard III., chap. 4, which fixes the qualification of a juror at twenty shillings a year in freehold, or twenty-six and eight-pence copyhold, clear of all charges. That is to say, a clear yearly income from real property of at least twenty pounds a year of our money! And yet the Scotch historians would make us believe that our ancestors were a set of beggars! These things prove beyond all dispute that England was in Catholic times a real wealthy country; that wealth was generally diffused; that every part of the country abounded in men of solid property; and that, of course, there were always great resources at hand in cases of emergency. If we were now to take it into our heads to dislike to have men of "small behavior set over us"; if we were to take a fancy to justices of the peace of four hundred a year, and jurors of twenty pounds a year; if we were, as in the days of good King Henry, to say that we "would not be governed or ruled" by men of "small behavior," how quickly we should see Botany Bay! When Cardinal Pole landed at Dover, in the reign of Queen Mary, he was met and escorted on his way by two thousand gentlemen of the country on horseback. What! two thousand country gentlemen in so beggarly a country as Chalmers describes it! Aye, and they must have been found in Kent and Surrey too. Can we find such a troop of country gentlemen there now? In short, everything shows that England was then a country abounding in men of real wealth, and that it so abounded precisely because the king's revenue was small; yet this is cited by Hume and the rest of the Scotch historians as a proof of the nation's poverty! Their notion is that a people are worth what the government can wring out of them and not a farthing more. And this is the doctrine which has been acted upon ever since the "Reformation," and which has at last brought us into our present wretched condition.

As to the POWER of the country compared with

what it is now, what do we want more than the fact that for many centuries before the "Reformation" England held possession of a considerable part of France; that the "Reformation" took, as we have seen, the two towns of Boulogne and Calais from her, leaving her nothing but those little specks in the sea, Jersey and Guernsey? What do we want more than this? France was never a country that had any pretensions to cope with England until the "Reformation" began. Since the "Reformation" she has not only had such pretensions, but she has shown to all the world that the pretensions are well founded. She, even at this moment, holds Spain in despite of us, while in its course the "Reformation" has wrested from us a large portion of our dominions, and has erected them into a state more formidable than any we have ever before beheld. We have, indeed, great standing armies, arsenals, and barracks, of which our Catholic forefathers had none; but they were always ready for war, nevertheless. They had the resources in the hour of necessity. They had arms and men; and those men knew what they were to fight for before they took up arms. It is impossible to look back to see the respect in which England was held for so many, many ages, to see the deference with which she was treated by all nations, without blushing at the thought of our present state. None but the greatest potentates presumed to think of marriage alliance with England. Her kings and queens had kings and princes in their train. Nothing petty ever thought of approaching her. She was held in such high honor, her power was so universally acknowledged that she had seldom occasion to assert it by war. And what has she been for the last hundred and fifty years? Above half the time at war; and with a Debt never to be paid, the cost of that war, she now rests her hopes of safety solely on her capacity of persuading her well-known foes that it is not their interest to assail her. Her warlike exertions have been the effect, not of her resources, but of an anticipation of those resources. She has mortgaged, she has spent beforehand the resources necessary for future defence. And there she now is inviting insult and injury by her well-known weakness, and, in case of attack, her choice lies between foreign victory over her, or internal convulsion. Power is relative. You may have more strength than you had, but if your neighbors have gained strength in a greater degree, you are in effect weaker than you were. And can we look at France and America, and can we contemplate the inevitable consequences of war without feeling that we are fast becoming, and, indeed, that we are already become a low and little nation? Can we look back to the days of our Catholic ancestors, can we think of their lofty tone and of the submission instantly produced by their threats, without sighing, alas! those days are never to return!

And, as to the FREEDOM of the nation, where is the man who can tell me of any one single advantage that the "Reformation" has brought, except it be freedom to have forty religious creeds instead of one? FREEDOM is not an empty sound; it is not an abstract idea; it is not a thing that nobody can feel. It means, and it means nothing else, the full and quiet enjoyment of your own property. If you have not this; if this be not well secured to you, you may call yourself what you will, but you are a slave. Now, our Catholic forefathers took special care upon this cardinal point. They suffered neither kings nor parliaments to touch their property without cause clearly shown. They did not read newspapers, they did not talk about debates, they had no taste for "mental enjoyment"; but they thought hunger and thirst great evils, and they never suffered anybody to put them to board on cold potatoes and water. They looked upon bare bones and rags as indubitable marks of slavery, and they never failed to resist any attempt to affix these marks upon them. You may twist the word freedom as long as you please; but, at last, it comes to quiet enjoyment of your property, or it comes to nothing. Why do men want any of those things that are called political rights and privileges? Why do they, for instance, want to vote at elections for members of Parliament? Oh! because they shall then have an influence over the conduct of those members. And of what use is that? Oh! then they will prevent the members from doing wrong. What wrong? Why, imposing taxes, that ought not to be paid. That is all; that is the use, and the only use, of any right or privilege that men in general can have. Now, how stand we in this respect, compared with our Catholic ancestors? They did not, perhaps, all vote at elections. But do we? Do the fiftieth part of us? And have the main body of us any, even the smallest, influence in the making of laws and in the imposing of taxes? But the main body of the people had the Church to protect them in Catholic times. The Church had great power; it was naturally the guardian of the common people; neither kings nor Parliaments could set its power at defiance; the whole of our history shows that the Church was invariably on the side of the people, and that, in all the much and justly boasted of triumphs, which our forefathers obtained over their kings and nobles, the Church took the lead. It did this because it was dependent on neither kings nor nobles; because, and only because, it acknowledged another head; but we have lost the protection of the Church, and have got nothing to supply its place; or rather, whatever there is of its power left has joined, or has been engrossed by, the other branches of the State, leaving the main body of the people to the mercy of those other branches. "The liberties of England" is a phrase in every mouth; but what are those liberties? The laws which regulate the descent and possession of property; the safety from arrest, unless by due and settled process; the absence of all punishment without trial before duly authorized and well-known judges and magistrates; the trial by jury; the precautions taken by the divers writs and summonses; the open trial; the impartiality in the proceedings. These are the "liberties of England." And, had our Catholic forefathers less of these than we have? Do we not owe them all to them? Have we one single law that gives security to property or to life, which we do not inherit from them? The tread-mill, the law to shut men up in their houses from sunset to sunrise, the law to banish us for life if we utter anything having a tendency to bring our "representatives" into contempt; these, indeed, we do not inherit, but may boast of them, and of many others of much about the same character, as being, unquestionably, of pure Protestant origin.

PoVERTY, however, is, after all, the great badge, the never-failing badge of slavery. Bare bones and rags are the true marks of the real slave. What is the object of government? To cause men to live happily. They can not be happy without a sufficiency of food and of raiment. Good government means a state of things in which the main body are well fed and well clothed. It is the chief business of a government to take care that one part of the people do not cause the other part to lead miserable lives. There can be no morality, no virtue, no sincerity, no honesty, amongst a people continually suffering from want; and it is cruel, in the last degree, to punish such people for almost any sort of crime, which is, in fact, not crime of the heart, not crime of the perpetrator, but the crime of his all-controlling necessities.

To what degree the main body of the people in England are now poor and miserable; how deplorably wretched they now are; this we know but too well; and now, we will see what was their state before this vaunted "Reformation." I shall be very particular to cite my authorities here. I will infer nothing; I will give no "estimate"; but refer to authorities, such as no man can call in question, such as no man can deny to be proofs more complete than if founded on oaths of credible witnesses, taken before a judge and jury. I shall begin with the account which Fortesque gives of the state and manner of living of the English in the reign of Henry VI., that is, in the 15th century, when the Catholic Church was in the height of its glory. Fortesque was Lord Chief-Justice of England for nearly twenty years ; he was appointed Lord High Chancellor by Henry VI. Being in exile, in France, in consequence of the wars between the Houses of York and Lancaster, and the King's son, Prince Edward, being also in exile with him, the Chancellor wrote a series of Letters, addressed to the Prince, to explain to him the nature and effects of the Laws of England, and to induce him to study them and uphold them. This work, which was written in Latin, is called *De Laudibus Legum Angliæ;* or, Praise of the Laws of England. This book was, many years ago, translated into English, and it is a book of Law Authority, quoted frequently in our courts at this day. No man can doubt the truth of facts related in such a work. It was a work written by a famous lawyer for a Prince ; it was intended to be read by other contemporary lawyers, and also by all lawyers in future. The passage that I am about to quote, relating to the state of the English, was purely incidental; it was not intended to answer any temporary purpose. It must have been a true description of the English, at that time; those "priest-ridden" English, whom Chalmers and Hume, and the rest of that tribe, would fain have us believe, were a mere band of wretched beggars: "The King of England can not alter the laws, or make new ones, without the express consent of the whole kingdom in Parliament assembled. Every inhabitant is at his liberty fully to use and enjoy whatever his farm produceth, the fruits of the earth, the increase of his flock, and the like; all the improvements he makes, whether by his own proper industry, or of those he retains in his service, are his own, to use and to enjoy, without the let, interruption, or denial of any. If he be in any wise injured, or oppressed, he shall have his amends and satisfactions against the party offending. Hence it is, that the inhabitants are rich in gold, silver, and in all the necessaries and conveniences of life. They drink no water, unless at certain times, upon a religious score, and by way of doing penance. They are fed in great abundance, with all sorts of flesh and fish, of which they have plenty everywhere; they are clothed throughout in good woollens; their bedding and other furniture in their houses are of wool, and that in great store. They are also well provided with all other sorts of household goods and necessary implements for husbandry. Every one, according to his rank, hath all things which conduce to make life easy and happy."

Go, and read this to the poor souls who are now eating sea-weed in Ireland; who are detected in robbing the pig-troughs in Yorkshire; who are eating horse-flesh and grains (draff) in Lancashire and Cheshire; who are harnessed like horses, and drawing gravel in Hampshire and Sussex; who have 3d. a day allowed them by the Magistrates in Norfolk; who are, all over England, worse fed than the felons in the jails. Go, and tell them, when they raise their hands from the pig-trough, or from the grainstub, and, with their dirty tongues cry, "No-Popery," go, read to the degraded and deluded wretches this account of the state of their Catholic forefathers, who lived under what is impudently called "Popish superstition and tyranny," and in those times which we have the audacity to call "the dark ages."

Fortesque's authority would, of itself, be enough; but I am not to stop with it. White, the late

Rector of Selbourne, in Hampshire, gives, in his history of that once famous village, an extract from a record, stating, that, for disorderly conduct, men were punished by being "compelled to fast a fortnight on bread and beer"! This was about the year 1380, in the reign of Richard II. Oh! miserable "dark ages"! This fact must be true. White had no purpose to answer. His mention of the fact, or, rather, his transcript from the record, is purely incidental; and trifling as the fact is, it is conclusive as to the general mode of living in those happy days. Go, tell the harnessed gravel-drawers, in Hampshire, to cry "No-Popery!" for that if the Pope be not put down, he may, in time, compel them to fast on bread and beer, instead of suffering them to continue to regale themselves on nice potatoes and pure water.

But, let us come to Acts of Parliament, and, first, to the Act above quoted, in 453, which see. That Act fixes the price of meat. After naming the four sorts of meat, beef, pork, mutton, and veal, the preamble has these words: "These being the food of the poorer sort." This is conclusive. It is an incidental mention of a fact. It is in an Act of Parliament. It must have been true; and, it is a fact that we know well, that the judges have declared from the bench, that bread alone is now the food of the poorest sort. What do we want more than this to convince us that the main body of the people have been impoverished by the "Reformation"?

But I will prove, by other Acts of Parliament, this Act of Parliament to have spoken truth. These Acts declare what the wages of workmen shall be. There are several such Acts, but one or two may suffice. The Act of 23d of Edward III. fixes the wages without food, as follows. There are many other things mentioned, but the following will be enough for our purpose:

	s.	d.
A woman hay-making, or weeding corn for the day,	0	1
A man filling dung-cart,	0	3¼
A reaper,	0	4
Mowing an acre of grass,	0	6
Threshing a quarter of wheat,	0	4

The price of shoes, cloth, and of provisions throughout the time that this law continued in force, was as follows:

	l.	s.	d.
A pair of shoes,	0	0	4
Russet broad-cloth, the yard,	0	1	1
A stall-fed ox,	1	4	0
A grass-fed ox,	0	16	0
A fat sheep unshorn,	0	1	8
A fat sheep shorn,	0	1	2
A fat hog, two years old,	0	3	4

		l.	*s.*	*d.*
A fat goose,	- - - - - - -	0	0	2¼
Ale, the gallon, by Proclamation,	- - -	0	0	1
Wheat, the quarter,	- - - - -	0	3	4
White wine, the gallon	- - - - -	0	0	6
Red wine,	- - - - - - -	0	0	4

These prices are taken from the PRECIOSUM of Bishop Fleetwood, who took them from the accounts kept by the bursers of convents. All the world knows that Fleetwood's book is of undoubted authority.

But the Popish people might work harder than "enlightened Protestants." They might do more work in a day. This is contrary to all the assertions of the *feelosofers;* for they insist that the Catholic religion made people idle. But, to set this matter at rest, let us look at the price of the job-labor; at the mowing by the acre, and at the threshing of wheat by the quarter; and let us see how these wages are now, compared with the price of food. I have no parliamentary authority since the year 1821, when a report was printed by order of the House of Commons, containing the evidence of Mr. Ellman, of Sussex, as to wages, and of Mr. George, of Norfolk, as to price of wheat. The report was dated 18th June, 1821. The accounts are for twenty years, on an average, from 1800 inclusive. We will now proceed to see how the "popish priest-ridden" Englishman stands in comparison with the "No-Popery" Englishman.

	Popish man.	No-Popery man.
	s. d.	s. d.
Mowing an acre of grass,	- 0 6	3 7¼
Threshing a quarter of wheat,	- 0 4	4 0

Here are "waust improvements, Mau'm!" But now let us look at the relative price of the wheat, which the laborer had to purchase with his wages. We have seen that the "popish superstition slave" had to give fivepence a bushel for his wheat, and the evidence of Mr. George states that the "enlightened Protestant" had to give 10 shillings a bushel for his wheat; that is 24 times as much as the "popish fool" who suffered himself to be "priest-ridden." So that the "enlightened" man, in order to make him as well off as the "dark ages" man was, ought to receive twelve shillings instead of 3s. 7¼d. for mowing an acre of grass; and he, in like manner, ought to receive, for threshing a quarter of wheat, eight shillings, instead of the four shillings which he does receive. If we had the records, we should, doubtless, find that Ireland was in the same state.

There! That settles the matter; and, if the Bible Society, and the "Education" and the "Christian-knowledge" gentry would, as they might, cause this little book to be put into the hands of all their millions of pupils, it would, as far as relates to this kingdom, settle the question of religion for ever and ever! I have now proved that Fortesque's description of the happy life of our Catholic ancestors was correct. There wanted no proof; but I have given it. I could refer to divers other Acts of Parliament, passed during several centuries, all confirming the truth of Fortesque's account. And there are, in Bishop Fleetwood's book, many things that prove that the laboring people were most kindly treated by their superiors, and particularly by the clergy; for instance, he has an item in the expenditure of a convent, "30 pair of autumnal gloves for the servants." This was sad "superstition." In our "enlightened" and Bible-reading age, who thinks of gloves for ploughmen? We have ministers as well as the "dark ages" people had; ours ride as well as theirs, but theirs fed at the same time; both mount, but theirs seem to have used the reign more, and spur less. It is curious to observe that the pay of persons in high situations was, as compared with that of the present day, very low, when compared with the pay of the working classes. If you calculate the year's pay of the dung-cart man, you will find it, if multiplied by 20 (which brings it to our money), to amount to

91 pounds a year; while the average pay of the Judges did not exceed 60*l.* a year of the then money, and, of course, did not exceed 1,200*l.* a year of our money. So that a Judge had not so much pay as fourteen dung-cart fillers. To be sure, Judges had, in those "dark ages," when Littleton and Fortesque lived and wrote, pretty easy lives; for Fortesque says that they led lives of great "leisure and contemplation," and that they never sat in court but three hours in a day, from 8 to 11! Alas! if they had lived in this "enlightened age," they would have found little time for their "contemplation!"—they would have found plenty of work; they would have found, that theirs was no sinecure, at any rate, and that ten times their pay was not adequate to their enormous labor. Here is another indubitable proof of the great and general happiness and harmony and honesty and innocence that reigned in the country. The Judges led lives of leisure! In that one fact, incidentally stated by a man who had been twenty years Chief-Justice of the King's bench, we have the true character of the so long calumniated religion of our fathers.

As to the bare fact, this most interesting fact, that the main body of the people have been impoverished and degraded since the time of the

Catholic sway; as to this fact there can be no doubt in the mind of any man who has, thus far, read this little work. Neither can there, I think, exist in the mind of such a man any doubt that this impoverishment and this degradation have been caused by the event called the "Reformation," seeing that I have, in former Numbers, and especially in Number XIV., clearly traced the debt and the enormous taxes to that event. But I can not bring myself to conclude, without tracing the impoverishment in its horrible progress. The well-known fact, that no compulsory collections for the poor; that the disgraceful name of pauper; that these were never heard of in England, in Catholic times; and that they were heard of the moment the "Reformation" had begun; this single fact might be enough, and it is enough; but we will see the progress of this Protestant impoverishment.

The Act, 27 Henry VIII., chap. 25, began the poor laws. The monasteries were not actually seized on till the next year; but the fabric of the Catholic Church was, in fact, tumbling down; and, instantly, the country swarmed with necessitous people, and open begging, which the Government of England had always held in great horror, began to disgrace this so lately happy land. To put a stop to this, the above Act authorized sheriffs, magistrates, and churchwardens to cause voluntary alms to be collected; and at the same time it punished the persevering beggar, by slicing off part of his ears, and for a second offence put him to death as a felon! This was the dawn of that "Reformation" which we are still called upon to admire and to praise!

The "pious young Saint Edward," as Fox, the Martyr-man, most impiously calls him, began his Protestant reign, 1st year Edward VI., chap. 3, by an Act punishing beggars by burning with a red-hot iron, and by making them slaves for two years, with power in their masters to make them wear an iron collar, and to feed them upon bread and water and refuse meat! For even in this case, still there was meat for those who had to labor; the days of cold potatoes and of bread and water alone were yet to come; they were reserved for our "enlightened" and Bible-reading days; our days of "mental enjoyment." And as to horse-flesh and draff (grains), they appear never to have been thought of. If the slave ran away, or were disobedient, he was, by this Protestant Act, to be a slave for life. This Act came forth as a sort of precursor of the Acts to establish the Church of England! Horrid tyranny. The people had been plundered of the resource, which Magna Charta, which justice, which reason, which the law of nature, gave them. No other resource had been provided; and they were made actual slaves, branded and chained, because they sought by their prayers to allay the cravings of hunger!

Next came " good Queen Bess," who, after trying her hand eight times, without success, to cause the poor to be relieved by alms, passed that compulsory Act which is in force to the present day. All manner of shifts had been resorted to, in order to avoid this provision for the poor. During this and the two former reigns, licenses to beg had been granted. But at last, the compulsory assessment came, that true mark, that indelible mark, of the Protestant Church, as by law established. This assessment was put off to the last possible moment, and it was never relished by those who had got the spoils of the Church and the poor. But it was a measure of absolute necessity. All the racks, all the law-martial, of this cruel reign could not have kept down the people without this Act, the authors of which seem to have been ashamed to state the grounds of it; for, it has no preamble whatever. The people, so happy in former times; the people, described by Fortesque, were now become a nation of ragged wretches. Defoe, in one of his tracts, says that "good Bess," in her progress through the kingdom, upon seeing the miserable looks of the crowds that came to see her, frequently exclaimed, "*pauper ubique jacet*"; that is, the poor cover the land. And this was that same country in which Fortesque left a race of people "having all things which conduce to make life easy and happy!"

Things did not mend much during the reign of the Stuarts, except in so far as the poor law had effect. This rendered unnecessary the barbarities that had been exercised before the passing of it; and, as long as taxation was light, the paupers were comparatively little numerous. But, when the taxes began to grow heavy, the projectors were soon at work to find out the means of putting down pauperism. Amongst these was one Child, a merchant and banker, whose name was Josiah, and who had been made a knight or baronet, for he is called Sir Josiah. His project, which was quite worthy of his calling, contained a provision, in his proposed Act, to appoint men, to be called "Fathers of the Poor"; and one of the provisions relating to these "Fathers" was to be, "that they may have power to send such poor, as they may think fit, into any of his Majesty's plantations!" That is to say, to transport and make slaves of them! And, gracious God! this was in Fortesque's country. This was in the country of *Magna Charta!* And this monster dared to publish this project! And we can not learn that any man had the soul to reprobate the conduct of so hard-hearted a wretch.

When the "deliverer" had come, when a "glorious revolution" had taken place, when a war had been carried on, and a debt and a bank created, and all for the purpose of putting down popery forever, the poor began to increase at such a frightful rate that the Parliament referred the subject to the Board of Trade to inquire and to report a remedy. Locke was one of the commissioners, and a passage in the report of the board is truly curious: "The multiplicity of the poor, and the increase of the tax for their maintenance is so general an observation and complaint that it can not be doubted of; nor has it been only since the last war that this evil has come upon us; it has been a growing burden on the kingdom this many years, and the last two reigns felt the increase of it as well as the present. If the causes of this evil be looked into, we humbly conceive it will be found to have proceeded, not from the scarcity of provisions, nor want of employment for the poor, since the goodness of God has blessed these times with plenty no less than the former, and a long peace during three reigns gave us as plentiful a trade as ever. The growth of the poor must therefore have some other cause;

and it can be nothing else but the relaxation of discipline and corruption, virtue and industry being as constant companions on the one side as vice and idleness are on the other."

So the fault was in the poor themselves! It does not seem to have occurred to Mr. Locke that there must have been a cause for this cause. He knew very well that there was a time when there were no paupers at all in England; but, being a fat placeman under the "deliverer," he could hardly think of alluding to that interesting fact. "Relaxation of discipline!" What discipline? What did he mean by discipline? The taking away of the church and poor's property, the imposing of heavy taxes, the giving of low wages compared with the price of food and raiment, the drawing away of the earnings of the poor to be given to paper-harpies and other tax-eaters. These were the causes of the hideous and disgraceful evil. This he knew very well, and therefore it is no wonder that his report contained no remedy.

After Locke, came in the reign of Queen Anne; Defoe, who seems to have been the father of the present race of projectors, Malthus and Lawyer Scarlett being merely his humble followers. He was for giving no more relief to the poor. He imputed their poverty to their crimes, and not their crimes to their poverty; and their crimes he imputed to "their luxury, pride, and sloth." He said the English laboring people ate and drank three times as much as any foreigners! How different were the notions of this insolent French Protestant from those of the Chancellor Fortesque, who looked upon the good living of the people as the best possible proof of good laws, and seems to have delighted in relating that the English were "fed in great abundance with all sorts of flesh and fish!"

If Defoe had lived to our "enlightened age," he would at any rate have seen no "luxury" among the poor, unless he would have grudged them horse-flesh, draff (grains), sea-weed, or the contents of the pig-trough. From his day to the present there have been a hundred projects and more than fifty laws to regulate the affairs of the poor; but still the pauperism remains for the Catholic Church to hold up in the face of the Church of England. "Here," the former may say to the latter, "here, look at this: here is the result of your efforts to extinguish me; here in this one evil, in this never-ceasing, this degrading curse, I am more than avenged, if vengeance I were allowed to enjoy. Urge on the deluded potato-crammed creatures to cry 'No-Popery' still, and when they retire to their straw, take care not to remind them of the cause of their poverty and degradation."

Hume, in speaking of the sufferings of the people in the first Protestant reign, says that at last those sufferings "produced good," for that they "led to our present situation." What, then, he deemed our present situation a better one than that of the days of Fortesque! To be sure Hume wrote fifty years ago; but he wrote long after Child, Locke, and Defoe. Surely enough the "Reformation" has led to "our then present and our now present situation." It has "at last" produced the bitter fruit of which we are now tasting. Evidence given by a clergyman, too, and published by the House of Commons in 1824, states the laboring people of Suffolk to be a nest of robbers too deeply corrupted ever to be reclaimed; evidence of a sheriff of Wiltshire (in 1821) states the common food of the laborers in the field to be cold potatoes; a scale published by the magistrates of Norfolk in 1825 allows threepence a day to a single laboring man; the judges of the Court of King's Bench (1825) have declared the general food of the laboring people to be bread and water; intelligence from the northern counties (1826), published upon the spot, informs us that great numbers of people are nearly starving, and that some are eating horseflesh and grains, while it is well known that the country abounds in food, and while the clergy have recently put up from the pulpit the rubrical thanksgiving for times of plenty, a law recently passed, making it felony to take an apple from a tree tells the world that our characters and lives are thought nothing worth, or that this nation, once the greatest and most moral in the world, is now a nation of incorrigible thieves; and, in either case, the most impoverished, the most fallen, the most degraded that ever saw the light of the sun.

I have now performed my task. I have made good the positions with which I began. Born and bred a Protestant of the Church of England, having a wife and numerous family professing the same faith, having the remains of most dearly beloved parents lying in a Protestant church-yard and trusting to conjugal or filial piety to place mine by their side, I have in this undertaking had no motive, I can have had no motive but a sincere and disinterested love of truth and justice. It is not for the rich and the powerful of my countrymen that I have spoken, but for the poor, the persecuted, the proscribed. I have not been unmindful of the unpopularity and the prejudice that would attend the enterprise; but when I considered the long, long triumph of calumny over the religion of those to whom we owe all that we possess that is great and renowned; when I was convinced that I could do much toward the counteracting of that calumny; when duty so sacred bade me speak, it would have been baseness to hold my tongue, and baseness superlative would it have been if, having the will as well as the power, I had been restrained by fear of the shafts of falsehood and of folly. To be clear of self-reproach is amongst the greatest of human consolations; and now, amidst all the dreadful perils with which the event that I have treated of has at last surrounded my country, I can, while I pray God to save her from still further devastation and misery, safely say that neither expressly nor tacitly am I guilty of any part of the cause of her ruin.

WILLIAM COBBETT,
Protestant Reformation.

www.ingramcontent.com/pod-product-compliance
Lightning Source LLC
Chambersburg PA
CBHW020741020526
44115CB00030B/728